# Naming and Othering in Africa

This book examines how names have been fashioned to create dominance and subjugation, inclusion and exclusion, others and self in Africa.

Taking examples from Africa, particularly Zimbabwe, the author demonstrates how names are used in class, race, ethnic, national, gender, sexuality, religious and business struggles in society as weapons by ingroups and outgroups. Using othering theory as a framework, the chapters explore themes such as globalised names and their demonstration of the other; onomastic erasure in colonial naming and the subsequent decoloniality in African name changes; othering of women in onomastics; and crude and sophisticated phaulisms in the areas of race, ethnicity, nationality, disability and sexuality.

Highlighting social power dynamics through onomastics, this book will be of interest to scholars of onomastics, social anthropology, sociolinguistics and African culture and history.

**Sambulo Ndlovu** is a Humbolt Research Fellow at the Institut fur Ethnologie und Afrikanstudien at Johannes Gutenberg-Universitat, Germany and a Professor at Great Zimbabwe University.

## Routledge African Studies

41. **African Transnational Mobility in China**
    Africans on the Move
    *Roberto Castillo*

42. **Mennonites and Post-Colonial African Studies**
    *Edited by John M. Janzen, Harold F. Miller and John C. Yoder*

43. **Oral Literary Performance in Africa**
    Beyond Text
    *Edited by Nduka Otiono and Chiji Akọma*

44. **Decolonising Childhoods in Eastern Africa**
    Literary and Cultural Representations
    *Oduor Obura*

45. **Black – Arab Encounters in Literature and Film**
    *Touria Khannous*

46. **The De-Africanization of African Art**
    Towards Post-African Aesthetics
    *Denis Ekpo and Pfunzo Sidogi*

47. **Memories of Violence in Peru and the Congo**
    Writing on the Brink
    *G. S. Ndi*

48. **Naming and Othering in Africa**
    Imagining Supremacy and Inferiority through Language
    *Sambulo Ndlovu*

49. **The Pan-African Imperative**
    Revisiting Nkrumah's Vision for African Development
    *Michael Williams*

For a full list of available titles please visit: www.routledge.com/African-Studies/book-series/AFRSTUD

# Naming and Othering in Africa

## Imagining Supremacy and Inferiority through Language

**Sambulo Ndlovu**

Routledge
Taylor & Francis Group
LONDON AND NEW YORK

First published 2022
by Routledge
2 Park Square, Milton Park, Abingdon, Oxon OX14 4RN

and by Routledge
605 Third Avenue, New York, NY 10158

*Routledge is an imprint of the Taylor & Francis Group, an informa business*



*British Library Cataloguing-in-Publication Data*
A catalogue record for this book is available from the British Library

*Library of Congress Cataloging-in-Publication Data*
Names: Ndlovu, Sambulo, author.
Title: Naming and othering in Africa : imagining supremacy and inferiority through language / Sambulo Ndlovu.
Description: Abingdon, Oxon ; New York, NY : Routledge, 2022. | Includes bibliographical references and index.
Identifiers: LCCN 2021028743 (print) | LCCN 2021028744 (ebook) | ISBN 9780367773106 (hardback) | ISBN 9780367773151 (paperback) | ISBN 9781003170761 (ebook)
Subjects: LCSH: African languages—Etymology—Names. | Names, African—Social aspects. | Onomastics. | African languages—Social aspects. | Dominance (Psychology) | Other (Philosophy)
Classification: LCC PL8005 .N35 2022 (print) | LCC PL8005 (ebook) | DDC 929.9/7096—dc23
LC record available at https://lccn.loc.gov/2021028743
LC ebook record available at https://lccn.loc.gov/2021028744

ISBN: 978-0-367-77310-6 (hbk)
ISBN: 978-0-367-77315-1 (pbk)
ISBN: 978-1-003-17076-1 (ebk)

DOI: 10.4324/9781003170761

Typeset in Bembo
by Apex CoVantage, LLC

# Contents


*Acknowledgements* vii
*List of figures* viii
*List of tables* ix

1 Introduction 1

**SECTION ONE**
**Global, cultural and ethnophaulic nomen othering of Africa** 15

2 Africa and global onomastic othering dichotomies 17
3 Names as cultural othering of Africa 38
4 Ethnophaulisms as crude nomen othering in African contexts 59

**SECTION TWO**
**Selfing and othering in colonial and de-colonial onomastics in Africa** 85

5 *UMlungu/Mzungu/Oborofo* decoloniality and coloniality nuances 87
6 Onomastic attestations of coloniality in Africa 105
7 Colonial othering of African anthroponymy 129

SECTION THREE
**Names as exhibits of gendered, disablist, exclusion and sexist subalternities in African contexts** 149

8 The woman other in African names and naming 151

9 Disablist, homophobic and sexist nomen othering in Africa 168

10 Socio-political onomastic exclusions in Africa 186

11 Conclusions and recommendations 199

*Index* 204

# Acknowledgements

I acknowledge with gratitude the opportunity I was granted by the Alexander von Humboldt Foundation to work on this book. I also extend my acknowledgements to the Department of Anthropology and African Studies and colleagues at Johannes Gutenberg University in Mainz, Germany, and the Department of African Languages and Culture at the Great Zimbabwe University. Thank you very much to my data sources, across Africa and to my family for the support.

# Figures


| | | |
|---|---|---|
| 2.1 | The development factor in the naming of Global North countries | 26 |
| 2.2 | Characterisation of developed, developing and underdeveloped country nomenclature | 31 |
| 4.1 | Eugenics' imagined degeneration of Mongoloids and Negroids from the perfection in Caucasoids | 64 |
| 5.1 | Implications of divine race hierarchies in naming White people in Africa | 101 |
| 5.2 | Amelioration of names of White people in Africa | 102 |

# Tables


3.1 Disparaging names given to African flora 42
3.2 Names that animalise and savage African flora 43
3.3 Naming African fauna for European ownership and honour 45
3.4 Implied traditional-modern dichotomy in naming African systems 47
3.5 Indigenised African culture vs globalised European culture 48
3.6 Names satanising African religious concepts and selfing Christian concepts 51
3.7 African (Ndebele) self othering cultural names 54
4.1 Flagrant ethnophaulic transphonologies between the Ndebele and the Shona of Zimbabwe 72
5.1 *AbeLungu* relational frame metaphor analysis 91
5.2 *Aboforo/abeLumbi/vaRumbi* metaphor mappings 96
6.1 Colonial toponyms indicating ownership of Africa by European countries 109
6.2 Colonial figures in African hodonymy 113
6.3 Hodonyms glorifying colonial institutions in Africa 114
6.4 Colonial renaming of African water bodies 115
6.5 Meaningless English transphonologies of indigenous Zimbabwean toponyms 116
6.6 Weird semantic inferences in some English transphonologies of Zimbabwean toponyms 117
6.7 Coloniality of African currencies 120
6.8 Indigenous African names of currency 121
6.9 Names attesting to African resource coloniality 121
6.10 Imperial toponymy in some Zimbabwean church names 124
7.1 Euro-American toponyms used as anthroponyms in Zimbabwe 137
7.2 Nguni anthroponyms derived from African culture and colonial culture 138
7.3 Slavery and colonial connotations in naming Africans as *boy* or *girl* 139
7.4 English translations of some African names 142
8.1 The agentive status for men and object position of women in Nguni social verbs 154
8.2 Active and passive names in naming boys and girls in Nguni 155

8.3 Names of Zimbabwean family businesses which exclude daughters 158
8.4 Zimbabwean business nomenclature indicating brother partnerships 159
8.5 Gendered naming of key streets of Abuja, Nigeria 160
8.6 Patriarchal naming of Nairobi's major streets Kenya 161
8.7 Male domination in naming Harare's main streets – Zimbabwe 162
8.8 Some African universities named after men 163
8.9 The woman other in naming African international airports 164
9.1 Names of non-disabled people used to name disability centres in Zimbabwe 175
9.2 Begging implications in the meaning of some names of disability centres in Zimbabwe 177

# 1 Introduction

## 1.0 Introduction

Language, including names, expresses culture and identity. Okello (2020, p. 78) opines that 'a name is one of the most explicit pointers of identity.' This is because naming can include or exclude one or a group from certain identities. Naming the self is usually motivated by the need to assert self value or ingroup membership, and naming the other is usually associated with stereotypes and lower comparisons. The self ego embedded in self naming is clearly demonstrated in motivations for renaming, while the intensity of stereotypical naming of the other is demonstrated in the proliferation of nomen slurs. Stereotypes weaponise names and naming, creating expressive content to exalt the self and demean the other. Darwish (2010, p. 191) makes the claim that 'Names used during conflicts are not mere labels; they are able to influence public thinking, beliefs, and political standpoints. They can also be used to change facts.' Power can also be exhibited through naming; Richardson (1991, p. 1) posits that 'From Charlemagne to the Tsars, from British imperialism to Italian fascism, the language and symbols of the Roman republic and the Roman emperors have been essential elements in the self-expression of imperial powers.' This book identifies strategies of othering deployed within names and naming in global, continental, national, ethnic, economic, political and social colonialities of power. This introductory chapter highlights the nexus between names, naming and various colonialities in political, social, economical, gender and philosophical contexts in Africa. The chapter also highlights the theories engaged in the book, methodological issues and the organisation of the book.

## 1.1 Names and the other

The language-culture nexus has been described extensively in literature, and names, as part of language and discourse, are embedded in culture, and they are in fact culture. As Hall (1959) postulates that culture hides more than we can see, so does language. Strani and Szczepaniak-Kozak (2018, p. 162) opine that 'Language, inextricably linked with culture, works in the same way, as it may mask (or betray) hegemonic relations as relics of colonialism, racialisation and

DOI: 10.4324/9781003170761-1

othering in the context of societies that foster monoculture.' The conflation of biology and politics in understanding human social power and its structures gave rise to othering language to separate the powerful from the powerless in discourse, as in reality. Fritsche (2019) traces colonialities of power back to Aristotle's biological justification of slavery in politics, when he opined that society is made up of Greeks, then European Barbarians, followed by Asian Barbarians. Suffice it to note that the biological and regional gradings excluded Africa and Africans. As early as Aristotle, the world was ranked from Greek to European to Asian; here Greek is the self and the Barbarian the other, with layers of otherness all named to rank the otherness. On the one hand, names represent otherness, which already obtains in power structures, while on the other, they can influence othering. Names are part of language, and they operate to communicate and shape thinking and world views. Lake (2003, p. 2) observes that 'the examination of names and naming draws attention to the fact that language not only gives us a medium to express our thoughts but also influences what we are capable of thinking.'

Controversies surrounding the name *Mlungu* for White persons in post-apartheid South Africa are indicative of the politics and emotions that can be loaded into a name. Loewe (2016), writing for *Dispatchlive*, notes that White people are offended by being called *Mlungu* and that they even equate the emotional damage they suffer from being called so to that of the 'K' word. The name has sparked intense debate based on different etymologies, and he further quotes South African language and culture experts Wababa and Kaschula as indicating that words are just letters; it is the emotions attached to them by humans which give them their power for good and evil and that language does not create the Holocaust, apartheid or racism – it is humans who do that. Language simply underpins the attitude. This development in South Africa motivated the author to examine the etymologies, meanings, implications and representations of various names in the African and global contexts so as to extricate how these relate to and influence various forms of inequalities and colonialities in Africa. The fact that people can debate the name *Mlungu* and give differing etymologies to justify their claims points to the fact that people manipulate reality so as to describe themselves favourably and others unequally.

Analysing the normative aspects of Plato's *Cratylus*, Barney (2001) observes that for Plato, names should be analysed on how truthfully they reflect the nature of the thing named. However, seeking the exact truth in names and other such analogies may be futile given the subjectivities associated with the making of history. Facts of history are not entirely scientific (that is, if they can be scientific at all); they are socially constructed manipulative ideologies to control the present and the future. The motives and facts of history are dependent on each other to serve the historian or his or her handlers' ideologies. Names and their etymologies cannot be spared by this subjectivity; the motives justify the facts of etymology in names. Bhatia (2005, p. 9) argues that 'A name will place emphasis on certain aspects and characteristics of an object, while neglecting or omitting other key areas.' Names are part of orature, and orality and lore utilise the power of words to preserve history and culture. Matson (1956, p. 63) argues that 'words are full of history.' Kirby (1954, p. 2) states that 'language does not exist in a vacuum, but in a lived reality.' History and politics are loaded into names so as to facilitate their discriminatory power. This is why Mangena and Ndlovu (2013, p. 441) argue that 'the approach to the study of names is multidimensional; names are discussed from linguistic, historical as well as political standpoints.' Such an approach to the analysis of names reveals those selfed by names and their others. The unequal power relations in human aggregates represent different colonialities of power (Ndlovu-Gatsheni, 2013). some names represent and enforce colonialities, while others challenge them.

There are various colonialities which work to produce the various forms of subalternity. Coloniality is the machine that reproduces subalternity (Mignolo, 2001). Names in Africa are deployed to describe various forms of subalternity. Coloniality outlived colonisation and post-enlightenment structures and discourses such as postmodernism and postcoloniality. Globalisation and modernity are globalised forms of structuring the world into global masters and colonials. The structuring of power to dominate the other is the coloniality of power, and it was conceived together with Euro-American supremacy and race supremacy (Quijano, 2007). Globalised coloniality is achieved through dominance and subjugation by coercion, collaboration and persuasion (Mignolo, 2001). Some names represent the lives and afterlives of unequal power relations within and between human aggregates. Those in power and with power appropriate to themselves the divine right to name, and with this power, they inferiorise the other. Martinot (2011, p. 5) states that 'The power to define is the power to objectify, and thus inferiorise; by defining an otherness for the Africans as property and wealth, the English defined themselves as superior.' The fact that humans name other animals is a good example of how naming represents power relations. Borkfelt (2011, p. 117) points out that 'naming, thus, is symbolic of the unequal power relations inherent to our relationship with other species.' Naming also betrays the unequal power relations inherent to human relations.

The manipulation of power to create subalternity is present in all human organisations. This book explores the various powers and their subalternity described and expressed through names; these are globalised, political, economical, gendered, sexualised, ethnic, racial, regional and national colonialities expressed onomastically in Africa or to and by Africa. Borkfelt (2011, p. 118) argues that:

> Naming is thus not only the first and most basic of linguistic processes; it is also an excellent example of the power or control that is in many ways inherent to language use. Whether what is named are lands, people or animals, the process of naming reflects the worldview of the one who names rather than the view of what is named.

Being named by others comes with a high risk of being misnamed. Bekerie (2004) identifies this misnaming as a process of devaluation. This superiority of the name givers is challenged through decolonial renaming as resistance to unequal social power, creating new forms of selfing and othering. Mendoza (2015) alludes to the coloniality of gender in patriarchal social structures which various feminist discourses seek to address. McNeill (1997, p. 521) reasons thus: 'Superiority, real and perceived, and inferiority, real and perceived, are the substance of human intercourse and the major stimulus to social change throughout the course of history.' Dominance and resistance have, over time, created othering and counter-othering names. Typically, names describing the other are usually offensive by their reference to stereotyped identity markers. Gilroy (2004, p. 104) observes that 'when identity refers to an indelible mark or code somehow written into the bodies of its carriers, otherness can only be a threat.' Names therefore, can be expressions of power and subalternity or talking back to power, and they can also be outright slurs.

## 1.2 Theoretical framework

The book engages postcolonial theory as it analyses the coloniality of power through names and naming. The power inequalities in names depict images of the self and the other. This makes othering theory central in all chapters. Various sub-theories of postcolonial theory and othering are deployed depending on the nature of the colonialities of power addressed by individual chapters. The book engages coloniality and decoloniality as frames to analyse global onomastic colonialities affecting Africa, while colonisation and decolonisation are engaged for the analysis of colonial naming and anti-colonial renaming, respectively. Feminist political economy frames arguments around the coloniality of gender in names, while historical trauma is engaged in the discussion of psychological effects of bad names such as ethnophaulisms and slavery-motivated naming of Africans by colonial powers.

Colonialist discourse was underpinned by imperial stewardship, a belief that western civilisation was superior and the standard which was to be spread to regenerate the degenerate people of colour in the world (Said, 2004). Othering philosophies that accompanied imperial stewardship included social Darwinism, eugenics and apartheid. These were forced on Africa and other spaces to create the self-other dichotomy which favours Euro-American racism and coloniality. These foreign colonialities of power had in them embedded social colonialities such as gender and sexualities; these blended with patriarchy in Africa to create tiers of political and social colonialities which were and are still expressed and established through names and naming. Postcolonial theory is engaged here as cultural critique to expose coloniality and how colonials are affected and in turn respond to coloniality. Postcolonial theory has been accused or at least identified with elitism and imperial spaces. It is a theory which can be identified as a leftist empathy on absent colonial subjects within the centre. Elitist characterisation of postcolonial theory makes it an otherising rather than othering theory. It is a case of having oppressors get into the shoes of the oppressed and speak out for them. It has been identified with elite colonials or former colonials domiciled in the empire and speaking for people who are, through systems of empire, still imperial subjects. This uneasy position of postcolonial theorists creates mistrust from the people they seek to liberate through their school of thought. However, othering theory as a sub-theory of postcolonial theory engages power inequalities in analysing names, as othering can be both imperialism and resistance to it.

Othering theory originates with Hegel's (1807) master-slave dialectic, where identity is created through distancing oneself from others. The concept of the other was later popularised by De Beauvoir (1949), who argued that the notion of the other opposes and helps create the self. While othering is natural to human cognition, Tajfel (1974) observes that identifying with self creates ingroups and outgroups, and these groups create identity through ingroup favouritism and outgroup derogation (Billig, 1973). Such a situation sets up identities in an unequal relationship (Crang, 1998). Strani and Szczepaniak-Kozak (2018, p. 163) reason that:

> What is fundamental in processes of othering is that categorisation takes place and is established by the dominant group, which constructs group boundaries and assigns subordinate characteristics to other groups, devaluing and demoting them to a lesser category, thus establishing a hierarchy. . . . This hierarchical categorisation leads to the assumption that difference from the dominant group signifies weakness or subordination.

Globally, certain races and their spaces are accorded superiority over others; some cultures are more equal than others. Languages, religions, gender, abilities and sexualities are also ranked in power tiers. Names operate to enforce these colonialities of power, creating the self and the other in unequal power dichotomies. Canales (2000) states that the identified other is defined as inferior due to some of its (real or imaginary) traits. Othering overlaps with other concepts such as stereotyping, prejudice and discrimination (Çelik et al., 2017). Othering sets out to create social hierarchies, where identities are created to be unequal (Crang, 1998). Brons (2015, p. 70) posits that:

> Othering is the simultaneous construction of the self or in-group and the other or out-group in mutual and unequal opposition through identification of some desirable characteristic that the self/in-group has and the other/out-group lacks and/or some undesirable characteristic that the other/out-group has and the self/in-group lacks. Othering thus sets up a superior self/in-group in contrast to an inferior other/out-group, but this superiority/inferiority is nearly always left implicit.

Hitchcock (1993) highlights that European colonisation and globalisation are processes of othering the so-called third world. He further notes that western cultural critique fosters othering of the so-called third world subjects. Brons (2015) extends the notion of othering by developing two types of othering, sophisticated and crude othering. Sophisticated othering, he argues, is less hostile to the encountered other, who is treated as the other self, while crude othering does not only distance the self but also dehumanises the other by over-inflating the otherness. However, it is difficult for relations within colonialities of power to exhibit sophisticated othering. What may appear as sophisticated othering could be veiled crude othering. Over-inflated otherness also results in outright insults aimed at the other; this creates slurs or ethnophaulisms. Ndlovu (2017, p. 119) states that 'ethnophaulism derives from Greek terms that mean disparaging an ethnic other . . . since 1944 the term has been used to refer to insulting language or action aimed at an ethnic or racial group.' While some names do not explicitly insult, they are implied insults on race, culture, space, ethnicity, disability, sexuality and gender. Othering has psychological effects of trauma just like any insult (Ndlovu & Mangena, 2014). Names are not only used in discourse to establish mental otherness and self; they are also used physically to mark identity and space.

Names have been used to colonise and decolonise. Nhemachena (2016) argues that colonialism goes beyond othering to incorporate other vices such as dispossession, assimilation and incorporation. The theories of coloniality and decoloniality are engaged to analyse the coloniality and decoloniality of names and naming in Africa; these espouse postcoloniality and othering. Decoloniality is a postcolonial theory. Bhabha (2003) declares that postcolonial theory is a testimony and discourse of subalternity. It aims at shedding colonialities by addressing topical questions in unequal relations in history, culture, identity, ethnicity, gender, language and education. Naming and renaming in Africa are within the frame of postcolonial theory. Ndlovu-Gatsheni (2015) argues that decoloniality is not only a political and epistemological movement aimed at liberating former colonised people from global coloniality but also a way of thinking, knowing and doing. Names and naming relate to thought, knowledge and doing within contexts of colonialities of power. Mpofu (2017) alludes to the fact that decoloniality has more urgent business and is framed on the reality of being Black in a world governed by a racial constitution and contract that consigns Blacks to the toilet of history. Naming and renaming are part of the strategies for rescuing Black history from the toilet of history and making it compete with other global cultures on linguistic heritage. Decoloniality is also realised in the philosophy of Afrikology espoused by Nabudere (2011), which is a search for wholeness by Africa after years of minimisation and reduction.

Maldonado-Torres (2016) argues that coloniality and decoloniality are different from the processes of colonisation and decolonisation because, while the later are historical, the former refer to the logic, metaphysics, ontology and matrix of power created by the massive processes of colonisation and decolonisation. The processes of coloniality and decoloniality are tied to hegemonic discourses and institutions of western civilisation and western modernity.

Maldonado-Torres (2016) further proffers three taxonomies of coloniality and decoloniality which are premised on power, knowledge and being. The colonial power matrices obtain in any unequal relationship of power, which is why Mignolo and Walsh (2018) state that there are hidden forces of the colonial matrix of power, and for colonials to disentangle from colonial power, their decoloniality should seek to answer the critical questions of how, what, why, with whom and for what. Coloniality of the mind is aptly described by Fanon (2008) in the image of Black people who wear white masks to fit into the global norms of western civilisation and modernity. Decoloniality is therefore a consciousness and state of mind (Biko, 1978). Colonialism created an imbalance in the naming traditions characterised by the coloniser as the namer. Suffice it to note that after political freedom, inclinations towards colonial naming remain, as the former colonies suffer from coloniality of being, power and knowledge. Decoloniality is related to Africana *Existentia* as espoused by Gordon (2008), who describes it as the deep and painful thinking by people whose humanity has been doubted. It is not only the humanity of Africans that has been doubted by imperial power, but patriarchy doubts the humanity of women, ethnic majorities doubt the humanity of others, heterosexuals doubt the humanity of homosexuals, nationals doubt the humanity of foreigners and non-disabled people doubt the humanity of disabled people, and all these inhumanities are also expressed through names and naming.

## 1.3 Data and analysis

The chapters are generally qualitative, and the quantitative data are used to support qualitative arguments. The book is a descriptive and interpretive analysis of names. Rehman and Alharthi (2016, p. 56) state that 'interpretive researchers employ methods that generate qualitative data, and data collecting methods that yield qualitative data include open ended interviews in their various structures, observations, field notes, documents and discussions.' Borg and Gall (1989) posit that descriptive studies are aimed at finding out 'what is'; as a result, observations and surveys are generally used to collect descriptive data. Descriptive research designs use both qualitative and quantitative data; however, this book uses limited quantitative data, as it is predominantly qualitative. The names analysed in the chapters were collected through intuition, unstructured interviews, participant and nonparticipant observations and document analysis. Some of the data were collected through document analysis of literature relevant to the type of names discussed in the chapter and some through telephone interviews conducted with resource persons in 12 African countries. Google maps, atlases, newspapers, magazines, news networks, journals, dictionaries, encyclopaedia and books were sources of some names and their etymologies. Interviews were done with key informants on some names and their etymologies in the African countries of Zimbabwe, South Africa, Eswatini, Zambia, Malawi, Botswana, Senegal, Nigeria, Ivory Coast, Kenya and Gambia. The specific data are outlined in the individual chapters.

The names are analysed qualitatively to reveal their meanings and the intentions of the namers. This makes most of the discussions critical discourse analysis (CDA) of the names. To get the meaning and implications of the names, content, etymological, metaphor, semantic, linguistic landscape (LL) and phonological analyses are deployed within the confines of CDA. Discourse analysis (DA) focuses on the purposes and effects of different types of language. According to Johnstone (2017), DA is an open-ended set of techniques which include critical discourse analysis, which, according to Fairclough (2012), subsumes a variety of approaches to the social analysis of discourse. Johnstone (2017) demonstrates how discourse is shaped by the world, language, participants, prior discourse, medium and purpose and how discourse also shapes these factors in turn. Fairclough (2013, p. 35) argues that:

> CDA brings the critical tradition of social analysis into language studies and contributes to critical social analysis a particular focus on discourse and on relations between discourse and other social elements (power relations, ideologies, institutions, social identities, and so forth). Critical social analysis can be understood as normative and explanatory critique.

CDA is an interdisciplinary approach to the study of discourse. Fairclough (1995) establishes that non-linguistic social practice and linguistic practice constitute one another; he argues that power relations are established and reinforced through language use. The language is used for manipulation and exploitation in situations of power asymmetries. CDA is a methodology to extricate how discourse reproduces (or resists) social and political inequality, power abuse or domination, and names are part of the language used in situations of power asymmetries.

The history of the names is important for both semantic and areal analysis, and etymological analysis is employed as methodology to trace the origins and histories of names. Etymological analysis is the study of the origin of words, looking at historical formations and meaning. Svensen (1993, p. 189) defines etymological analysis and notes that 'information about the etymology of words tell us their history. Etymological facts lie along the time axis, and cut straight across the other information categories, . . . combining things and events outside language.' Looking at the historicity of names, Allan and Burridge (1991) observe that names immortalise historical evidence and become key reference points for future debates and discussions. Schadeberg (1989, p. 105) observes that 'people like to speculate about where their words come from and how they have changed.' He further suggests that 'this interest stems from the conviction that in the history of each word, there is hidden a tiny piece of the history of the community that speaks this language today.'

To determine the meanings and pragmatics of names, this book engages semantic, pragmatic and metaphor analyses. The book employs Altheide's (1987) ethnographic content analysis (ECA), which posits that meaning can be deduced from a text's format and positioning of information within the text. The emphasis is on describing and conceptualising data. In outlining a methodology for ECA, Altheide and Schneider (2013) note that researchers need to learn about the production process and context of texts and understand formatting and patterns of the text and imagery. They further argue that ECA is conceptually oriented rather than categorically oriented. ECA does not use data to tell stories but rather to expose the meaning and effects texts have through grounding them in the social world and social processes. Wimarth (2019) contends that content analysis is a research tool used to determine the presence of certain words or concepts within texts or sets of texts. Researchers quantify and analyse the presence, meanings and relationships of such words and concepts, then make inferences about the messages within the texts, the writer(s), the audience and even the culture and time of which these are a part. Krippendorff (1989, p. 403) argues that:

> Content analysis is indigenous to communication research and is potentially one of the most important research techniques in the social sciences. It seeks to analyse data within a specific context in view of the meanings someone – a group or a culture – attributes to them. Communications, messages, and symbols differ from observable events, things, properties, or people in that they inform about something other than themselves; they reveal properties of their distant producers or carriers, and they have cognitive consequences for their senders, their receivers, and the institutions in which their exchange is embedded.

In this book, names are analysed to reveal properties of both the name givers and bearers. The names demonstrate colonialities of power in the realms of colonialism, race, ethnicity, globalisation, disability, sexualities, gender, culture and cognition. Content analysis also caters to the analysis of the descriptive and expressive content in names and their cognitive effects. The meaning or lack of it in names can be affected by phonology; this makes phonological analysis important in analysing some names and their transphonologies. Phonological analysis of names, which reveals othering, looks at the process of transphonologisation, which can be intentional or unintentional mispronunciation of names by both coloniser and colonials (Ndlovu, 2017). The process can give away coloniality and decoloniality by looking at why the colonisers could not get indigenous names right and vice versa (Neethling, 2005; Du Plessis, 2009).

Names are also used in power relations to mark spaces and exclude other identities from space and concepts, such power asymmetries, which require an LL analysis. Names that are part of the public space are also analysed using LL. Landry and Bourhis (1997, p. 25) define the linguistic landscape as:

> The language of public road signs, advertising billboards, street names, place names, commercial shop signs, and public signs on government buildings combines to form the linguistic landscape of a given territory, region, or urban agglomeration.

LL is engaged in the analysis of names used to name space, because naming space is part of identifying with it and owning it (Ndlovu, 2018). Bruns (1984, p. 29) posits that 'Certainly it has always been understood that the world belongs to the one who names it.' Naming spaces, streets, buildings and institutions is one way societies commemorate their past struggles and victories, creating heritage from history. Light (2004, p. 154) concurs and claims:

> Those names which commemorate key events or personalities from a country's history are a manifestation of political order, and can be significant expressions of national identity with a powerful symbolic importance. They represent a particular view of the national past which is directly mapped onto urban geography.

Power dynamics play out in commemorative naming, and some identities are excluded from the onomastic heritage.

## 1.4 Organisation of this book

The book has eleven chapters. Chapter 1 is the introductory chapter, and Chapter 11 is composed of conclusions and recommendations. Chapters 2 to 10 are divided into three thematic sections, and each section has three chapters. Section One focuses on global colonialities in names that involve Africa in the areas of global politics and economy, culture and race relations. Chapter 2 analyses global names of spaces, countries and cooperation and how these self the West, East and North America while othering and undermining Africa. Chapter 3 juxtaposes African and Euro-American culture and demonstrates that names and naming are used to portray African culture as the inferior culture. The chapter draws names from ecological, social and material culture. Chapter 4 is dedicated to discussing ethnophaulisms. It addresses racial and ethnic slurs from global, regional and national perspectives. Section Two, comprising Chapters 5 to 7, focuses on colonial and decolonial onomastics in Africa. Chapter 5 analyses the names for White people in Africa and the colonial and anticolonial nuances in the names. Chapter 6 focuses on onomastic colonial attestations in Africa, looking at the names of countries, towns, streets, water bodies, currencies and churches. Chapter 7 is dedicated to the coloniality of African personal names and surnames and the coloniality of African naming conventions. Section Three, comprising chapters 8 to 10, is on political and social othering in Africa. The section deals with colonialities of power within the continent and individual states, focusing on patriarchy, sexualities and political exclusions. Chapter 8 addresses coloniality of gender in African names and naming, looking especially at political, economic and cultural representations of women and men in the LL. Chapter 9 addresses disablist, homophobic and sexist nomenclature in African languages and cultures, and Chapter 10 focuses on socio-political exclusions of some people and cultures in African commemorative naming.

## References


Allan, K., & Burridge, K. (1991). *Euphemism and dysphemism: Language used as shield and weapon*. Oxford University Press.

Altheide, D. L. (1987). Ethnographic content analysis. *Qualitative Sociology, 10*, 65–77.

Altheide, D. L., & Schneider, C. J. (2013). *Qualitative media analysis* (2nd ed.). Sage.

Barney, R. (2001). *Names and nature in Plato's Cratylus*. Routledge.

Bekerie, A. (2004). Ethiopica: Some historical reflections on the origin of the word Ethiopia. *International Journal of Ethiopian Studies*, 110–121. www.jstor.org/stable/27828841

Bhabha, H. K. (2003). Postmodernism/postcolonialism. In R. S. Nelson & R. Shiff (Eds.), *Critical terms for art history* (pp. 435–451). University of Chicago Press.

Bhatia, M. V. (2005). Fighting words: Naming terrorists, bandits, rebels and other violent actors. *Third World Quarterly, 26*(1), 5–22. https://doi.org/10.1080/0143659042000322874

Biko, S. (1978). *I write what I like: Selected writings*. University of Chicago Press.

Billig, M. (1973). Normative communication in a minimal intergroup situation. *European Journal of Social Psychology, 3*(3), 339–343. https://psycnet.apa.org/record/1975-07275-001

Borg, W. R., & Gall, M. (1989). *Education research: An introduction* (4th ed.). Longman Publisher.

Borkfelt, S. (2011). What's in a name? Consequences of naming non-human animals. *Animals, 1*(1), 116–125. https://doi.org/10.3390/ani1010116

Brons, L. L. (2015). Othering, an analysis. *Transcience, 6*(1), 69–90. https://philpapers.org/rec/BROOAA-4

Bruns, G. L. (1984). Language and power. *Chicago Review, 34*(2), 27–43.

Canales, M. K. (2000). Othering: Toward an understanding of difference. *Advances in Nursing Science, 22*(4), 16–31.

Çelik, A. B., Bilali, R., & Iqbal, Y. (2017). Patterns of "othering" in Turkey: A study of ethnic, ideological, and sectarian polarisation. *South European Society and Politics, 22*(2), 217–238.

Crang, M. (1998). *Cultural geography*. Routledge.

Darwish, I. (2010). Pre-peace and post-peace referring in Jordanian journalistic Arabic. *Names, 58*(4), 191–196.

De Beauvoir, S. (1949). *Le deuxième sexe*. Gallimard.

Du Plessis, T. (2009). Language visibility and the transformation of geographical names in South Africa. *Language Matters, 40*(2), 215–238.

Fairclough, N. (1995). *Media discourse*. Edward Arnold.

Fairclough, N. (2012). Critical discourse analysis. *International Scientific Researchers*, 7, 452–487.

Fairclough, N. (2013). Critical discourse analysis. In *The Routledge handbook of discourse analysis* (pp. 35–46). Routledge.

Fanon, F. (2008). *Black skin, white masks* (R. Wilcox, Trans.). Grove Press.

Fritsche, J. (2019). Aristotle's biological justification of slavery in politics I. *Rhizomata*, 7(1), 63–96.

Gilroy, P. (2004). *Between camps-nations, cultures and the allure of race*. Routledge.

Gordon, R. L. (2008). *An introduction to Africana philosophy*. Cambridge University Press.

Hall, E. T. (1959). *The silent language*. Fawcett.

Hegel, G. W. F. (1807). *Phänomenologie des Geistes*. Suhrkamp.

Hitchcock, P. (1993). The othering of cultural studies. *Third Text*, 7(25), 11–20.

Johnstone, B. (2017). *Discourse analysis*. John Wiley & Sons.

Kirby, P. R. (1954). Gquma, Mdepa and the Amatshomane clan: A by-way of miscegenation in South Africa. *African Studies*, *13*(1), 1–24.

Krippendorff, K. (1989). Content analysis. In E. Barnouw, G. Gerbner, W. Schramm, T. L. Worth, & L. Gross (Eds.), *International encyclopedia of communication* (pp. 403–407). Oxford University Press.

Lake, O. (2003). *Blue veins and kinky hair: Naming and color consciousness in African America*. Greenwood Publishing Group.

Landry, R., & Bourhis, R. Y. (1997). Linguistic landscape and ethnolinguistic vitality: An empirical study. *Journal of Language and Social Psychology*, *16*, 23–49.

Light, D. (2004). Street names in Bucharest, 1990–1997: Exploring the modern historical geographies of post-socialist change. *Journal of Historical Geography*, *30*(1), 154–172.

Loewe, M. (2016, November 21). Experts say uMlungu is not negative in meaning [correspondent]. *Dispatch Live*. www.dispatchlive.co.za/news/2016-11-21-experts-say-umlungu-is-not-negative-in-meaning/

Maldonado-Torres, N. (2016). *Outline of ten theses on coloniality and decoloniality*. Frantz Fanon Foundation.

Mangena, T., & Ndlovu, S. (2013). Decolonization-oriented naming of selected "satellite" schools in Zimbabwe. In O. Felecan (Ed.), *Names and naming: Onomastics in contemporary public space* (pp. 440–446). Editura Mega.

Martinot, S. (2011). *The coloniality of power: Notes toward de-colonization*. San Francisco State University. www.ocf.berkeley.edu/~marto/coloniality.htm#:~:text=The%20%22coloniality%20of%20power%22%20is,the%20Americas%20to%20the%20present

Matson, J. N. (1956). History in Akan words: Transactions of the Gold Coast & Togoland. *Historical Society*, *2*(2), 63–70.

McNeill, W. (1997). What we mean by the West. *Orbis*, *41*(4), 513–524.

Mendoza, B. (2015). Coloniality of gender and power: From postcoloniality to decoloniality. In L. Disch & M. Hawkesworth (Eds.), *The Oxford handbook of feminist theory* (pp. 100–121). Oxford University Press.

Mignolo, W. D., & Walsh, C. E. (2018). *On decoloniality: Concepts, analytics, praxis*. Duke University Press.

Mignolo, W. D. (2001). Coloniality of power and subalternity. In I. Rodríguez (Ed.), *The Latin American subaltern studies reader* (pp. 424–445). Duke University Press.

Mpofu, W. (2017). *Decoloniality as travelling theory: Or what decoloniality is not*. Retrieved June 22, 2020, from https://wiser.wits.ac.za/system/files/seminar/Mpofu2017.pdf

Nabudere, D. W. (2011). *Afrikology, philosophy and wholeness: An epistemology*. Africa Institute of Africa.

Ndlovu, S. (2017). Transphonologisation as ethnophaulism between the Ndebele and the Shona of Zimbabwe in selected toponyms and ethnonyms. *Nomina Africana: Journal of African Onomastics*, *31*(2), 117–125.

Ndlovu, S. (2018). Characterisation and social impact of urban youth languages on urban toponymy: S'ncamtho toponomastics in Bulawayo. *Literator (Potchefstroom. Online)*, *39*(1), 1–7.

Ndlovu, S., & Mangena, T. (2014). Articulations of "othering" through ethnic names and naming: Selected Zimbabwean cases. *Nomina Afrikana*, *28*(2), 75–82.

Ndlovu-Gatsheni, S. J. (2013). *Coloniality of power in postcolonial Africa*. African Books Collective.

Ndlovu-Gatsheni, S. J. (2015). Decoloniality as the future of Africa. *History Compass*, *13*(10), 485–496.

Neethling, B. (2005). *Naming among the Xhosa of South Africa*. Edwin Mellen Press.

Nhemachena, A. (2016). Animism, coloniality and humanism: Reversing the empire's framing of Africa. In M. Mawere & A. Nhemachena (Eds.), *Theory, knowledge and politics: What role for the academy in the sustainability of Africa* (pp. 13–54). Langaa RPCIG.

Okello, B. (2020). What's in a name? Reinventing Luo naming system in Kenya's ethnopolitical landscape. *African Identities*, *19*(1), 77–90. https://doi.org/10.1080/14725843.2020.1791687

Quijano, A. (2007). Coloniality and modernity/rationality. *Cultural Studies*, *21*(2–3), 168–178.

Rehman, A. A., & Alharthi, K. (2016). An introduction to research paradigms. *International Journal of Educational Investigations*, *3*(8), 51–59.

Richardson, J. S. (1991). Imperium Romanum: Empire and the language of power. *The Journal of Roman Studies*, *81*, 1–9.

Said, E. (2004). Orientalism once more. *Development and Change*, *35*(5), 869–879.

Schadeberg, T. C. (1989, November 7–8). *Historical inferences from Swahili etymologies*. Unwritten Testimonies of the Past, Proceedings of the International Symposium, Ojrzanów n. Warshaw. www.afrykanistyka.uw.edu.pl/pliki/files/publikacje/12_schadeberg.pdf

Strani, K., & Szczepaniak-Kozak, A. (2018). Strategies of othering through discursive practices: Examples from the UK and Poland. *Lodz Papers in Pragmatics*, *14*(1), 163–179.

Svensen, B. (1993). *Principles and methods of dictionary making*. Oxford University Press.

Tajfel, H. (1974). Social identity and intergroup behaviour. *Social Science Information*, *13*, 65–93.

Wimarth, P. (2019). *Content analysis*. Retrieved July 10, 2021, from www.umsl.edu/~wilmarthp/mrpc-web-resources/content-analysis.pdf

Section One

# Global, cultural and ethnophaulic nomen othering of Africa

# 2 Africa and global onomastic othering dichotomies

## 2.0 Introduction

Cartographical cardinal points and qualitative and quantitative grading scales deployed globally as nomen references to space are in fact realisations of the centre-periphery dichotomy. History has been shaped and is shaping the gradings, and the centre remains in Europe and the United States, with some countries being qualified or disqualified to join these centres. Direction, industry and commerce and numerical grades are used as names to refer to geopolitical spaces as means of distinguishing and separating global regions. Naming can be used to divide people. Foucault (1980) observes that mechanisms of power and its capillary existence seep into people; permeate their culture; and shape how they speak, live and work with other people. Edelman (1977) states that names can be used to make status distinctions and reinforce ideologies. The world has been divided between East and West; North and South; Left and Right; developed, developing and underdeveloped, and these divisions are not physical but ideological. Mestrovic (2004), for example, posits that the boundaries between East and West are cultural rather than geographical; this explains why Australia, which is geographically in the East, is grouped in the West, and all Muslim countries can only be East.

Scholars have argued that globalisation and spatial restructuring have eliminated the structural divide between the First and Third worlds (Hardt & Negri, 2000; Hoogvelt, 1997). Arrighi et al. (2003, p. 3) opine that 'global restructuring in the early 1990s collapsed the Second world,' and they speak of the First and Third worlds as former designations of an economic structure which has since been overtaken by global financial and industrial restructuring. Amsden (2001) also characterises the closing of the economic divide between First, Second and Third worlds as 'The rise of the rest', while Burbach and Robinson (1999, p. 27) argue that 'worldwide convergence, through the global restructuring of capitalism, means that the geographic breakdown of the world into North-South, core-periphery or First and Third worlds, while still significant, is diminishing in importance.' They believe geopolitical polarisation to be on the decline at the global level. Hoogvelt (1997, p. 145) concurs by stating that the core-periphery discourse 'is becoming a social relationship, and no longer

DOI: 10.4324/9781003170761-3

a geographical one.' However, while economists may argue that the divide is narrowing or has narrowed for some countries, the ideology and the names remain. The names are not just remnants of a former unequal development, but reality points to current inequalities. Arguing that First and Third world are obsolete categories, Harris (1986, p. 200) notes that 'Those notions bore some relationship to an older economy, one marked by the exchange of raw materials for manufacturing goods.' In the case of Africa, the exchange of raw materials with the so-called First world is still the norm, and it is now even worse because those formerly or presently in the Second world category are also courting Africa for its resources and not industrialising it. Claims of a change of global exploitative structures are, in my view, centre economic rhetoric to pacify and justify continued 'peripherising' of Africa. Whether economists in the idealised centre or its periphery downplay the symbolic effects of these labels or not, it is evident that these names are problematic referents and symbols. McFarlane (2006) concurs that the validity of categories such as First and Third world or North and South has been increasingly questioned. He calls for a consistent interrogation of the epistemic and institutional basis and implications of the North-South divide.

Said (1993, p. 28) alludes to a pervasive 'Eurocentric and totalising view' of the world. He imagines the West and America as a whale and Whites as insiders to the whale and the rest outside. Wa Thiongo (1993) sees this proverbial whale as the imperial centre of the world, which should be deconstructed and moved to various points and regions to create a variety of centres. McNeill (1997, p. 524) advises that:

> insofar as a concept of the West excludes the rest of humanity, it is a false and dangerous model. Situating the West within the totality of humankind is the way to go, and we should in our classrooms move as best we can in that direction.

Lacerda et al. (2020, p. 4) also argue that 'the division North versus South results from an abstraction that should be repelled with the denial, but to some extent also acceptance, of universal standards that animate situated behaviour.' However, reactionary scholarship to the global metropoles in Europe and North America also uses the same problematic labels to create names for their theories, such as Southern Theory (Connell, 2007) and the Global South and North (Mignolo, 2008). Levander and Mignolo (2011, p. 1) observe that recent literature 'collectively suggests that the term "Global South" seems to be a new and powerful ordering system for academic disciplines as well as for geographies, politics, and cultures.' However, it remains problematic to still use imperial cartography symbols to label global inequalities, even when you are in fact trying to fight the inequalities.

This chapter deploys the theory of coloniality, southern theory and postcolonial theory to critique global nomenclature as used to refer to spaces on the globe, in politics, sociology, economics, history and other fields which use geopolitical designations for global spaces and nations. These theories are deployed within the framework of othering theory and Orientalism. Using critical discourse analysis and etymological analysis, the chapter aims to investigate the meanings and implications of toponyms in global geopolitics. The chapter also uses metaphor analysis to analyse the associations people conjure up when they hear the names. The study was motivated by the glaring otherness and self in names used on global regions and the current efforts to deal with global inequalities. While theorists have tried to fight imperial inequalities, they tend to fail when it comes to naming their theories and naming inequalities within their theories. Names appear to be a powerful tool of coloniality, and they perpetuate social, economic and political subalternity. The names were collected through document analysis, and the documents consisted of literature on global politics, development, economics and social studies. The names are analysed thematically along the themes of cartography, grading and enumeration. The analysis answers the question of whether these names are geographical and referential or they communicate more than what they ordinarily mean.

## 2.1 Globalised directional selfing and othering onoma

People and their spaces have been referred to from certain points of cartography on the globe. Jolly (2008) states that North and South, just like West and East, uneasily connect geographical cardinal points with geopolitical potencies. The starting point of contention is: to whose south and whose east?, for example. Calling global regions using cardinal points of cartography assumes a central self, pointing to others in relation to their direction from the centre. This section analyses the toponyms North, South, East, West, Far East, Middle East, Global North and South and sub-Saharan to expose their imperial othering and selfing innuendoes. The section also looks at the othering and selfing implications and practices in the ergonyms Left and Right of the political spectrum.

### *2.1.1 The East-West dichotomy*

Global space and culture are imagined along the East-West dichotomy. McNeill (1997, p. 514) traces the origins of the East-West dichotomy and alludes to the fact that:

> The birth of a concept of a West as opposed to an East can be dated exactly to events that occurred on either side of the Aegean Sea in the years 480 and 479 B.C. That may seem exceedingly strange – to wit, that the West of Anglo-French imagination sprang from a Persian imperial invasion of Greece.

The animosity and othering originate from the East's imperial aggression to its West, creating the directional self East and its other the West. This history can help explain why the West of Asia loathes Asian culture and has over the years attempted to dominate Asia, pathologised and orientalised everything Asian as eastern uncivilisation so as to create a civilised self to the West of Asia. According to Jolly (2008), the Euro-America metropoles have always seen parts of Asia and the Middle East as rival loci of civilisations. The East–West dichotomy was consummated during Europe's domination of global geopolitics through imperialism, colonialism and empire. The imperial feuding between Asia and Europe has become global categories which include Africa and other centres far outside the Eurasia east-west cartography.

Europe uses the toponym East to designate inferior environs and culture. Said (1995, p. 71) links this inferiorisation of the East to Othered colonial race relations whereby there is 'an imagined geography separating the Orient from the West.' The Orient is an alien, while the European is a global autochthon. Through colonialism, Europe designated self to itself and othered the rest, starting with its East. Ndlovu and Mangena (2014, p. 76) aver that 'the Orient is projected as Europe's "other"; the colonised subject. The colonised are orientalised for purposes of justifying such domination.' The concept West was recreated in imperial Europe and North America to reference the global selves, and the rest are grouped together using cultural and development scales as part of the East and the rest. Ironically, the east of Europe includes some spaces to its west, and some to its east are graded and qualified to be to the west. Mestrovic (2004) states that the West now has three categories; the core, the marginal and the area of western influence. The core consists of western Europe, Australia, New Zealand, the United States and Canada, while the marginal west consists of Eastern Europe, Latin America, the Caribbean and South Africa. Areas of western influence include most African countries. This malleability and manipulation of fixed cardinal points indicates that they are used as tags for selfing and othering, not for indicating physical direction. In Africa, South Africa, which is a haven for White supremacy as remnants of apartheid, and of course much more developed than the rest of the continent according to capitalist grading scales, is uprooted from the continent and transplanted to the imagined western development. The East connotes segregated Europe's other, Hayward (2020, p. 281) argues that concepts of west, rest, race and culture have been used to explain human difference from a western world view. 'All of these concepts are implicated in the hierarchical and segregationist worldviews and policies that have shaped and legitimised colonialism.' The East is a category or toponym for othering by Europe; this is evidenced by the fact that there is Middle East and Far East. These classes of East are in relation to Europe as the namer and self actor in global geopolitics.

While physical blocking of the northern hemisphere into East and West may appear to have subsided with the end of the Cold War, Tuathail and Luke (1994) observe the emergence of new mental geographical divisions, dividing the tame West from the wild and violent East. Moderation and reason are imbued to the West, while fanaticism and unreason are held to characterise the East; this is clearly a continuation of imperial dichotomy (Ignatieff, 1997). The east is where the sun rises, and it sets in the west. This natural terrestrial order seems to explain the progression of civilisation and development. It would appear from social practice that civilisation may have started in the East and was fulfilled or it matured in the West. Like the sun, development and civilisation move towards the West. McNeill (1997, p. 513) reasons thus:

> The first and most obvious point to make is that the meaning of the West is a function of who is using the word. Those who feel themselves to be part of the West – who think of the West as 'we' – will surely have flattering things to say about their civilization. Those who think of the West as the 'other' are likely to define it in less flattering terms. The basic meaning of the word is 'where the sun sets' – one of the cardinal directions.

The world is now divided into East and West, with the West believing in its superiority and civility, while the East challenges this position for equality or even turning the tables of power. The Orient is linked to 'unchristian' violent extremism of Islamist militants in the mould of Al-Qaida, Elshabab and Boko Haram. This also others Islam as a dominant religion of Europe's East. While this chapter cannot condone violence, suffice it to note that these terrorists are fighting empire, albeit using unorthodox means, assuming of course that they have not exhausted all orthodox means. In the case of Africa, the East-West tensions indicate an exclusion from global politics, Africa is the insignificant other in the global schemes and can only join the West when developed and cultured enough or join the East in its fight for equality with the West.

African countries have been identified with the West as areas of western influence through colonialism. The period of the Cold War gifted the East with an opportunity to 'buy' Africa through military support during the anti-colonial wars of the 1950s, 60s and 70s. This created an eastern influence in Africa. While East is now an African term for anti-empire, strategically othering the West, East itself is becoming empire. We need to examine the position of the East regarding Africa and the western whale. Ndlovu-Gatsheni (2020, p. 57) reasons thus:

> The post-1945 dispensation was not only entangled in politics of fake political decolonisation (flag independence and neo-colonialism) but with what is here termed Cold War coloniality, which polarised Africans ideologically and reduced the continent to a theatre of proxy hot wars. This is another important epoch that witnessed an Africa that was entrapped in a global ideological warfare that decimated any of the African authentic political and economic formulations and creations.

Africa needs to ask questions such as: Is the East still part of the West's periphery, or does it now stand as a self, othering Africa and the rest? Is Africa safe from the West inside the East? Are we part of the East against the West, or we are in between empires? Are we othered by one empire or both? As Africans celebrate the East as a category that opposes the western self, they should ask these pertinent questions about the eastern countries; for example: Do Chinese love Africa, and, if so, why? Do Russians love Africa, and, if so, since when and until when? Do Indians love Africa, and, if so, which ones? Does the Arab world love Africa, and, if so, which Africa? Europe's East has enticed Africa to other Europe by identifying with the East through global formations such as Brazil, Russia, India, China and South Africa (BRICS). South Africa supposedly represents Africa. However, the East dominating BRICS's vision for Africa is aptly described by Taylor (2014) as diversifying dependency. It is critical for Africa not to be drawn into East-West othering, as it is neither their east or west. Santos (2007, p. 78) states that:

> In search for alternatives to domination and oppression, how can we distinguish between alternatives to the system of oppression and domination and alternatives within the system or, more specifically, how do we distinguish between alternatives to capitalism and alternatives within capitalism? In sum, how do we fight against the abyssal lines using conceptual and political instruments that do not reproduce them?

Those fighting for the marginalised people, Africa included, have come up with names which they think replace imperial nomenclature or fight it, such as the Global South (Mignolo, 2008). Levander and Mignolo (2011) even argue that Global South as a tag and concept replaces Third World and reduces tensions between the East and the West. Africa has been used as a stepping stone to empire by the East, and the development of the East does not make Africa part of its improvement towards empire. The East now uses Africa as the appended other in its fight against its namer, the West.

### *2.1.2 The left-right political spectrum*

The east-west discourse is similar to the left-right political spectrum. While the political spectrum originates in the French parliament, it now fits well into the development discourses that other Africa and other people facing unequal treatment around the globe. According to Bobbio (1996), the designations left and right appeared during the French revolution in 1789. He states that those who supported the king sat to the right of the speaker of the assembly and those who supported the revolution to his left. The left is identified with uncivil behaviour from the institution of the left-right political spectrum, while the right epitomises civility and order. Hodgson (2018, p. 7) quotes one deputy president of the French Assembly as saying:

> We began to recognise each other: those who were loyal to religion and the king took up positions to the right of the chair so as to avoid the shouts, oaths, and indecencies that enjoyed free rein in the opposing camp.

From this etymology, the left is linked to the East in the East-West dichotomy; to be called left or leftist, is to be crudely othered as uncivilised, indecent and misbehaving, while those on the right wing are the epitome of western civility.

For some strange or maybe obvious reasons, the left, as opposed to the right, is the place of Africa and Africans in western and American politics. Africa and people of colour belong to the left, not the right; this makes White right and Colour left (wrong). Freire and Kivistik (2013) contend that left-right politics developed from an incident in the French Assembly during the French revolution, and since then the designations have characterised mass politics, starting in the West and spreading to other parts of the globe. They compare left-right politics globally and observe that in the West, the right is characterised by an affinity for support for law and order, traditional values, individual initiatives, privatisation, reduced taxes and materialism. On the other hand, they identify the left as characterised by defence for civil liberties, individual liberties such as the right to abortion, religious liberty, equal distribution of wealth, public ownership, improved public services and citizen participation. The left's inclinations within the African-American population in US politics other them as a lower class which is fighting the centre for equality. The right is an expression of self-indulgence and a realisation of social Darwinism whereby the state is not supposed to interfere with economic and social structures but leave them be. Kinder and Winter (2001) concur that in the United States, Blacks and Whites differ systematically and substantially because of class difference, political principles, social identity and audience. Here, social circumstances shape political ideology and choices. They indicate that the majority of Blacks in the United States identify with left-wing political ideologies.

It is common to see 'people of colour' (whatever that really means) supporting right-wing politics in Europe and North America because political choices are mutable. Carmines et al. (2012, p. 1633) argue that 'there is still significant disagreement among researchers as to whether partisan identification is a stable, unwavering belief or whether it is a mutable attitude that responds to changing circumstances.' Some scholars argue that allegiance to the left or the right is inculcated by parents in their children, remains remarkably stable throughout a person's life and shapes their political choices (Goren, 2004; Rahn, 1993). Some opine that left-right allegiances are mutable as influenced by political and economic changes and incidents such as scandals (Lockerbie, 2002; Bassili, 1995). Whatever individuals may choose or be manipulated to choose does not alter the argument of this chapter, that Rightwing politics is White supremacist and pro empire while Leftwing politics identifies with non-Whites and their global spaces and choices. Wiesehomeier and Doyle (2012) argue that we label political parties as left or right because they communicate their policies publicly. The policies they communicate clearly help others name them as right (White supremacy and empire) or left (the oppressed subjects of empire).

The political spectrum helps name people and ideas according to their attitude towards global inequalities. Jahn (2011) opines that positioning people and parties on the left or the right is based on political theory and philosophy, the key philosophy being the attitudes towards inequality. Bobbio (1996) argues that the left and the right both acknowledge the presence of inequality but treat it differently. Luna and Kaltwasser (2011, p. 6) characterise the political spectrum thus:

> The left is a political position which is characterised by the idea that the main inequalities between the people are artificial and thus seeks to overcome them by active state involvement. The right is a political position which is distinguished by the belief that the main inequalities between people are natural and outside the purview of the state.

The right's ideas on inequality are informed by ideologies of social Darwinism and White supremacy. The concepts left and right create sensations of power and disempowerment. In the body habitus, the right is imagined as having power over the left, since the majority of people are right-handed. This creates implications of being labelled powerless through the name left wing; this is true from the ideologies of left-wing politicians, because they are fighting for power, an indication that they are powerless, while the right is fighting to retain the power. Coincidences between the etymology of the left-right political spectrum and images of divine power in Judeo-Christian theology are conspicuous. Those on the right of the president of the French Assembly voted for Christianity and the power of the king, and in the Judeo-Christian Bible, the position of power is at the right hand of the deity. The name left wing on the political spectrum denotes the powerless political other, who seeks advancement towards the self on the right of the political spectrum. The names are not mere coincidences from the French parliament denoting physical sides of debate, but they denote the selves and others of global inequalities.

### *2.1.3 The North-South dichotomy*

In physical and social geography, the designations north and south refer to positions above and below the zero-degree line of latitude, the equator, respectively. However, in socio-political and developmental discourses, the relations between the North and the South create imageries of 'topia', utopia being the Global North and the Global South its dystopia. The South becomes a heterotopia of deviation for the North (Foucault, 1967) a place where people with behaviour outside the norm are found (kept). McNeill (1997, p. 516) concurs that the West has been idealised as the topia and the East its undesired dystopia when he says:

> In time, of course, an overlay of Christianity obscured the older megalithic cultures of Western Europe, but the dream of the West as a sort of heaven, the place one goes to escape the crowding, pain, and heartaches of mortal life in an imperfect East, lived on.

It would appear the East-West tensions of the northern hemisphere find a solution in diverting the civil and equality discourse to another dichotomy, which may unite these centres, and this dichotomy is the North-South dichotomy. The North is the economic and development self, and the South denotes the underdeveloped global spaces. Arrighi et al. (2003, p. 23) have observed that:

> The reproduction of the North-South income divide since 1960 has been based on two main mechanisms, one structural and one ideological. The structural mechanism consists of the tendency of profit-oriented innovations in the organisation of economic life to polarise space into zones of more or less permanent prosperity and zones of more or less permanent depression.

According to Lopez (2007, p. v), 'South becomes those parts of the world that have experienced the most political, social, and economic upheaval, and which have suffered the brunt of the greatest challenges, facing the world under globalisation.' Sparke (2007) envisages the North as equivalent to the capitalist elite class and South as equivalent to marginalised groups of people. Race relations, colonial power and money structures are infused in the toponyms North and South to create a rich North and a poor South. In his analysis of the name for White people in East Africa *(Mzungu),* Spitzer (2014, p. 1) argues:

> In my view, the term Mzungu is not racist, but it is certainly linked to both historical and contemporary relations between 'North' and 'South', between colonialists and those who were colonised, between Europeans and Africans. In this perspective, Mzungu can also denote a label for somebody who represents wealth, knowledge and power.

North and South map onto European and African, coloniser and colonised, powerful and powerless, rich and poor, respectively. The body habitus of north and south naturalises oppression of the South by the North. The North maps onto the head, which thinks and eats, while the South maps onto the limbs, which do the work to feed the head. Jolly (2008) concurs that our embodied associations of up and down help create the meaning of North and South as used to describe geopolitical phenomena. Such a metaphor creates superiority based on location, and it is true that high is the opposite of low and they both map onto North and South, respectively. The centre has created the dichotomy of North and South which resonates with high and low and maps onto the bodily habitus of head and limbs. The metaphors ironically describe what obtains today in global geopolitics: there is a conscious grading scheme that elevates some Southern spaces to the North because they bear the character of the North as opposed to that of the South. Africa is further divided along social and physical habitus of sub-; here, that under development is named sub-Saharan, which means below the Sahara Desert. The image of Africa as below a desert creates a hopeless place worse than a desert in the eyes of those in the Northern centre. They are looking at Africa from above the desert, and only South Africa has managed to emerge above the desert of development in sub-Saharan Africa.

The physical position of South being under the North is itself a problematic binary. The symbolism is telling, and the campus metaphor maps the South as 'under'. The symbolism of the South being under translates to its underdevelopment, and the North is the development above the underdeveloped south. Social practice confirms that the names North and South are not physical locatives depicting binary latitudes but socially constructed development indices to other Africa and other non-centre spaces. Countries like Australia which are latitudinally in the South but do not fit into the othered, underdeveloped South are elevated into the North. Countries in the physical north in Asia and the Middle East which do not fit into the Western centre model of self are demoted to the 'under' South. The North and South are not global locatives juxtaposed by lines of latitude but names fashioned by Euro-American ideology of northern supremacy and the southern other. The Euro-American metropoles of power have devised an un-cartographical formula of defining and designating global directionality along the North-South dichotomy, as exemplified in Figure 2.1.

North = + development +/– north, while South = – development +/– south

Therien (1999) discusses the North-South divide as a synonym for rich-poor and haves-have nots. He analyses the impact of globalisation on this divide and observes two competing paradigms, the Bretton Woods and the United Nations paradigms, the former arguing that the gaps are narrowing, while the later claims they are widening. The North-South divide has been used to denote rich and

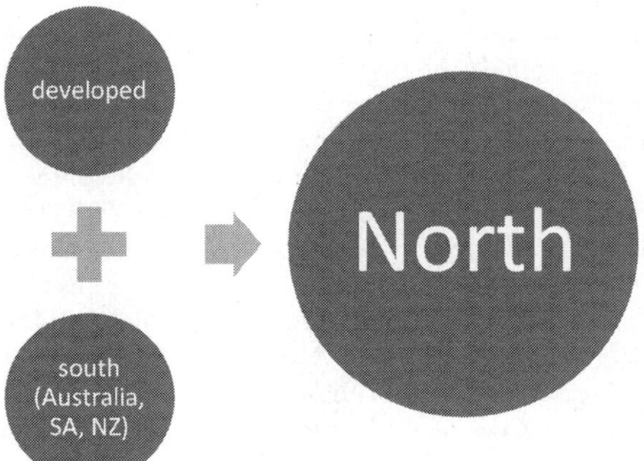


*Figure 2.1* The development factor in the naming of Global North countries

poor, respectively, in some local spaces within the centre. Martin (1988) observes that, up to 1970, England was itself divided into the industrialised and rich North and the poor, less-developed South, although this changed after 1970. The concept of a rich North and a poor South appears to have been constructed within empire and spread throughout the world. South is just another name for the other countries perceived to be different from Europe and North America. Levander and Mignolo (2011, p. 3) define the Global South as:

> not an existing entity to be described by different disciplines, but an entity that has been invented in the struggle and conflicts between imperial global domination and emancipatory and decolonial forces that do not acquiesce with global designs. Thus, it is well known – to start with – that 'Global South' is the geopolitical concept replacing 'Third World' after the collapse of the Soviet Union. From this perspective, the global South is the location of underdevelopment and emerging nations that needs the 'support' of the global North (G7, IMF, World Bank, and the like).

While the Global South can and may appear to be a collection of countries fighting for equality, the name positions them as opposites, not opponents, of empire. Pagel et al. (2014) posit that the Global South is presented in literature as being rural, chaotic, problematic and backward, while, on the other hand, the Global North is presented as urbanised, orderly and well planned. They further identify regions in Asia, Africa, Latin America and the Middle East as characterised under the Global South, and countries in the European Union, North America, Japan, Australia, New Zealand and South Africa are counted to be in the Global North. Naming of social and political theory aimed at tackling global inequalities has itself relied on the very same othered taxonomies. Connell (2007) rallies social science scholarship in the former colonies to fight for the knowledge of these places which was erased by imperial histories. However, she calls this theoretical fight for global equality the Southern Theory, falling into the very same imperial labelling. Jolly (2008) hazards that we need to reflect on the effects of our naming of global inequalities; she condemns Connell's (2007) labels of North and South, centre and periphery in her espousing of the Southern Theory. She further opines that using cardinal points of cartography to describe global inequalities naturalises and dehistoricises them and maps them to the body habitus of up and down, left and right. The designations North and South are imperially poisoned chalices which anti-empire scholarship is still using. The connotations and denotations of South are enough evidence to prove that the name is used crudely to other those on the disadvantaged side of global inequalities.

## 2.2 Names as global grades of self and other

While the use of cartographical cardinal points to name global spaces is clearly euphemistic for some meanings beyond the campus points, the use of grading descriptors is more direct. Development is the central theme in names given to the imagined centre and its periphery. However, the developed-developing country dichotomy is problematic and has been described as flawed (Neuwirth, 2020). The United Nations (UN), through its Creative Economy Reports, uses the developed-developing country dichotomy, and this is questioned by De Beukelaer (2014, p. 232), who proposes that 'a more correct, balanced, and disaggregated outlook on the classification of countries is needed.' He further alludes to the category Least Developed Countries as used in UN economic reports, which is a case of othering some countries using the fetish of development scales and indicators. Blaut (1993) advises that all human beings have equal capabilities, and there is psychological unity in all cultures and regions. Given these universal qualities of human civilisation, any inequalities have to be explained. This section analyses global names assigned to countries based on imagined or real development scales and how these names expose the othered nature of global development. The section argues that development is realised through lifestyles, industrialisation, technology and economic and military might and that these are harnessed to create nomenclature that creates power distinctions between world countries, and Africa is on the other side of global power, while Europe and North America are on the self side of power. The names are divided between those that describe development or lack of it and those that enumerate development into quantitative groupings of the selves to the exclusion of others.

### *2.2.1 The development scale in naming global space*

The United Nations (2010) acknowledges that:

> There is no established convention for the designation of 'developed' and 'developing' countries or areas in the United Nations system. In common practice, Japan in Asia, Canada and the United States in Northern America, Australia and New Zealand in Oceania, and Europe are considered 'developed' regions or areas.

Already, in a world of over 200 countries, only a few are elevated to the name 'developed', leaving the rest to lower nomen designations. Wackernagel and Rees (1998) observe that the developed-developing country dichotomy is not reflective of socio-political reality but thoughtless and destructive endorsement of gross domestic product (GDP) fetish. They argue for individual classification of countries because each has its own ways of dealing with reality. The underdeveloped and developing worlds are so named to indicate the problems they face and create of themselves. Development is stretched to include industrialisation, technological advancement and economic and weaponised power. The weaponisation of power culminates in nuclear power and weaponry being used to name and separate countries. Gusterson (1999, p. 114) posits, 'thus in western discourse nuclear weapons are represented so that "theirs" are a problem whereas "ours" are not.'

The developed country as a concept can be replaced with its synonyms such as industrialised country and advanced country. To show the othering nature of these categories, other names for developed and developing countries are more developed/advanced/economically developed and less/least developed/advanced/economically developed countries, respectively. A developed country is imagined to fit into the Global North, the West and the First World, while the developing country is its opposite. Developing and underdeveloped countries are spaces of the other human being who battles with daily problems which the self in the developed countries has overcome. To develop is to overcome problems affecting the developing and underdeveloped countries, and these problems include physical, social, political and intellectual ones. Steffen et al. (1987) associate developing countries with disease as they outline health problems which affect people of the developed world after visiting developing countries; they use Greece as a developed country control in their experiment. In similar manner, Hill (2000) researches health problems posed by developing countries to American travellers, while Chudi (2010) characterises developing countries as wrought with health care problems. The countries are also associated with problems in the agricultural sector (Baloch & Thapa, 2019), problems in their urbanisation (Van der Bruggen et al., 2010), economic problems (Eshag, 1983), problems of safety and governance (Chen et al., 2020) and problems of poverty (Grindle, 2004).

The self designation through development has created further dynamics of power and over-powering based on economic and military might. In a state of over-industrialisation, some countries have come openly to name themselves as having power over others through names such as superpower. Huntington (1999) reasons that a superpower exerts its influence on a global scale; to achieve this influence, these superpower countries combine military, diplomatic, economic, cultural and technological strength. The term superpower appeared during the Second World War (WW2) referring to the United States, the Soviet Union and Britain in recognition of their military might in overpowering their war opponents to end WW2. The superpower countries are the selves of the world, who get others to do what they want and stop others from doing what they want; they dominate the other economically and in many other ways. Subramanian (2011, p. 67) states that:

> Broadly speaking, economic dominance is the ability of a state to use economic means to get other countries to do what it wants or to prevent them from forcing it to do what it does not want. Such means include the size of a country's economy, its trade, the health of its external and internal finances, its military prowess, its technological dynamism, and the international status that its currency enjoys.

The superpower discourse is linked to superior weaponry. Africa and other spaces have been excluded from this military might, and the exclusion is evident in the naming of those with superior weapons. Nuclear power politics further divided the world into self and othered countries and regions. Gusterson (1999, p. 112) alludes to 'nuclear orientalism', whereby 'Western alarmism about the dangers of nuclear weapons in Third World hands was particularly evident when India and Pakistan set off their salvos of nuclear tests in May 1998.' The nuclear powers police other countries insofar as nuclear weapons and power are concerned so as to maintain their stranglehold on global power dynamics.

The selection of spaces on the globe and grouping them according to certain variables of selfing has been extended to Africa in a manner which divides the continent into global selves and others. South Africa, for example, is in league with other countries; Brazil, Russia, India and China, and other African countries are excluded from the acronym and the association BRICS. In defining BRICS, the Brazilian presidency (2019) states that 'BRICS is the group composed by the five major emerging countries; Brazil, Russia, India, China and South Africa, which together represent about 42% of the population, 23% of GDP, 30% of the territory and 18% of the global trade.' The name and what it stands for are a confrontation of the western self and centre; however, BRICS itself others Africa as not developing or at least not developed up to the stage of acceptance into this emerging middle self. BRICS furthers the gap between Africa and the West, creating a lower standard for Africa which ironically Africa still cannot reach. Semanticisation of the guiding concept in BRICS, 'emerging', creates problems for Africa, as drowning or being buried is implied. If BRICS is emerging, who is outside to witness the emergence? Obvious, the West, so BRICS is emerging out of the abyss Africa is still in, into the light of the West. Africa therefore experiences graded othering, first from BRICS, which is now better, and then from the West, which itself is far better than BRICS. The two-tiered effects of othering on Africa are such that it is first othered by the West together with BRICS for being below the West's standard and later othered by BRICS for failing to 'emerge', where BRICS, which includes an African country, emerged.

Categorising BRICS as emerging implies submersion of those countries which are not graded among the emerging BRICS. The terminology creates othering categories of the underworld of development (Africa and other 'poor' countries), the ground level of development (BRICS) and the heaven of development (Europe and the United States of America). BRICS does not solve the otherness of Africa but in fact worsens it. Ndlovu-Gatsheni (2014, p. 192) notes that:

> The entry of China, Russia, Brazil and India on the African market has boosted this sale of primary commodities. There is no change of the forms of integration of Africa into the ever-evolving capitalist economy, making the notion of 'Africa Rising' to exist as slogan trumpeted by benefitting global corporations. Such blocs as BRICS (Brazil, Russia, India,

China, and South Africa) are not about radical change of the world system and its global orders.

The development grades are clearly in three layers: the underdeveloped, the developing and the apex developed countries, and all these hinge on global development scales. The three layers of development are in relation to the centre, creating the centre periphery dimensions. Figure 2.2 illustrates the three layers of development used in global nomenclature and their characteristics in relation to the centre.

The significant progress made by the so-called developed countries in problem solving was and is based on creating problems for others. The developing countries in the mould of China and Russia are also solving their problems by creating more problems for Africa. The control of global markets gifts the so-called developed world with the opportunity to manipulate others through economic and military might, giving rise to the superpower terminology. The superpower discourse serves to name power and disempower those outside the scope of the name. It is a category that concentrates global power in a name and creates world power boundaries which are not accessible to Africa. Using economy, development scales and military force, the name superpower strategically excludes all African countries. The name superpower is imbued with fear to create the name nuclear power. The category nuclear power deploys intimidation as an othering strategy to exclude those without the intimidating resource (nuclear weapons) and creates a league of those who can destroy the other worlds. Gusterson (1999, p. 111) quotes Dan Quayle, US vice president 1988–92, as saying 'Think . . . what the world would be like if Saddam Hussein

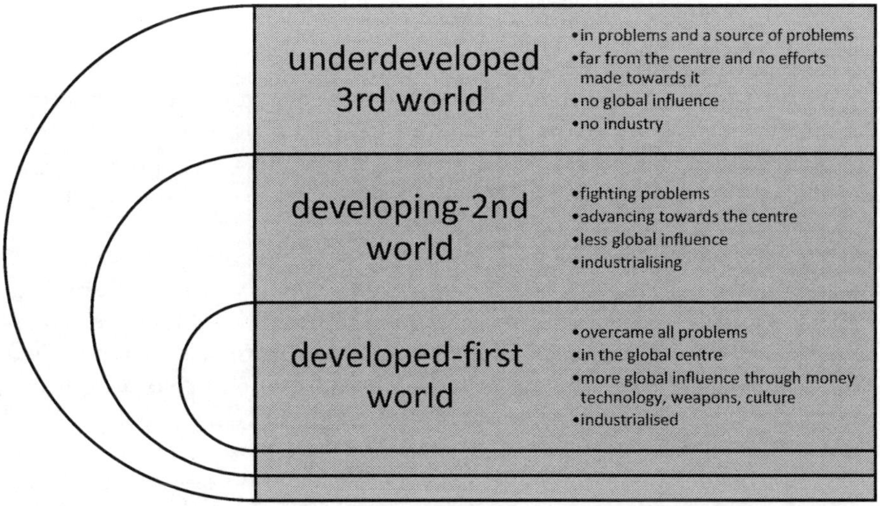


*Figure 2.2* Characterisation of developed, developing and underdeveloped country nomenclature

would have a nuclear weapon. First of all, it would change the balance of power. Second of all, he would use it. And that would be most disastrous.' This statement exposes the power dynamics in the names superpower and nuclear power. It also shows how the so-called developed countries view the other with utter contempt. African countries are also buying into the superpower discourse, and they are divided by the global powers with others designated by the imposed title of regional power. It is common to hear talk of South Africa as the regional superpower in Southern Africa, Nigeria in West Africa, Kenya in East Africa and Egypt in North Africa. These names and titles are all tailored to justify global dominance by these so-called superpowers and divide Africa by giving borrowed superpower status to 4 countries in a continent of 55 countries.

### *2.2.2 Numerical nomen grading of world countries*

The development pointers used by the UN, IMF, World Bank and other pro-centre organisations create names whereby countries are named numerically to indicate development or association with development. Numerically grading countries was developed to mark a distinction between civilised and well-planned economies as opposed to uncivilised and unplanned ones. Harris (1986, p. 200) alludes to this crude othering in numerical grading nomenclature:

> The conception of an interdependent, interacting, global manufacturing system cuts across the old view of a world consisting of nation-states as well as one of groups of countries, more or less developed and centrally planned – the First, the Third and the Second Worlds.

Arrighi et al. (2003, p. 8) attest that:

> Several studies have shown that the North (or former First World) constitutes a 'convergence club' at the high end of the world income distribution. Joining this club (that is, catching up with the income that on average accrues to its members) has been the primary objective of the developmental efforts of the countries of the South (or former Third World).

Africa is grouped under the designation Third World, although some argue that this is an obsolete designation. Numerically grading countries is similar to the development tier whereby the First World maps onto the developed countries, the Second World maps onto the developing countries and the Third World maps onto the underdeveloped countries. Classifying global countries into first, second and third resonates with linguistic narratives of the self and others. In linguistic analysis, first, second and third person are used to give points of view (Lyons et al., 2018). The world is viewed from the perspective of the first person, the I/we point of view. Human beings speak in the first person when they talk about themselves and their positions; the first world in this case becomes the selves who own ideas and the globe, and all topics are about them and their world views. In the second person, which maps on to the second world or the developing world, we have the 'you' point of view. The 'I's and 'we's of the first world can address the 'you's of the second world. Interestingly, Africa is in their third world, mapping to the third person point of view. These are people who have no opinion, who cannot be addressed but can only be talked about in their absence. The third person is characterised by pronouns such as she, he, them, they, it (Nevins, 2007), which are clear indications of othering. Africa is talked about, not talked to or talking to the world in the majority of cases, and the analogy of linguistic analysis fits well into the numerical grading of global development into first-, second- and third-world countries.

Countries have been grouped together according to the likeness and levels of their development at the exclusion of those countries perceived to be lower on the global scales of development. They accord pride to themselves through enumerated nomenclature. Raffer and Singer (2002) identify the G5 and the G7 as controlling the global economy. They further state that in 1942, Keynes formulated the basis for the International Monetary Fund and the World Bank to be the grandmothers of global finance, but the grandmothers only have a human face to the North; their face is inhuman to the South. They argue that the relationship between the North and the South or the centre and the periphery is globally and economically unequal. This unequal development creates global pacts whereby countries group and name themselves to show economic and military might at the exclusion or frustration of the others. Numerically grading countries for inclusion and exclusion has been extended to the East and Africa. In a world with over 197 countries, choosing only 7 and calling them G7 others over 190 countries who cannot be accepted into the 7. The G series is extended to G20, and this is a far cry from including all countries; it is a case of 20 selves against others, and South Africa is part of the 20.

The othered African countries have been grouped together with other 'poor' countries on the globe under the numerical banner of the G77 and the G77 and China. The name G77 is counter-othering by African countries against the West, and China takes advantage of this African selfing to oppose the West. However, China cannot be part of the G77 because it is a self outside African 'poverty'; hence, the name can only be 'G77 and China', not 'G78', if China is to join. China others Africa in its very partnership with Africa; if it did not disdain partnering with Africa and saw itself as a 'humble' power compared to the segregationist West, it should have no problem joining Africa and its other partners, and the union would be called G78. However, China would rather be the big brother to 77 countries. How can 77 countries be equated to 1? A union of say, Uganda and Botswana would be ideally named 'Uganda and Botswana', but '77 and 1' is a problematic category which serves to empower China and belittle Africa. China is clearly imposing itself on the other 77, because had it been part of the 77, the name would logically increase numerically to 78 in order to accommodate the new member. The name as it is suggests a power mathematical formula whereby the 77 of Africa, and other countries deemed like Africa by the development scales, are equal to or less than 1 developed or developing country. Africa and others are equal to or less than China; *Africa and others ≤ China, 77 ≤ 1.* This irrational math can only be rationalised through power matrices that undermine the 77 and empower the 1.

## 2.3 Conclusion

The global labels used to name countries and regions are instances of names used actively to distinguish the desired from the undesired, the centre from the periphery, the self from the other. Global inequalities are expressed and subtly celebrated as trophies of colonialism and imperialism. Institutions inside the centre which are instruments of the centre are used to create globalised apparatus for the measurement and maintenance of inequality. While it is clear that all human beings are equal in terms of natural potential, the inequalities used to name and shame some global species such as Africa are evidence of the real and imagined superiority of the centre as compared to its periphery. Physical geography and its campus cardinal points are exploited to aid the naming of global space, and this is done with respect to directionality from Europe. However, the countries included and excluded in these directional names betray the sinister motives behind the naming. What is East or South is measured from the point of European development and civilisation, which are the true North on the campus of global inequalities? The centre is always the West and the North, and all else fits into the periphery. There are other names that are more explicit in describing global selves and others using the realities and fallacies of global development indices as espoused by institutions such as the IMF and World Bank. Africa is named to reveal its problems, its lack of effort towards the centre and how it is a burden to the centre. The names reveal a trend whereby there are three tiers of development, and Africa falls into the lowest category. Some of the names express global inequalities numerically; in this class of toponyms, countries are numerically ranked from one down to three, and they group or are grouped into quantitative and qualitative groupings. In all these gradings and groupings, the names reveal an unequal global order, and Africa is among the disadvantaged nomen others.

## References

Amsden, A. (2001). *The rise of "the rest"*. Oxford University Press.

Arrighi, G., Silver, B. J., & Brewer, B. D. (2003). Industrial convergence, globalization, and the persistence of the North-South divide. *Studies in Comparative International Development, 38*(1), 3–31.

Baloch, M. A., & Thapa, G. B. (2019). Review of the agricultural extension modes and services with the focus to Balochistan, Pakistan. *Journal of the Saudi Society of Agricultural Sciences, 18*(2), 188–194.

Bassili, J. N. (1995). On the psychological reality of party identification: Evidence from the accessibility of voting intentions and of partisan feelings. *Political Behavior, 17*, 339–358.

Blaut, J. M. (1993). *The coloniser's model of the world: Geographical diffusionism and Eurocentric history*. Guilford Press.

Bobbio, N. (1996). *Left and right: The significance of a political distinction*. University of Chicago Press.

The Brazilian Presidency. (2019). *What is BRICS*. http://brics2019.itamaraty.gov.br/en/about-brics/what-is-brics#:~:text=BRICS%20is%20the%20group%20composed,18%25%20of%20the%20global%20trade

Burbach, R., & Robinson, W. I. (1999). The fin de siècle debate: Globalization as global shift. *Science and Society, 63*(1), 10–39.

Carmines, E. G., Ensley, M. J., & Wagner, M. W. (2012). Who fits the left-right divide? Partisan polarization in the American electorate. *American Behavioral Scientist, 56*(12), 1631–1653.

Chen, H., Hou, C., Zhang, L., & Li, S. (2020). Comparative study on the strands of research on the governance model of international occupational safety and health issues. *Safety Science, 122*, 104513. www.sciencedirect.com/science/article/pii/S092575351930534X

Chudi, I. P. (2010). Healthcare problems in developing countries. *Medical Practice and Reviews, 1*(1), 9–11.

Connell, R. (2007). *Southern theory: The global dynamics of knowledge in social science*. Allen and Unwin.

De Beukelaer, C. (2014). Creative industries in "developing" countries: Questioning country classifications in the UNCTAD creative economy reports. *Cultural Trends, 23*(4), 232–251. https://doi.org/abs/10.1080/09548963.2014.912043

Edelman, M. (1977). *Political language: Words that succeed and politics that fail*. Academic Press.

Eshag, E. (1983). *Fiscal and monetary policies and problems in developing countries*. Cambridge University Press.

Foucault, M. (1967). *Madness and civilisation*. Tavistock.

Foucault, M. (1980). *Power/knowledge: Selected interviews and other writings, 1972–1977*. Harvester Press.

Freire, A., & Kivistik, K. (2013). Western and non-western meanings of the left-right divide across four continents. *Journal of Political Ideologies, 18*(2), 171–199.

Goren, P. (2004). Political sophistication and policy reasoning: A reconsideration. *American Journal of Political Science, 48*, 462–478.

Grindle, M. S. (2004). Good enough governance: Poverty reduction and reform in developing countries. *Governance, 17*(4), 525–548.

Gusterson, H. (1999). Nuclear weapons and the other in the western imagination. *Cultural Anthropology, 14*(1), 111–143.

Hardt, M., & Negri, A. (2000). *Empire*. Harvard University Press.

Harris, N. (1986). *The end of the third world: Newly industrializing countries and the decline of an ideology*. Penguin Books.

Hayward, J. (2020). Orality in the digital age. In R. H. Kaschula & H. E. Wolff (Eds.), *The transformative power of language: From postcolonial to knowledge societies in Africa* (pp. 277–303). Cambridge University Press.

Hill, D. R. (2000). Health problems in a large cohort of Americans traveling to developing countries. *Journal of Travel Medicine*, 7(5), 259–266.

Hodgson, G. M. (2018). *Wrong turnings: How the left got lost*. University of Chicago Press.

Hoogvelt, A. (1997). *Globalization and the postcolonial world: The new political economy of development*. Johns Hopkins University Press.

Huntington, S. P. (1999). The lonely superpower. *Foreign Affairs*, 35–49.
Ignatieff, M. (1997). *The warrior's honor: Ethnic war and the modern conscience*. Metropolitan Books.
Jahn, D. (2011). Conceptualizing left and right in comparative politics: Towards a deductive approach. *Party Politics*, *17*(6), 745–765.
Jolly, M. (2008). The South in southern theory: Antipodean reflections on the Pacific. *Australian Humanities Review*, *44*(1), 75–99.
Kinder, D. R., & Winter, N. (2001). Exploring the racial divide: Blacks, whites, and opinion on national policy. *American Journal of Political Science*, 439–456.
Lacerda, D. S., Meira, F. B., & Brulon, V. (2020). Spatial ethics beyond the North-South dichotomy: Moral dilemmas in favelas. *Journal of Business Ethics*, 1–13. https://link.springer.com/article/10.1007/s10551-020-04467-8
Levander, C., & Mignolo, W. (2011). Introduction: The global South and world dis/order. *The Global South*, *5*(1), 1–11. https://muse.jhu.edu/article/449213/summary
Lockerbie, B. (2002). Party identification: Constancy and change. *American Politics Research*, *30*(4), 384–405.
Lopez, A. J. (2007). Preface and acknowledgments. *The Global South*, *1*(1), v–vi.
Luna, J. P., & Kaltwasser, C. R. (2011, July 29–30). *The right in contemporary Latin America: A framework for analysis*. Paper prepared for the WZB workshop Bringing the Right Back In.
Lyons, M., Aksayli, N. D., & Brewer, G. (2018). Mental distress and language use: Linguistic analysis of discussion forum posts. *Computers in Human Behavior*, *87*, 207–211.
Martin, R. (1988). The political economy of Britain's North-South divide. *Transactions of the Institute of British Geographers*, 389–418.
McFarlane, C. (2006). Crossing borders: Development, learning and the North – South divide. *Third World Quarterly*, *27*(8), 1413–1437.
McNeill, W. H. (1997). What we mean by the West. *Orbis*, *41*(4), 513–524.
Mestrovic, S. (2004). *The Balkanization of the West: The confluence of postmodernism and postcommunism*. Routledge.
Mignolo, W. D. (2008). Racism as we sense it today. *PMLA*, *123*(5), 1737–1742. www.jstor.org/stable/25501980
Ndlovu, S., & Mangena, T. (2014). Articulations of "othering" through ethnic names and naming: Selected Zimbabwean cases. *Nomina Afrikana*, *28*(2), 75–82.
Ndlovu-Gatsheni, S. J. (2014). Global coloniality and the challenges of creating African futures. *Strategic Review for Southern Africa*, *36*(2), 181–202.
Ndlovu-Gatsheni, S. J. (2020). Four journeys of capital and their consequences for Africa. In *The Palgrave handbook of African political economy* (pp. 45–61). Palgrave Macmillan.
Neuwirth, R. J. (2020). The end of "development assistance" and the BRICS. In *International development assistance and the BRICS* (pp. 15–33). Palgrave Macmillan.
Nevins, A. (2007). The representation of third person and its consequences for person-case effects. *Natural Language & Linguistic Theory*, *25*(2), 273–313.
Pagel, H., Ranke, K., Hempel, F., & Köhler, J. (2014, July 11). *The use of the concept "global South" in social science & humanities*. Symposium of the Global South, Humboldt University. www.academia.edu/download/38188278/pdf
Raffer, K., & Singer, H. W. (2002). *The economic North-South divide: Six decades of unequal development*. Edward Elgar Publishing.
Rahn, W. M. (1993). The role of partisan stereotypes in information processing about political candidates. *American Journal of Political Science*, *37*, 472–496.
Said, E. W. (1993). *Culture and imperialism*. Alfred A. Knopf.
Said, E. W. (1995). *Orientalism*. Penguin Books.

Santos, B. S. (2007). Beyond abyssal thinking: From global lines to ecologies of knowledge. *Review, XXX*(1), 45–89.

Sparke, M. (2007). Everywhere but always somewhere: Critical geographies of the global South. *The Global South, 1*(1), 117–126.

Spitzer, H. (2014). *Mzungu, how are you? Reflections on the human element of North-South partnerships.* https://appear.at/fileadmin/Dokumente/appear.at/implementation_and_reporting/Gender/article_HelmutSpitzer_2014.pdf

Steffen, R., Rickenbach, M., Wilhelm, U., Helminger, A., & Schär, M. (1987). Health problems after travel to developing countries. *Journal of Infectious Diseases, 156*(1), 84–91.

Subramanian, A. (2011). The inevitable superpower: Why China's dominance is a sure thing. *Foreign Affairs, 90*(5), 66–78.

Taylor, I. (2014). *Africa rising: BRICS-diversifying dependency*. James Currey.

Therien, J. P. (1999). Beyond the North-South divide: The two tales of world poverty. *Third World Quarterly, 20*(4), 723–742.

Tuathail, G. O., & Luke, T. W. (1994). Present at the (dis)integration: Deterritorialisation and reterritorialisation in the new wor(l)d order. *Annals of the Association of American Geographers, 84*(3), 394–395.

United Nations. (2010, March 6). *Composition of macro geographical (continental) regions, geographical sub-regions, and selected economic and other groupings.* http://unstats.un.org/unsd/methods/m49/m49regin.htm

Van der Bruggen, B., Borghgraef, K., & Vinckier, C. (2010). Causes of water supply problems in urbanised regions in developing countries. *Water Resources Management, 24*(9), 1885–1902.

Wackernagel, M., & Rees, W. (1998). *Our ecological footprint: Reducing human impact on the earth* (Vol. 9). New Society Publishers.

Wa Thiongo, N. (1993). *Moving the centre: The struggle for cultural freedoms*. Heinemann.

Wiesehomeier, N., & Doyle, D. (2012). Attitudes, ideological associations and the left-right divide in Latin America. *Journal of Politics in Latin America, 4*(1), 3–33.

# 3 Names as cultural othering of Africa

## 3.0 Introduction

Africa has been juxtaposed with Europe to conjure it as the Dark Continent compared to the advancement in Europe. Wolf (1982, p. 22) describes European culture as set against 'other' cultures, and he terms this 'a false construction of reality.' The periphery is envisaged as Europe's opposite which lacks civilisation and light. Early artists such as Conrad (1902) portray Africa as the heart of darkness. However, Frimpong-Ansah (1996) points out that the Akan of Ghana, for example, were state organised in the 13th century, and their gold production and weighing methods were sophisticated by the standards of the period. DuBois (1935) describes the ancient Ethiopian civilisation as the oldest and wisest, with a just social system. European civilisation later became hegemonic through colonialism. Oyedemi (2020, p. 401) contends that:

> The ideology of the supremacy of European culture is another element of coloniality. Eurocentrism defines the notion of western culture as exceptional and its global propagation as unavoidable for modernity and civilisation. The European culture and ways of producing knowledge and meanings became imposed on the dominated and the colonised, and all existing patterns of knowledge creation were relegated. The Euro-American patterns of knowledge creation and culture were mystified and eventually became hegemonic as global cultural practices.

Ndlovu-Gatsheni (2014, p. 197) concurs that:

> African subjectivity that emerged from these processes of racialisation and inferiorisation of blackness is one that has a diminished ontological density. It became a subjectivity that was said to be characterised by a catalogue of deficits and a series of lacks.

Ndlovu-Gatsheni (2013) identifies the lacks colonialism attributed to Africans as consisting of a lack of civilisation, writing, history, souls, democracy, human rights, ethics and development. The collection of these lacks imagines an

DOI: 10.4324/9781003170761-4

anthropos in tandem with Darwinist Christologies of Ham, Shem and Japheth theologies. The perceived lacks create animals out of Africans and a justification for coloniality, colonisation and acculturation. African culture is therefore perceived as the culture of uncultured animals; hence, the names given to aspects of the culture are themselves indicative of the perceived lacks. This chapter looks at how Europe named African culture. Evidently, according to Bekerie (2004), an exonym has a high potential of being a mis-name, creating onomastic devaluation and hierarchisation. Billig (1973) describes this hierarchisation of difference as ingroup favouritism and outgroup derogation.

The chapter focuses more on the crude othering of elements of African culture as they are named by Europeans, English in Zimbabwe being the case in point. The main argument is that racism against Africans is also expressed in how their culture is given crude and sophisticated othering nomenclature. Borkfelt (2011, p. 118) posits that:

> Naming is thus not only the first and most basic of linguistic processes; it is also an excellent example of the power or control that is in many ways inherent to language use. Whether what is named are lands, people or animals, the process of naming reflects the worldview of the one who names rather than the view of what is named. Thus, when Europeans have wanted to describe or name something in parts of the world outside Europe, this has most often been done through some form of reference to something already found on the European subcontinent, even in cases where the likeness implied by the new names do not seem altogether straightforward. This applies to lands and people, but is perhaps most obvious in the descriptions and names of animals.

Some of the names here express difference crudely, insulting the ethnic other. Çelik et al. (2017) argue that this type of othering is characterised by dislike, mistrust and unwillingness to associate with another social group. Racism in Africa is also characterised by the European's disdain for African culture. Williams (1999, p. 177) describes racism as an:

> ideology of inferiority that is used to justify unequal treatment (discrimination) of members of groups defined as inferior, by both individuals and societal institutions. This ideology of inferiority may lead to the development of negative attitudes and beliefs towards racial outgroups (prejudice).

Bonilla-Silva (1996) opines that racism lies within organised institutional structures, not in individual attitudes or behaviours; individuals react and conform to institutionalised racism. Lake (2003) argues that European racist luminaries such as Hume and Voltaire laid the foundation for the Euro-American ideology that ranks Africans closer to animals than to humans.

Functional African systems have been named and othered to the level of affecting the African intellectual ego. African knowledge is identified in retronyms as indigenous or traditional, creating implied and explicit references to European knowledge as modern and global. Ndlovu (2011) has argued that in the derivation of retronyms, the use of a particular adjective to derive a retronym implies the existence of its antonym or opposite. The names antagonise African culture, which has been proven to be working for Africans despite the exotic onslaught. Omotayo and Aremu (2020), for example, discuss how indigenous fruits are sold in both urban and rural markets and provide a substantial income to small-scale farmers across Africa. However, the adoption of large-scale cultivation of indigenous fruits by farmers will remain low until the economic returns on investment associated with the cultivation of underutilised fruit trees are profitable. African fauna and flora are othered and ostracised by the now-dominant colonial cultures in Africa, and they struggle to compete with exotic cultures despite having climatic and home advantage.

Madsen and Vallentin (2018, p. 1) note that:

> while extant research tends to associate othering with pejorative meaning, in a more balanced account of othering it is a matter of not only self-other distantiation, but also self-other identification. Apart from seeing othering as a form of social dysfunction, we argue that it can also have functional value.

The functional value of difference is exploited by African and other suppressed cultures to create brands out of their othered cultures, especially in tourism to attract Europeans and Americans. To do so, innocent-seeming descriptors such as traditional, indigenous, African, black, tribal and ethnic are used to brand African culture as authentic. However, this chapter proves that these, too, are also loaded, crude othering descriptors due to their intrinsic meanings and social practice. The name Africa itself has been othered to connote backwardness, ruralness, tribalness, locality and poverty (Ndlovu, 2018).

The chapter is an interpretivist analysis of cultural names, as it looks at socially constructed realities (Guba & Lincoln, 2005). Colonial othering ideas can be deduced from the naming of the other's culture. Ogbulogo (1999, p. 61) states that 'names are veritable resources for decoding ideology.' Names are analysed along the themes of ecological names, social and material names, names as branding African authenticity and, last, names as exhibits of African self-othering. The researcher has lived with the names within Southern African cultures and, as such, intuitive knowledge was one of the sources of data. Grix (2004, p. 83) argues that in interpretive inquiry, 'researchers are inextricably part of the social reality being researched.' The study is a critical discourse analysis and semantic analysis of the names Europeans gave to elements of African culture. Data for the analysis were collected through semi-structured, open-ended questionnaires sent online to purposively sampled respondents in different African countries. Unstructured telephone interviews were also done to collect and verify some meanings and etymologies. The study also deploys document analysis as a qualitative method for data and meaning analysis (Patton, 2002).

Texts used in the analysis were purposively sampled from journals, the media, books and online sites. This chapter deploys CDA as a method for analysing the imperial othering nuances in the naming of African culture by Europeans, as Poole (2010) states that CDA is an established interdisciplinary approach to texts in terms of their wider social and political significance.

## 3.1 Names and crude othering of African ecology

Ecology is the basis of a people's culture, as it provides them with resources. Ecological culture includes, among other elements, fauna and flora. Ndlovu (2012, p. 154) argues that 'concepts in ecology are mostly retro-named due to a new concept from another culture, while social and material concepts can be from another culture or from within the same culture.' Ecologically, Africa is different from Europe, and this creates cultural differences, which is not a problem. The problem arises when naming each other's culture confirms unequal social relations. This section analyses names of African fruits, vegetables and animals as they are described in European languages, especially English. Some of these names exhibit European disgust of African ecology, while some are loaded with nuances of animalising African culture, and, last, some actually appropriate African ecology to European individual owners.

There are some names that were given to elements of African culture in Zimbabwe and in other countries which are outright insults, and the insulted culture is alienated from the development process and its people left to languish in onomastically induced mental and physical poverty. This type of onomastic othering is what is classed as crude othering. Brons (2015) argues for the existence of crude othering whereby the self does not subscribe to equality to the other; the difference between the self and the other is the undesirable characteristic of the other, which is presumed absent in the self. Some elements of African culture have been named to express that they are undesirable for human beings.

Trees form part of people's culture, they are used for shelter, tools, food, ornaments and medicine. All communities adapt to their flora, and lives are based on it, as it includes the crops they live on. It is therefore impossible for such key commodities in livelihood to be without names. The fallacy that they were discovered and later on named by explorers is imperial (witch) craft to advantage imperial history over autochthon realities. Using data from Goredema (2013), Shava (2005) and botanical journals, Table 3.1 demonstrates how African flora is described using ecological slurs which disparage it as useless and detestable compared to European flora of the same species or genus.

The adjectives snot, smelly and false are instances not only of othering but also of outright insults to African ecological culture. They depict the fruits as undesired dirt, and the use of false implies a true genus in Europe, while Africa has the fake. All fruits and animals were domesticated from the wild; to classify European elements as belonging to the home as if they originated in homes is a fallacy. To designate African fruits, vegetables and teas as wild and bush is not

*Table 3.1* Disparaging names given to African flora

| *Botanical name* | *African names* | *Disparaging English name* | *Disparaging adjective and meaning* |
|---|---|---|---|
| *Azanza garckeana* | *Uxakuxaku* – Ndebele, *matohwe* – Shona | *Snot* apple | *Snot* – dried nasal mucus, or contemptible and worthless |
| *Vitez mombassae* | *Umtshwankela* – Ndebele, *tsubvu* – Shona | *Smelly* berry | *Smelly* – pungent and unpleasant smell; stinking/odour/foul |
| *Aspalathus linearis* | *Rooibos* – Afrikaans | *Bush* tea | *Bush* – wild uncultivated wilderness |
| *Lannea* | *Tsambatsi* – Shona | *Wild* grape | *Wild* – untamed, fierce, uninhabited, unmanaged |
| *Vangueria infausta* | *Umthofi* – Ndebele | *False* wild medlar | *False* – incorrect imitation, fallacious and flawed |

entirely true; it serves to savage African ecology in favour of exotic ecology. Characterising African ecology as wild is also observed by Tavuyanago, Mutami and Mbenene (2010, p. 2), who declare that the Shona of Zimbabwe grew 'finger millet, bulrush millet, and sorghum' before European contact. Suffice it to note that a bulrush is a wild swampy area, and the authors argue such a name contributed to the people abandoning the crop to propagate exotic maize. Nhemachena (2017) identifies a similar trend with what is named wild cotton, which is ignored because it is named 'wild', and western cotton is preferred. Some popular beverages today were first named as bush and wild to alienate them from English civilisation: the African tea rooibos from South Africa was called bush tea, and for years it was not promoted and western teas were. There are several African trees and shrubs which make beverage and medicinal teas, and these are called bush teas, classifying them as wild and not fit for plantations. However, after realising the value of some African vegetables and fruits, seed companies in Zimbabwe are now packaging and selling these seeds. This is evidence that, if Africans do away with the savaging names and attitudes, African fruits, teas and vegetables can be used to alleviate African poverty. Omotayo and Aremu (2020) state that indigenous fruit trees can contribute to small-scale and commercial agriculture in Africa because, despite their othered status, they still contribute a significant percentage to fruit markets in many African countries. Ham et al. (2007) posit that various organisations across Africa are venturing into African fruit tree juices and propagating the trees.

Names that insult African culture do not depict it as wild only, but some brazenly describe aspects of African culture as animalistic, implying humanness in European ones. Tavuyanago et al. (2010) describe the precolonial Shona people in Zimbabwe growing leguminous crops, chief of which was cowpeas (*nyemba*); suffice it to note that they did not grow the peas for cows but for people, yet the Europeans came and insisted on the name cowpeas. Ndlovu (2011) also identifies animalised English retronyms for Ndebele culture in Zimbabwe, such as monkey oranges for *umkhemeswane* (hard-shelled African fruit), monkey nuts for *indlubu* (round nuts) and kangaroo court for *inkundla yenduna* (chief's court). Nhemachena (2016) argues that animalism is a colonial strategy to make Africans sub-human, Table 3.2 gives examples of some African fruits and vegetables named as belonging to animals, not people.

All genera in Table 3.2 are based on European valued and selfed concepts except weed in the name pig weed. The genus weed implies something that grows where it is not wanted, yet the vegetable is wanted by Africans, as it forms part of their diet where it is found. It is ironic for people to come from elsewhere and declare a vegetable unwanted in its own ecosystem. Animalising African culture has intended effects of justifying occupation; the assumption is that the ecology belongs to animals, and there are no humans to manage the ecosystem, hence colonialism. Such justifications have been implied, for example, in the apartheid ideologies expressed in apartheid South Africa's national anthem whereby the Dutch who occupied the Cape claimed to have found no people on the land but animals. While this claim has been challenged by historians and geographers, and it is of course challenged by common sense, apartheid later became explicit that the category animal included Africans to them.

The act of naming is believed in human societies to exhibit authority over the named. Naming animals is a human way of asserting authority over them Borkfelt (2011, p. 117) argues that:

> This naming of the animals clearly shows a divide between Man and the other animals. Adam, gifted with the language and understanding to name what he sees, is given the power for his very first act of control over the animals by God: the act of naming and thereby defining the beings named. An act that is second only to creation.

*Table 3.2* Names that animalise and savage African flora

| *Botanical name* | *Genus* | *African names, Ndebele/Shona* | *Animalising English name* |
|---|---|---|---|
| *Stychnos* | Fruit | *Umkhemeswane/ matamba* | *Monkey* orange |
| *Piliostigma thonniningii* | Fruit | *Ihabahaba/musekesa* | *Monkey* bread |
| *Berchemia discolor* | Fruit | *Umnyi/nyii* | *Bird* plum |
| *Amazanthus hybridus* | Vegetable | *Imbuya* | *Pig* weed |
| *Cheome gynandra* | Vegetable | *Ulude/nyevhe* | *Spider* flower |
| *Vigna unguiculata* | Bean/vegetable-leaves | *Indumba/nyemba* | *Cow* peas |

Fudge (2004, p. 24) concurs that:

> it is as if the animals had no identity, no presence without Adam, and their inherent powerlessness, perhaps most easily described as their inability to name themselves, has persisted in human relations with animals. An animal cannot think, we argue, and therefore it is down to us to think for it.

The fact that Europeans arrived in Africa and discovered and named animals implies that there were no namers on the continent and hence no people or that the people could not think, just like animals. Africans are relegated to that level of beings who do not have the God-given right to name others. African fauna is named using European fauna as the root or genus, which creates taxonomies only in Africa, while the real animals are in Europe. Borkfelt (2011, p. 118) postulates that:

> Both the anthropocentrism and eurocentrism of animal names like Thomson's gazelle or Lichtenstein's hartebeest is quite obvious, but a certain eurocentrism is in fact inherent to many other names of non-European animals as well, due to the references to animals already known in Europe, which are included in the names.

The etymology of the name gazelle, for example, is traced to the Arabic word Ghazal, meaning love poetry (Winslow, 2015; Necipoğlu & Bailey, 2005). However, its use in Africa came with Europeans. The genus gazelle itself is linked to the religion of imperial Europe; the Name-Doctor (2020) notes that:

> The name Dorcas derives from the Ancient Greek 'dorkás (δορκᾰ́ς)', meaning 'gazelle, deer, buck'. Dorcas (also known as Tabitha) was a disciple who lived in Joppa, referenced in the Book of Acts 9:36–42 of the Bible. The name Dorcas is Greek translation of the Aramaic name Tabitha, meaning 'gazelle'. One species of gazelle is now known as the Dorcas Gazelle. The Dorcas gazelle, also known as the Ariel gazelle, is a small and common gazelle.

Europeans came to an Africa which had its own names for animals both domesticated and undomesticated. Instead of using or adopting these names, as Africans did with European cultural elements, these newcomers 'discovered' the animals as new and used their names on the animals to record the histories of their 'discoveries'. Table 3.3 gives some African animals named using nomen constructions that give ownership to Europeans.

The names given to these animals undermine African abilities and authority over animals, and, most sinisterly, they are commemorative of colonial power in Africa. This constitutes crude nomen othering. Wilson and Reeder (2005) indicate that the name Dorcas gazelle originates with Swedish zoologist Carl Linnaeus, who first described the animal in 1758. They further indicate that

*Table 3.3* Naming African fauna for European ownership and honour

| *Scientific name* | *Possessive English taxonomy* | *Etymology of English name* |
|---|---|---|
| *Gazella dorcas* | *Dorcas* gazelle | Ancient Greek – dorkás (δορκᾰ́ς) means gazelle, deer or buck |
| *Eudorcas thomsonii* | *Thomson's* gazelle | Joseph Thomson – Scottish explorer |
| *Nanger granti* | *Grant's* gazelle | James Grant – British explorer |
| *Nanger soemmerringii* | *Sömmerring's* gazelle | Samuel Thomas von Sömmerring – German physist and explorer |
| *Gazella gazella/cuvieri* | *Cuvier's* gazelle | Georges Cuvier – French naturalist and zoologist |
| *Gazella spekei* | *Speke's* gazelle | John Hanning Speke – British explorer |
| *Alcelaphus lichtensteinii* | *Lichtenstein's* hartebeest | Martin Hinrich Carl Lichtenstein – German zoologist |
| *Raphicerus sharpei* | *Sharpe's* grysbok | Richard Bowdler Sharpe – English zoologist and ornithologist |

the German mammologist Theodor Haltenorth in 1953 described taxonomies of the Dorcas gazelle as Eritrean, Egyptian, Moroccan and Saharawi. The *Merriam-Webster Dictionary* (2020) declares that Thomson's gazelle is named after the Scottish explorer Joseph Thomson; the first recorded use of the name dates to 1897. Another common name for the gazelle is tommy. The *WordSense Dictionary* (2021) defines Speke's gazelle as a species of gazelle from the Horn of Africa, named after John Hanning Speke, a British explorer of Central Africa, while Arctander et al. (1996) posit that Grant's gazelle is found in Eastern Africa from the Sudan and Ethiopia to Kenya and Uganda and was named after the British explorer James Grant. Amir (2006) further divides Grant's gazelle into sub-taxonomies of; Bright's, Southern, Northern, Peter's, and Robert's. Wilson and Reeder (2005) identify the Sömmerring's gazelle as named after German physist Samuel Thomas von Sömmerring.

Gazelles are known in various African languages by names such as *impala, mpaa, mhara* and *swara*, and these are clearly homo-semantic cognates from one proto-form. The naming of these African animals using European anthroponymy devalues the African names in literature, and what are now perceived as scientific names are also derivatives of these European possessive constructions. To possess animals such as gazelle is tantamount to possessing people, because the animals own and are a symbol of people's identities in most African societies. Strandberg (2009) states that gazelles featured in ancient Egyptian art, they formed part of a religion associated with death and rebirth and they served as a model of a feminine deity. This implies that an aspect of African religion is now named to express its belonging to people who do not share in the history and the faith; this is othering at the levels of profanity and desecration of the African gods who abide in the gazelle. The gazelle identifies many people across Africa. Chidester et al. (1997) indicate that the gazelle is in the totemic system of many people in Africa, and the researcher can relate to this assertion, as there are many people of the gazelle totems in Southern Africa realised in various totems such as Mpala (Nguni) and Mhara (Nyai).

Literature on the gazelle exhibits some country-based taxonomies, but these are applied more to non-African countries. Myers et al. (2021) identify Indian, Arabian, Saudi, Tibetan, Mongolian and Iranian gazelles, and there are few references to Tunisian, Moroccan, Western Saharan and Algerian gazelles. Suffice it to say that the African areas identified in nomenclature as having gazelles are closer to Europe and are part of the Arab world of the former Persian empire. As you go down from Arab Africa, gazelles are named using names of Europeans in possessive constructions. This distinction further divides Africa into Arab and the other.

## 3.2 African knowledge and social systems in the onomastic self-other dichotomy

African knowledge, science and social systems are named indigenous knowledge systems (IKSs) in pro-European and American scholarship, which pits them against what is now popularly known and mis-named as western science. Knowledge cannot be regional – there is no global hemisphere that has greater natural capabilities of producing science than others, except in the delusions of social Darwinism and eugenics. African knowledge has been othered by years of colonialism and imperialism; during this time, social hierarchies were created to give an impression that intellect is also hierarchised in favour of certain human beings. The terms 'traditional' and 'indigenous' are deployed for African science and systems to create the intended effects of demoting and localising this science. The concepts traditional and indigenous have the semantic effect of localising and freezing in time and space, respectively. This section demonstrates how the naming of African concepts and knowledge as traditional or indigenous creates domination and ostracisation of African culture from modern and global knowledge. Othering African knowledge is part of epistemic injustice. Keet (2014, p. 23) states that 'epistemic othering constitutes epistemic injustice, which is inscribed in the disciplinary formations of knowledge.' He further notes that this 'epistemic injustice within disciplines renders the collective interpretive resources required for epistemic justice structurally prejudiced.' 'Traditional' and 'indigenous' are used as pejorative adjectives in naming African culture to achieve devaluation. Strani and Szczepaniak-Kozak (2018, p. 165) observe that:

> What is fundamental in the processes of othering is that categorisation takes place and is established by the dominant group, which constructs group boundaries and assigns subordinate characteristics to other groups, devaluing and demoting them to a lesser category, thus establishing a hierarchy.

Cesaire (2000, p. 43) describes the devaluation of African culture and states that 'I am talking about societies drained of their essence, cultures trampled underfoot, institutions undermined, lands confiscated, religions smashed, magnificent artistic creations destroyed, extraordinary possibilities wiped out of raw material.' The word 'traditional' denotes originality if analysed analytically; however, its association with and use for African culture by the coloniser has seen it assume the stigma associated with Africa by westerners. Its use for African crops, medicine and social systems others these, and the othering creates authenticity for western concepts and markets them as the working systems. Table 3.4 exemplifies how traditional is used to other African culture as obsolete and European culture as modern and relevant.

The African concepts are named 'traditional' so as to mark them as archaic, making them anachronistic in the modern era. The systems are only good as an example of the history of human development; naming Africa 'traditional' justifies other othering tags such as underdeveloped, unindustrialised and less advanced. African concepts cannot offer the world of science anything, as they have been overtaken by time. European or American concepts are usually prefixed with 'modern' to differentiate them from African concepts of the same genus. It is not surprising to hear people talk of modern doctors and leaders. The category of traditional places African systems behind Euro-American ones along the time axis.

To designate African culture as traditional may appear a neutral differentiation, as the term is not intrinsically negative. However, in colonial relations, it is difficult to envisage a situation of sophisticated othering. Words such as 'traditional', 'African', 'rural', 'customary', 'tribe', 'ethnic' and 'subsistence' are some of the adjectives used by the coloniser to derive retronyms for African culture. The words are not innocent adjectives in the way they are used to name African culture, because historically, they have been associated with disparaging African culture so as to make English culture superior. These adjectives localise

*Table 3.4* Implied traditional-modern dichotomy in naming African systems

| *Traditionalised African concept* | *Examples* | *Modernised European counterpart* | *Examples* |
|---|---|---|---|
| Traditional food | *Sadza, ugali, yarms, umxhanxa, uphuthu, fufu* | Food/dish | Spaghetti, rice, bread, sushi |
| Traditional healer | *Sangoma, mukoti* | Doctor | Physician, paediatrician, dentist, optician, gynaecologist |
| Traditional leader | Chief, headman, kraal head, village head, clan head | Leader/manager | President, prime minister, councillor, MP, senator |
| Traditional clothing | Hides, kente, sandals | Modern wear | Suits, t-shirts, blouses, trousers |

African culture and mark it as unfit for global markets. The term 'tribal' also divides African culture so that there is no collective effort to develop these systems to world standards and markets. 'Tribe' and 'ethnic' are derogatory to Africans. Lentz (1995) argues that their Greek roots mean 'heathen' or 'uncivilised person'. Ndlovu (2011) identifies that terms such as 'ethnic people' for Africans and 'tribal chief' for *induna* (royal African leader) in Zimbabwe are intended to indicate they are uncivilised.

African systems are also named 'indigenous', and this adjective is used to prefix names such as indigenous medicine, clothes, utensils, food, languages and knowledge systems. Semantically, the opposite of 'indigenous' is 'exotic', and the expectation is that where African concepts are named indigenous, European ones will be named exotic to Africa. However, this is not the case; in fact, 'indigenous' juxtaposes global/universal. Affixing African identity concepts with the adjective 'indigenous' excludes them from global identities. African medicine, for example, is called 'indigenous medicine', and this confines its relevance to Africa, yet western medicine is globalised as universal science and technology. While 'traditional confines' African knowledge to past time, 'indigenous' confines it to localised 'tribal or ethnic' spaces. Table 3.5 gives some examples of indigenised African knowledge versus globalised Euro-American knowledge.

While African concepts are always prefixed with 'indigenous', European imported concepts are not referred to as 'exotic' or 'foreign' to Africa; in fact, they replace the African concepts as the genus, and the African concepts are then retronamed to indicate their localised functions. In the case of languages, African languages were othered out of the global space so that they only operate within the indigenes, not further. The global languages are the dominant languages in African countries, and this language othering has attracted many researchers and theorists to question the use of European languages in Africa.

*Table 3.5* Indigenised African culture vs globalised European culture

| *Indigenised African concept* | *Examples* | *Globalised European counterpart* | *Examples* |
|---|---|---|---|
| Indigenous crops | Millet, finger millet, sorghum | Crops | Corn, wheat, rice |
| Indigenous medicine | Balms from tree barks, roots, leaves, bloodletting, *ukuchatha/peyita* | Scientific medicine | Pills, injections, theatre |
| Indigenous domestic animals | Thuli, Nguni, hard Mashona type (cattle), road runner (chicken) | High breeds | Brahman, Friesland, Herford |
| Indigenous languages | Zulu, Ndebele, Shona, Kirundi, Chewa, Tswana | Global languages | English, French, Spanish, Portuguese |

However, even the very same pro-African language theorists are compelled to express their anti-European language theories in European languages: such has been the extent of the othering of African languages over time.

The naming of some cattle breeds as 'indigenous' or 'African' compares them to the idealised European standard. While the African breeds are well suited for the ecology and hence are cheaper to breed, Africans are psyched into breeding expensive exotic breeds such as Brahman, for example. Western medicine is very expensive for most Africans, yet they have their own medicine which they cannot fully trust because it has been named 'indigenous' or 'traditional' and othered. As a result, it has not been developed to serve many people. In Zimbabwe, there is a popular medicinal bulb plant named the African potato in English. This medicinal plant is identified with the genus potato, implying food rather than medicinal qualities. This negatively impacts research into its medicinal qualities, which could develop into useful global drugs. Natural remedies to ailments are gaining popularity across the world. In fact, there is a renaissance and globalisation of herbal medicine. DeFilipps and Krupnick (2018) report on the popularity of medicinal tree bark in Myanmar. African systems have been proven beneficial to global development. Battiste (2005, p. 2) argues that:

> Indigenous scholars discovered that indigenous knowledge is far more than the binary opposite of western knowledge. As a concept, indigenous knowledge benchmarks the limitations of Eurocentric theory; its methodology, evidence, and conclusions re-conceptualise the resilience and self-reliance of indigenous peoples, and underscores the importance of their own philosophies, heritages, and educational processes.

History has many examples of African civilisation influencing and spreading globally. However, this African knowledge is subsumed into empire knowledge. Lacerda et al. (2020, p. 2) attest to the idealised superiority of western knowledge and note that 'Decolonial efforts critique the subaltern position of indigenous perspectives, which are tolerated only when they acquiesce to the knowledge conventions of the Global North and its semiotic codes.' Parker (1918), for example, identifies Ethiopia as the mother of all civilisation and Egypt as its first-born. While this claim has had much support from Afrocentric and postcolonial liberals, it over-authenticates Africa and simultaneously divides it into civilised Ethiopia and Egypt juxtaposed with a whole continent of darkness. The West imagines Ethiopia and Egypt as part of empire, as their history and civilisation are different from and anachronistic to the rest of the continent. Levine (1974) opines that in the West, Ethiopians and Egyptians have been subsumed into empire and are referred to by accommodating names such as 'dark-skinned Caucasians'. Bekerie (2004) laments a development whereby many Ethiopians believe in and pride themselves on this false supremacy bestowed on them by hegemonic Eurocentricity. Links to a recorded history of civilisation have seen western ideologies and scholarship work to 'de-Africanise' Ethiopia and Egypt.

The concepts traditional, indigenous and African are also used to name African religion and adaptations of Christianity in Africa. The names used in these formations also exhibit othering, and, in the case of African religion, crude slurs are at times used to name it. Ndlovu (2019, p. 21) observes that 'Westerners and western churches have exhibited dislike for African religion and African Initiated Churches (AICs) much that they refer to these using savaging and at times insulting names to create a superior western self-religion and a savage African religion.' Precolonial Africa had its own religion, and the advent of colonialism came with the missionary churches. These churches had to undo African religion by portraying it as local and savage through the names they used for it. To call African religion 'African traditional religion' (ATR) is a way of othering it as backward and local as opposed to modern and universal Christianity. Mbiti (2004, p. 221) notes that, 'Among other injustices that it did, colonial occupation eclipsed African peoplehood. Colonial presence, domination, ignorance and arrogance, plus a certain amount of (sometimes, cheap) missionary teaching, projected an attitude towards Africans as though they were no people.' Ndlovu (2019, p. 25) further states that:

> The name ATR has been popularised but a content analysis of the name reveals that it is an othering name when compared to names given to western churches. The meaning of traditional is the same as that of orthodox but they use traditional which is associated with being backward instead of calling it African Orthodox religion which closely associates with sticking to the original rules of a religion. African religion is sometimes referred to as ancestor worship which is opposed to the worship of God in western churches; the ancestors are framed on the concept of evil so that the religion becomes an evil religion juxtaposed to the holy missionary churches.

Practitioners of African religion are also called agents of the devil propagating a religious cult of evil. Some English and European languages' names for African religion satanise African religion and crudely other it while selfing European religions as holy. Table 3.6 gives some examples of onomastically satanised African religious concepts and juxtaposes them with the perceived holiness in European religions.

Many Africans were converted from their orthodox religion to European religions, and many scholars have linked this to mental coloniality. One of the strategies used to alienate the African from his religion was to name and portray it as savage and evil, a cult led by the devil. The naming of western marriage as holy matrimony, for example, presupposes that non-western marriage is an unholy matrimony. Such demonisation of African institutions creates an inferiority complex which leaves the African suspicious of his own systems which have sustained him/her over centuries before the advent of colonialism.

This crude othering is extended to African adaptations of Christianity, which are commonly referred to as AICs, these formations are called by various crude names such as 'tribal religious movements', 'separatists', 'syncretistic

*Table 3.6* Names satanising African religious concepts and selfing Christian concepts

| *Satanised African religious concept* | *Righteous Christian counterpart* | *Satanising semantics* |
|---|---|---|
| Ancestor worship | Followers of *Christ* – The Son of God | Ancestor – dead remote forbearers |
| Magic | *Miracle* – welcome and remarkable event of divine agency | *Magic* – mystical and of occult agency, such as necromancy |
| Sorcerer | *Prophet* – inspired teacher and proclaimer of the will of God | *Sorcerer* – inspired by a malignant devil to harm people |
| Ancestor | *Saint* – holy virtuous dead believed to be in heaven | *Ancestor* – dead remote forbearer |
| Evil/unclean spirit | *Clean spirit* – godly benevolent possession | *Evil spirit* – satanic malevolent possession with the occult |

movements', 'splinter groups' and 'native cults', while European churches are called 'mainline' churches (Walls, 1979; Sidima, 1994). Chitando (2005, p. 92) concurs that 'missiologists, keen to distinguish them from "authentic" versions of Christianity certainly used such negative labels.' Ndlovu (2019, p. 27) opines that 'The naming of AICs as separatist implies that they are rebels and they should be exterminated as they are fighters fighting the normal main church. They are also identified by indigenous names such as *Amabhazuka* (rebels) in Ndebele.' The othering of AICs in Africa divides Africans along taxonomies of foreign religions, and they other each other on a concept used to other their own religion. African culture from ecology, materials, social relations, science and belief systems has been named crudely by imperial namers to create an othered African culture versus a selfed, modern and global European culture.

## 3.3 Authenticity and the quest for African cultural selves

Africa and other victims of European imperialism have tried to fight back in the realm of cultural othering. Here, they seek to portray a sophisticated type of othering whereby Africa and Europe are named to be different and can appreciate each others' difference through tourism. Madsen and Vallentin (2018, p. 1) opine that 'the processes of othering can take other, more sophisticated and appreciative forms.' To recreate cultural selves, Africa has used names that create authenticity in African culture and artificiality in other European culture. The otherness created is ironically aimed at attracting tourists from Europe and North America. This section demonstrates that sophisticated othering of European culture by Africa does not in any way self African culture, as the whole process is driven by those very Europeans. The attempts at othering European culture through authenticating African culture are themselves problematic. Analysing the notion of authenticity as used in branding Fiji as a tourist destination, White (2007, p. 27) indicates that:

> The Fiji Visitors Bureau (FVB) caters to tourists' presumed quest for authenticity through othering mechanisms that hinge on differentiation. At one level this differentiation represents a derivative of colonial discourse on noble savagery that engages western constructions of Polynesian and Melanesian people and places.

Western creations of African culture as traditional and indigenous are used to recreate African culture and name it authentic. Tourism, cultural revival and postcolonial discourses in Africa and elsewhere have sought to recreate African culture from the ashes of colonial and imperialist othering to create a cultural self by othering imperial cultures. Africa and other former colonies attract tourists from imperial centres by branding their cultures as authentic (MacCannell, 1999). This movement is from reflecting on otherness. Mowforth and Munt (2003, p. 73) postulate that:

> otherness clearly involves a process of reflection. Other cultures and environments are everything that our cultures and environments are not. Thus, western lifestyles can be denigrated as empty, culturally unfulfilling, materialistic, meaningless, while on the contrary, Third World cultures are bestowed with meaning, richness, simplicity and, of course, authenticity.

White (2007) argues that when the so-called Third World markets its self to European tourists, it appeals to authentic backward lives, real villages, real poverty and real lives.

Tracing cultural steps back to reconnect is a necessary part of cultural emancipation and selfing. However, it can negatively impact the cultural renaissance drive, as it celebrates primitivity, which is the underlying category in the cultural othering of Africa by Europe and other global metropoles. Mowforth and Munt (2003, p. 74) observe that 'otherness and authenticity are united in a desire to ensure that culture and ethnicity are preserved and aestheticised. It is the promotion of primitiveness within which authenticity becomes the principal commodity.' However, Olsen (2002) espouses that the notion of authenticity itself is essentialising the cultures made to embody an authenticity belonging to a previous stage of human development which others have lost. White (2007, p. 34) further opines: 'The crude objectification of early tourism promotion has given way to barely more subtle essentialist discourse where a noble "primitivism" of natives is rendered less elusive.' Naming African culture and othering European culture as meaningless and materialistic actually works to authenticate European culture as modern and global, while African culture is confirmed as traditional and local. Li (1995, p. 169) postulates that:

> The relegation of cultural authenticity to the past in effect freezes or halts the process of historical and cultural change and denies that a culture may

> be open to new ideas and new ways of doing things or that it may develop and grow through intercultural addition, adoption, or even appropriation. The attempt to salvage cultural authenticity can turn into the censorship of cultural innovation.

Authenticity is celebrating backwardness, and Europeans are interested in this difference, as it confirms their superiority over rural, traditional, indigenous, tribal, ethnic and subsistent Africa. Wilson (1998, p. 416) describes the world view of those in the whale (West and United States of America) as Eurocentric and diffusionist, 'in which Europe is inventive and progressive and passes on its innovations to others who are traditional and static.' Adverts that call tourists to come to Africa and experience real culture undefiled by materials, urbanisation, industrialisation and money actually other Africa inversely as the opposite of global development.

## 3.4 Onomastic evidence of African cultural self-othering

The effects of colonialism are so deeply rooted in the African psyche that Africans even name their own systems to favour western ones in a process of self othering. It is not only names derived in European languages that denigrate African culture, but there are cases whereby African names are coined to other African culture. Ndlovu (2011) demonstrates that the Ndebele of Zimbabwe name some elements of their own culture using names which other it and self European culture. Colonial experiences and ideologies of White supremacy have made Africans internalise negative self-images (DuBois, 1920; Mazrui, 1986). Colonial ideas created a barbaric Africa which was saved from animalism by the intervention of western colonialism. Fanon (1968) argues that colonial domination was so designed to convince the natives that colonialism came to lighten their darkness and that without Whites, they could fall back into their former beastly life.

Mental coloniality can be read in language usage because language usage and development are linked to culture. Hall (1959, p. 53) contends that 'culture hides much more than it reveals, and strangely enough what it hides, it hides most effectively from its own participants.' The coloniality of African languages and culture is given away by some African names for their culture. Strani and Szczepaniak-Kozak (2018, p. 164) postulate that 'Language, inextricably linked with culture, works in the same way, as it may mask (or betray) hegemonic relations as relics of colonialism, racialisation and othering.' Africans have internalised the adjectives used to other their culture, such as traditional, indigenous, rural, tribal, ethnic and African. They translate these and use them to name elements of their own culture. In Zimbabwe and indeed other African countries, all these terms inflect backwardness on concepts in contrast with the advanced concepts described as English or European languages. Table 3.7 demonstrates how some African names perpetuate mental coloniality by degrading African concepts and upgrading European ones.

*Table 3.7* African (Ndebele) self othering cultural names

| *Ndebele self othering name* | *Gloss and examples* | *Selfed European counterpart* | *Gloss and examples* |
|---|---|---|---|
| *Inkukhu yemakhaya* | Rural chicken – free-range African chicken | *Inkukhu yesikhiwa* | European chicken – broiler and layer hens |
| *Igaki leganga* | Wild (gurke) cucumber – African thorn cucumber | *Igaki lesikhiwa* | European gurke – English cucumber |
| *Utshwala besibhoyi* | Boy beer – opaque African brew | *Utshwala besikhiwa* | European beer – clear beers, wines |
| *Izinto zabantu* | Black people's things – witchcraft, magic, occult | *Izinto zamakhiwa* | White people's things – technology |

These names confirm the cultural superiority of Europe, and they derive from a mentally colonised cognition, as Fanon (1967, p. 40) contends that 'it is not possible to enslave men without logically making them inferior through and through.' The noun 'boy', used to name African beer, for example, was a derogatory reference to African men working as gardeners in colonial Rhodesia. The men were boys, as they were forced to leave their families and survive like bachelor boys away from their wives and children, who remained in the rural areas or tribal trust lands.

Describing a concept as a boy-concept others it as a slave concept, as opposed to the master concept. Master concepts are identified as European and thought to be urban compliant and better. This self othering is evidence of the deep-rooted mental colonialism which impoverishes Africans mentally, leading to their physical poverty. Black is used to express evil in the West, and some African cultures also describe evil using black as a symbol. This is why evil and witchcraft are called Black people's things, while technology and science are referred to as White people's things. Ndlovu (2011, p. 64) states that:

> while the Ndebele associate advanced concepts with the English culture by using the secondary stem *isikhiwa* (English), the English associate despised, wild and evil concepts with Ndebele and other Africans by using secondary stems such as monkey, wild, black, rural, and tribal.

The concepts of rural and wild feature prominently in European names for African cultural concepts, and they also feature in names created by Africans to create retronyms. Any concept perceived to be better or new is given to European culture; ironically, even pod okra, which is from West Africa, is called *idelele lesikhiwa*, 'European okra', in Ndebele. Europe is given credit for some concepts that are not even European. Mental coloniality creates the black skin-white mask mentality in Africans, leading them to conceptualise their own cultures through colonial lenses.

## 3.5 Conclusion

People live in different environments, and they name these environments using their languages. However, people are not confined to environments anymore in this global age, and this leads them to encounter different people and environments with their own names. Europeans came to Africa, encountered the various cultures on the continent and named elements within these African cultures. They named elements of ecological culture such as fauna and flora, elements of social and material culture, elements of science and knowledge systems and religion. The names Europeans chose for African culture are predominantly exotic ones which are qualified using different adjectives. Adjectives such as 'disgusting', 'smelly' and 'false' are some of the crudest instances of savaging names created by Europeans to name elements of African culture, while some flora are named 'wild' and 'bush'. Language ideologies are explicit in the nomen hierarchies exhibited by European names for African flora. Some African fruits and vegetables are named to imply possession or belonging to animals, not humans. In all these cases, the genus is identified as a European fruit or vegetable, creating European cultural flora selves and their inferior wild and animal varieties in Africa. The Europeans took imperial othering of African ecology a step further when they used their anthroponyms to name African fauna, constructing possessive names. Some names of African animals are identified scientifically and in literature with European people's names, and their African names have been forgotten. African knowledge and science are also named in othering terms, creating traditional-modern and indigenous-global dichotomies. The names portray African culture as frozen in time and space, while European culture is current and global. African religion is not spared; it also is satanised and aligned with evil through names. African adaptations of Christianity are also named as rebel and apostate. Efforts to self African culture through authenticity cannot be successful, because authenticity itself confirms African culture as backward. Imperialism has affected the African intellect, and Africans even name some elements of their own culture using derogatory names and use upgrading names to name European culture.

## References

Amir, O. G. (2006). Wildlife trade in Somalia. *Report to the IUCN/SSC Antelope Specialist Group*, 1–28. www.wmenews.com/newsletters/File/Volume-1/Issue-4/support_art/Wildlife_Trade_in_Somalia_20061.pdf

Arctander, P., Kat, P. W., Aman, R. A., & Siegismund, H. R. (1996). Extreme genetic differences among populations of *Gazella granti*, Grant's gazelle, in Kenya. *Heredity*, *76*(5), 465–475.

Battiste, M. (2005). *Indigenous knowledge: Foundations for first nations*. Purish Publishing.

Bekerie, A. (2004). Ethiopica: Some historical reflections on the origin of the word Ethiopia. *International Journal of Ethiopian Studies*, 110–121.

Billig, M. (1973). Normative communication in a minimal intergroup situation. *European Journal of Social Psychology*, *3*(3), 339–343.

Bonilla-Silva, E. (1996). Rethinking racism: Toward a structural interpretation. *American Sociological Review*, *62*, 465–480.

Borkfelt, S. (2011). What's in a name? Consequences of naming non-human animals. *Animals*, *1*(1), 116–125. https://doi.org/10.3390/ani1010116

Brons, L. L. (2015). Othering, an analysis. *Transcience*, *6*(1), 69–90.

Çelik, A. B., Bilali, R., & Iqbal, Y. (2017). Patterns of "othering" in Turkey: A study of ethnic, ideological, and sectarian polarisation. *South European Society and Politics*, *22*(2), 217–238.

Cesaire, A. (2000). *Discourse on colonialism* (J. Pinkham, Trans. & R. D. G. Kelley, New Intro.). Monthly Review Press.

Chidester, D., Kwenda, C., Petty, R., Tobler, J., & Wratten, D. (1997). *African traditional religion in South Africa: An annotated bibliography*. ABC-CLIO.

Chitando, E. (2005). Naming the phenomena: The challenge of African independent churches. *Studia Historiae Ecclesiasticae*, *31*(1), 85–110.

Conrad, J. (1902). *Heart of darkness*. Penguin.

DeFilipps, R. A., & Krupnick, G. A. (2018). The medicinal plants of Myanmar. *PhytoKeys*, *102*, 1–341.

DuBois, W. E. B. (1920). Race intelligence. *The Crisis*, *20*(3), 118–119.

DuBois, W. E. B. (1935). Inter-racial implications of the Ethiopian crisis – a Negro view. *Foreign Affairs*, *14*(82).

Fanon, F. (1968). *Black skin, white masks* (C. Farrington, Trans.). Grove Press.

Fanon, F. (1967). *Toward the African revolution*. Monthly Review Press.

Frimpong-Ansah, J. H. (1996). *Flexibility and responsiveness in the Ghana economy: Reflections on post-decline atrophy syndrome*. Ghana Academy of Arts and Sciences.

Fudge, E. (2004). Animal lives. *History Today*, *54*(10), 21–26.

Goredema, B. (2013, October 28). *The indigenous fruits of Zimbabwe*. http://thesovereignstate.org/indigenous-fruits-of-zimbabwe/

Grix, J. (2004). *The foundation of research*. Palgrave Macmillan.

Guba, E. G., & Lincoln, Y. S. (2005). Paradigmatic controversies, contradictions, and emerging confluences. In N. K. Denzin & Y. S. Lincoln (Eds.), *The Sage handbook of qualitative research* (3rd ed., pp. 191–215). Sage.

Hall, E. T. (1959). *The silent language*. Fawcett.

Ham, C., Akinnifesi, F. K., Franzel, S., Jordaan, D. D. P. S., Hansmann, C., Ajayi, O. C., & De Kock, C. (2007). *Opportunities for commercialization and enterprise development of indigenous fruits in Southern Africa: Indigenous fruit trees in the tropics: Domestication, utilization and commercialization*. World Agroforestry Centre.

Keet, A. (2014). Epistemic "othering" and the decolonisation of knowledge. *Africa Insight*, *44*(1), 23–37.

Lacerda, D. S., Meira, F. B., & Brulon, V. (2020). Spatial ethics beyond the North-South dichotomy: Moral dilemmas in favelas. *Journal of Business Ethics*, 1–13.

Lake, O. (2003). *Blue veins and kinky hair: Naming and color consciousness in African America*. Greenwood Publishing Group.

Lentz, C. (1995). "Tribalism" and ethnicity in Africa. *Cah Science Human*, *31*(2), 303–328.

Levine, D. N. (1974). *Greater Ethiopia*. University of Chicago Press.

Li, V. (1995). Towards articulation: Postcolonial theory and demotic resistance. *ARIEL: A Review of International English Literature, 26*(1), 167–189.

MacCannell, D. (1999). *The tourist: A new theory of the leisure class*. University of California Press.

Madsen, S. O., & Vallentin, S. (2018). The processes of othering in public organization. *Academy of Management Proceedings, 1*, 17597. https://doi.org/10.5465/AMBPP.2018.17597 abstract

Mazrui, A. A. (1986). *The Africans: A triple heritage*. BBC Publications.

Mbiti, J. S. (2004). The role of the Jewish Bible in African independent churches 1. *International Review of Mission, 93*(369), 219–237.

Merriam-Webster. (2020, February 11). *Thomson's gazelle*. www.merriam-webster.com/dictionary/Thomson%27s%20gazelle

Mowforth, M., & Munt, I. (2003). *Tourism and sustainability: Development and new tourism in the third world*. Routledge.

Myers, P., Espinosa, R., Parr, C. S., Jones, T., Hammond, G. S., & Dewey, T. A. (2021, February 11). *The animal diversity web (online)*. https://animaldiversity.org

Name-Doctor. (2020). *Name – Dorcas meaning*. Retrieved February 10, 2021, from www.name-doctor.com/name-dorcas-meaning-of-dorcas-30039.html

Ndlovu, S. (2011). Colonial legacy in the Ndebele ethnocentric retronym. *Monash University Linguistics Papers*, 7(2), 59–67.

Ndlovu, S. (2012). Structural and philosophical aspects in isiNdebele retronym derivation. *South African Journal of African Languages, 32*(2), 153–160.

Ndlovu, S. (2018). *A comparative analysis of metaphorical expressions used by rural and urban Ndebele speakers: The contribution of S'ncamtho* [Doctoral dissertation, University of Cape Town].

Ndlovu, S. (2019). Colonial and brand tensions in some Zimbabwean religious nomenclature. In E. G. Konyana & D. Oguntola-Laguda (Eds.), *Religious violence and conflict management in Africa: Phenomenological and epistemological engagements* (pp. 117–133). Africa Institute for Culture, Peace, Dialogue and Tolerance Studies.

Ndlovu-Gatsheni, S. J. (2013). *Coloniality of power in postcolonial Africa: Myths of decolonization*. CODESRIA Book Series.

Ndlovu-Gatsheni, S. J. (2014). Global coloniality and the challenges of creating African futures. *Strategic Review for Southern Africa, 36*(2), 181–202.

Necipoğlu, G., & Bailey, J. (Eds.). (2005). *Muqarnas: An annual on the visual culture of the Islamic world* (Vol. 22). Brill.

Nhemachena, A. (2016). Animism, coloniality and humanism: Reversing the empire's framing of Africa. In M. Mawere & A. Nhemachena (Eds.), *Theory, knowledge and politics: What role for the academy in the sustainability of Africa* (pp. 13–54). Langaa RPCIG.

Nhemachena, A. (2017). *Relationality and resilience in a not so relational world: Knowledge, chivanhu and (de-) coloniality in 21st century conflict-torn Zimbabwe*. Langaa RPCIG.

Ogbulogo, C. (1999). Names as discourse: A study of Igbo female names. *Journal of Cultural Studies, 1*(1), 61–68.

Olsen, K. (2002). Authenticity as a concept in tourism research. *Tourist Studies, 2*(2), 159–182.

Omotayo, A. O., & Aremu, A. O. (2020). Underutilized African indigenous fruit trees and food – nutrition security: Opportunities, challenges, and prospects. *Food and Energy Security, 9*(3), e220.

Oyedemi, T. (2020). (De)coloniality and South African academe. *Critical Studies in Education, 61*(4), 399–415.

Parker, G. W. (1918). *The children of the sun*. Black Classic.

Patton, M. Q. (2002). *Qualitative research and evaluation methods*. Sage.

Poole, B. (2010). Commitment and criticality: Fairclough's critical discourse analysis evaluated. *International Journal of Applied Linguistics, 20*(2), 137–155.

Shava, S. (2005). Research on indigenous knowledge and its application: A case of wild food plants of Zimbabwe. *Southern African Journal of Environmental Education*, 73–86.

Sidima, H. J. (1994). *Drums of redemption: An introduction to African Christianity*. Greenwood.

Strandberg, A. (2009). *The gazelle in ancient Egyptian art: Image and meaning* [Doctoral dissertation, Uppsala University].

Strani, K., & Szczepaniak-Kozak, A. (2018). Strategies of othering through discursive practices: Examples from the UK and Poland. *Lodz Papers in Pragmatics, 14*(1), 163–179.

Tavuyanago, B., Mutami, N., & Mbenene, K. (2010). Traditional grain crops in pre-colonial and colonial Zimbabwe: A factor for food security and social cohesion among the Shona people. *Journal of Sustainable development in Africa, 12*(6), 1–8.

Walls, A. F. (1979). The anabaptists of Africa? The challenge of the African independent churches. *Occasional Bulletin of Missionary Research, 3*(2), 48–52.

White, C. M. (2007). More authentic than thou: Authenticity and othering in Fiji tourism discourse. *Tourist Studies*, 7(1), 25–49.

Williams, D. R. (1999). Race, socioeconomic status, and health: The added effects of racism and discrimination. *Annals of New York Academic Science, 896*, 173–188. https://deepblue.lib.umich.edu/bitstream/handle/2027.42/71908/j.1749-6632.1999.tb08114.x.pdf?sequence=1

Wilson, A. H. (1998). Oburoni outside the whale: Reflections on an experience in Ghana. *Theory & Research in Social Education, 26*(3), 410–429.

Wilson, D. E., & Reeder, D. M. (Eds.). (2005). *Mammal species of the world: A taxonomic and geographic reference* (Vol. 1). John Hopkins University Press.

Winslow, S. M. (2015). *Ethiopian manuscript culture: Practices and contexts*. University of Toronto.

Wolf, E. (1982). *Europe and the people without history*. University of California Press.

WordSense Online Dictionary. (2021, February 11). *Speke's gazelle*. www.wordsense.eu/Speke's_gazelle/

# 4 Ethnophaulisms as crude nomen othering in African contexts

## 4.0 Introduction

Ethnophaulisms are a form of crude identity formation. Gilroy (2004, p. 104) states that 'Seen or unseen, on the surface of the body or buried deep in its cells, identity forever sets one group apart from others who lack the particular, chosen traits that become the basis of typology and comparative evaluation.' Ethnophaulism is a neologism originating in Roback's (1944) characterisation of derogatory names for groups of people. Mullen (2001, p. 458) states that the term is 'from Greek roots meaning "a national group" and "to disparage".' Allen (1983) calls them *blazon populaire*, meaning ethnic slurs. Earlier on, Ericson (1939) characterised ethnic slurs as ethronyms, also from Greek roots meaning 'hostile' and 'name'. However, it is Roback's neologism, ethnophaulisms, which gained currency among linguists and sociologists. Ethnophaulisms are part of identity creation in all groups. Palmore (1962, p. 442) observes that 'it is probably safe to say that there is no known group which does not use ethnophaulisms', and Mullen (2001) opines that ethnophaulisms are common in sport, the media and works of fiction. Ethnophaulisms are also identified within the broader categories of hate speech and antilocutions, which are verbal expressions of prejudice (Bilewicz & Soral, 2020). Hate speech has no proper functional definition due to its potential infringements on freedom of speech and constructive intergroup criticism (Gelber, 2002). However, attempts to define it in political and legal contexts include expressions that spread, incite, promote or justify racial hatred, xenophobia and intolerance (Bilewicz & Soral, 2020). Other definitions narrow it from categories to individuals based on speech that disparages them based on their ethnicity, religion, race, gender, age, disability or sexuality (Sedler, 1992). Allport (1954) theorised that ethnophaulisms and all other forms of hate speech are the foundational step in a five-step continuum of evil othering; he hypothesised that the progression moves from antilocutions, to avoidance, to discrimination, to physical attack and finally to extermination.

Nuessel (2019, p. 185) argues that:

> an ethnophaulism derives from stereotypes of groups based on observable phenomena associated with them (skin colour, clothing,

DOI: 10.4324/9781003170761-5

culturally-determined eating and drinking customs, naming practices etc). This type of categorisation of groups is called metonymy which means the part stands for the whole.

The essence of a complex person is reduced to a single trait, and this has been established through research in racial and ethnic slurs (Bianchi, 2014; Croom, 2013; Rahman, 2012). Croom (2013) describes three uses of racial and ethnic slurs: (1) paradigmatic derogation to downgrade and create social hierarchies; (2) non-paradigmatic derogation, which only demeans the other outside social hierarchies; and (3) non-derogatory ingroup slurs – here targets of slurs fashion their identity around the slurs. This chapter argues that although the derogatory force of ethnophaulisms may be downplayed as non-paradigmatic and non-derogatory, the derogatory circumstances of their appellation remain.

Studies have been done in America and Europe on the reactions to ethnophaulisms by targeted groups and by observers (Pankiw & Bienvenue, 1990). Others have examined the valence of ethnophaulisms in Europe and America (Rice et al., 2010). This chapter disambiguates the meanings of some ethnophaulisms operating within Africa through etymological and semantic analyses to show how these ethnonyms and toponyms constitute crude outgroup othering based on imagined social and physical comparisons. The chapter discusses ethnophaulisms in the context of race, ethnicity and immigrants. While a lot of research has been done on the psychological and social effects of antilocutions in Europe and America, the area has not had robust engagement in Africa. Matsinhe (2011) engages narratives of antilocutions used in apartheid and post-apartheid South Africa, while Ndlovu (2017) engages phonological ethnophaulisms in Zimbabwe. This chapter is a content analysis (Croom, 2014; Hedger, 2012) of ethnophaulisms and deploys critical discourse analysis (Fairclough, 2012), metaphor analysis (Kövecses, 2017) and speech acts theory (Searle, 1975) on ethnophaulism to expose the etymologies and meanings behind the words which make the content of these ethnophaulisms.

The chapter engages the theories of post-coloniality and othering. According to Hickling-Hudson (2009, pp. 365–366):

> Postcolonial theory helps to uncover and rebuild the autonomous yet hybrid identity of those dispossessed by imperialist dominance through its exploration and probing of indigenous, local, and creole or blended knowledges. It challenges, counters, and can reshape political structures that have their roots in colonialism and imperialism.

Postcolonial theory helps to uncover the derogatory force in most ethnonyms used as descriptive content locutions in Africa. Bekerie (2004, p. 110) opines that 'naming plays a critical dual role either in defining or distorting one's identity, in articulating or blunting the essence of being human, and in evoking respect or disrespect from human community.' Othering theory help to demonstrate how the self-other dichotomy is created and maintained by these names. Othering is a faculty of human cognition. Cahoone (2003) argues that when humans encounter differences in people and culture, they use othering as a mental process of fashioning identity. People are bound to see difference and categorise it; it is only natural to do so. Madsen and Vallentin (2018, p. 1) concur, 'Indeed, othering is an inevitable part of language and how we relate to others. Othering as such is unavoidable. Crude and destructive forms of othering, however, are not.' However, Tilly (1999) argues that these categorise people see as differentiating them are, in fact, socially constructed to create the self identity and the other. Tajfel (1974) observes that these social categories give rise to the ingroup versus outgroup type of identity formation, and this creates othering, which, according to Crang (1998, p. 61), 'is a process through which identities are set up in an unequal relationship.' Ethnophaulisms are expressions of bigotry expressing robust intergroup hatred and, in the process, revealing social inequalities. Martinot (2011, p. 6) postulates:

> Bigotry is a collocation in one act of judgment of speaking for others, generalising them, gratuitously denigrating or assaulting them in so doing, being hypocritical in the act, and acting in bad faith. This is its structure. It does not matter whether it be anti-Semitism, anti-Black racism, homophobia, misogyny, redbaiting, or intra-movement polemic. It is always assaultive in its denigrations, dependent in its need for a threat, and gratuitously contemptuous toward its target. It is important to recognise this structure, because the political thinking of a person who finds this structure permissible, however progressive it may pretend to be, is suspect to the extent it contains a bigoted drive as its motivation.

The analysis of the meanings and implications of the names exposes colonial and ethnic hierarchies embedded in these antilocutions. Africa has had its own share of the antilocutions-violence continuum which culminated in mental and physical outgroup harm in the form of ethnic wars, colonialism, imperialism, discrimination, apartheid and xenophobia, among other ills. This chapter examines the impact of racialised slurs on Africa and Black people and how these seek to rank Africans on racial spectrums. The chapter also analyses Africa's reactionary antilocutionary naming and how the 'pandemic' of hate speech has affected Africans. The chapter seeks also to demonstrate how names are derived to be derogatory and fouling to their targets and how these meanings lead people along the hate speech continuum. Data for the analysis were collected through document analysis from journals and books that deal with slurs and ethnophaulisms, observations and intuitive knowledge.

The chapter is motivated by previous research on the semantics and pragmatics of racial and ethnic slurs (Hedger, 2012, 2013; Croom, 2014). Hedger (2012) deploys Kaplan's (1999) analysis of expressives and descriptives to qualify and disqualify known slurs. In his study, descriptive content represents the world as being a certain way and can be either true or false, while expressive content merely displays the attitude of the speaker and has no truth value. Such an analysis is oblivious to the socio-historical dynamics in language usage and may be intended to justify use of certain ethnophaulisms by stating that they are made up of descriptive content. To deploy truth values synchronically in the analysis of African ethnophaulisms covers up for the colonial and unjust historical conditions in which some truths were created. Croom (2014) opines that any argument for a definition of slurs based on a purely expressive content analysis is an attempt to account for the inoffensiveness of expressions, such as Chinese American. Kaplan's (1999) distinction between expressive and descriptive content cannot apply to ethnophaulisms because they are not motivated by linguistic content only to be derogatory; much of their derogatory force comes from non-linguistic intergroup conditions, not purely locution content conditions only. This chapter demonstrates how ingroups seek to self themselves by othering outgroups through crude nomen othering using the medium of ethnophaulisms.

The power of names derives from the social and historical contexts which give the namer the authority to name. Names also derive power from the semantic and pragmatic qualities of the words used in the names (Bosmajian, 1974). Nuessel (2019, pp. 186–187) argues that 'in defining another person by labelling that individual on the basis of race, gender, and ethnicity, that individual's identity is defined by another person who thereby controls how others perceive this human being.' The implications of ethnophaulisms on social relations and human psychology have led to an active drive to exclude them from all discourses in a process called prohibitionism (Anderson & Lepore, 2013). The United States has developed a Racial Slur Database to help enforce this prohibitionism.

## 4.1 Racialised ethnophaulisms

The politics of identity expressed in names and culture have been researched in anthropology (Scott, 1995; Dominguez, 1994). However, anthropologists are generally reluctant to address racial identity, as most believe race is a non-existent concept that is a mere social construction. This section discusses racism and anti-racism as expressed in how ingroups name outgroups. While it has been argued that race dose not exist, and this is true, science has been abused to accommodate derogation of other people and their spaces. Europeans named races, and that is already problematic. Martinot (2011, p. 5) posits 'The English (white) role as definers of race thus already contained an inherent pretence to superiority.' The names that have been allocated to non-Europeans by Europeans are based on prejudice in the majority. Nuessel (2019, p. 189) postulates that:

> it must be remembered that certain designations of racial, ethnic, religious, and gender groups are stereotypic, i.e., they use a metonymic process by which a single physical, behavioural, or psychological characteristic defines a person as belonging to a specific group thus denying the members of these groups their essential humanity.

In naming peoples of the world, the Europeans started by creating an imagined European beauty and authenticity which they used as a standard to prejudice others. The system of othering others was idealised and institutionalised, creating racism. It took the othered people time to react to this racist naming. They retaliated through anti-racist ethnophaulisms, too. Paradies (2005, p. 3) defines racism:

> as occurring at three conceptual levels (which overlap in practice): (i) internalised racism, the incorporation of racist ideologies within an individual's world view; (ii) interpersonal racism, racist interactions between people; and (iii) systemic/institutional racism, the racist production, control, and access to material, informational, and symbolic resources within society. Conversely, 'anti-racism' is any approach that reduces power differentials through advantaging subordinate racial groups and/or disadvantaging dominant racial groups.

Eugenics, the belief that human reproduction can be arranged to create desirable human breeds, (Galton 1904) is one fallacy of European racism which has been outmoded by science. However, it was only discredited after its racial biases were adopted to justify the Holocaust. Agar (1998) rightly states that eugenicists were following misguided views on human worth. These misguided views, unfortunately, left behind a legacy of divisive social, psychological and linguistic heritages, some of which are names that remind us of these views, although science has long proved them wrong. While scientific racism is outmoded as a domain of study, its categories are used today in medical and scientific research; for example, the Kaffir lime tree, *Citrus hystrix DC* (Wijaya et al., 2020). The psychological advantage these views gave to some people justified their abuse of others in physical and verbal forms. Galton's (1904) theory of eugenics proposes a people 'good in birth' who should be encouraged and bad ones discouraged. Social Darwinism and scientific racism resonate with such thinking. Mukhopadhyay (2008, p. 13) reminds us that:

> American scientists tried to prove that Caucasians had larger brains and were smarter than people of other races. Racial science dovetailed with nineteenth-century evolutionary theories, which ranked races from more 'primitive' 'savages' to more 'advanced' or 'civilised,' with Caucasians on top. Racial hierarchies were used to justify slavery and other forms of racial discrimination.

The taxonomies of humanity are named to imagine continued and consummated evolution of species. Eugenicists' preoccupation with beautiful human beings originated the inversely phaulic name Caucasian, which is the foundation taxonomy in the development of scientific racism. Perry (2016) states that in the late 1700s, German philosopher Christoph Meiners believed in the pseudo-scientific theory of scientific racism. He deified the skin of people from the Caucasus region (present-day central Russia, Georgia, Azerbaijan, Armenia and North Iran) as the whitest, most blooming and most delicate skin and that of non-Caucasians as inferior and animal-like. German scientist and skull collector Johann Blumenbach developed the 'good' Caucasian theory and identified Georgia as the cradle of humanity and as having the most beautiful people (Baum, 2006). Blumenbach's racial geometry created four othered categories of degenerate people: Malayan, 'the brown race'; Mongolian, 'the yellow race'; American, 'the red race'; and Ethiopian, 'the Black race' (Bhopal, 2007; Teo, 2009). Blumenbach, in his analysis and ordering of skulls, represented degeneration to be two directional, a degeneration to Mongolians with Malayans as the intermediate race and a degeneration to Ethiopians with Americans being the intermediate race. The ethnonym Caucasian creates a dual dichotomy of degenerates, the sickly and beastly in the ethnophaulisms Mongolian and Negroid, respectively (Bhopal, 2007). The degeneration implications in the names Mongolian and Ethiopian/Negroid are demonstrated in Figure 4.1.

The degeneration of Mongolians is used to name sickness in Caucasian culture; Down's syndrome is named mongolism (Miller, 1963). This is onomastic evidence that eugenics believe that Caucasians degenerate and become frail physically and mentally to become Mongolians. On the other hand, a degeneration towards being Ethiopian is imagined as human regression to animalism as evidenced by ethnophaulisms such as 'kaffir' and 'ape'. Mukhopadhyay (2008, p. 13) states that 'Blumenbach named four other races that he considered physically and morally "degenerate" forms of "God's original creation." He classified Africans (except lighter-skinned North Africans) as "Ethiopians" or "Black".' The division of Africa into Caucasians in the north and Ethiopians further south goes beyond derogation but also divides Africa, setting Africans

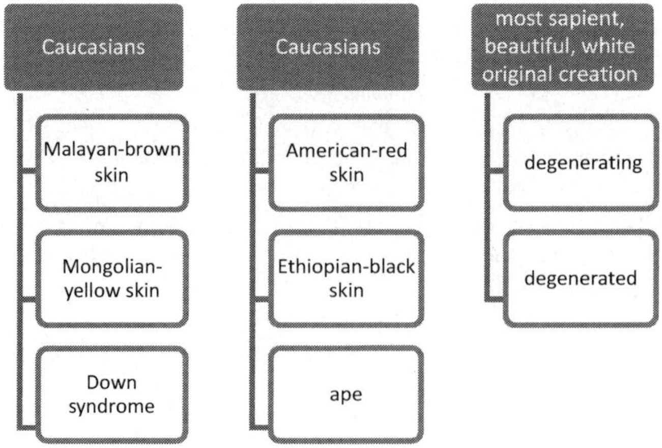


*Figure 4.1* Eugenics' imagined degeneration of Mongoloids and Negroids from the perfection in Caucasoids

against each other, and more ethnophaulisms have been created because of this foreign divide. Maart (2014) traces the origins of the word 'kaffir' to Arabic, meaning infidel, non-believer or non-Muslim. The ethnophaulism 'kaffir' is an instance of an African language, Arabic, derogating other Africans as animals because the namers are privileged to be Caucasian. Other ethnophaulisms that animalise Africans are 'Hottentot' and 'Bushmen' (Lindfors, 2001). The *Etymonline* Dictionary (2021) defines 'Hottentot' as a hunter gatherer, and the term derives from Portuguese, meaning 'nonsense words/sounds', referencing the click phonemes. These phonemes were misunderstood to be non-human speech sounds. Europeans even took some of these 'degenerate' Africans to showcase them in museums (Schmahmann, 2020).

The ethnophaulisms given to Africans rank them by closeness to Caucasian, Arab North Africa being the closest, followed by Ethiopia, then the rest, and at the bottom appears to be the Khoisan. There has been controversy as to the etymology of the name Ethiopia, with some advocating Eurasian etymologies aimed at disassociating Ethiopia from Africa, making it a conglomeration of western and eastern civilisations. Greek etymology of the toponym and ethnonym links Ethiopians to deformed Caucasians' 'burnt faces' because they are 'born under the sun's path' (Bekerie, 2004). He further posits that the name Ethiopia is derived by compounding *aitho*, αἴθω, which means burn, and *ops*, ὤψ, which means face. Under this etymology, the name creates humanity in White skin, and Black becomes 'damaged goods'. What this essentially means is that people are White and they only become burnt by the sun to be darker. Martinot (2011, p. 5) states, 'In defining others as non-White, they defined themselves as White.'

The colour spectrum in race identity is itself problematic in that human beings are not always black or white; they may not even be black or white in the first place. Colour schemes on human bodies are a variety of ranges that may ironically exclude black and white. People may be dark or light skinned, but the colour does not go beneath the skin to affect being. Parker (1918, p. 29) incorporates African identity into Greek and Roman genealogies and opines that, from Roman mythology, Aeneas, the founding father of the Romans, 'was a descendant of Dardanus the African founder of Troy.' However, being White is associated with purity and good; this is most likely the reason European namers chose this colour for themselves. In almost all human languages and cultures, white and black are iconographies for good and bad, respectively. In Ndebele, for example, bad luck is *umnyama*, 'blackness', and congratulations is *amhlophe*, 'white ones'. To call people Black is to associate them with being bad and evil, as confirmed by ethnophaulisms such as kaffir, while to call yourself White is to imagine yourself as good, beautiful and sapient, as in the ethnonym Caucasian. Martinot (2011, p. 3) argues that:

> The purity concept is an indispensable factor for the definition of race. Because human coloration exists on a continuum, there are no natural divisions in its spectrum. Between any two people of differing colour, a

> third can be found whose colour would lie between them. And there is no uniformity of colour in any human community. The purity of English parentage became the mark of the first division in the colour continuum, the basis on which, after 1690, the English defined themselves as 'White,' through their definition of others as non-White.

The association of the colour Black with Africans has created problematic ethnonyms such as Negro. Nuessel (2019) observes that the etymology of Negro derives from the Latin colour term *niger* (black). The term is an ethnophaulism for Africans, especially in the United States. Analysing the negative indices of the name Negro, Moore (1992) argues for a human right which bestows on all people the right to name themselves and define their own identity. While it is impossible to have only self namers, the crude names for others created by imperial Europe, which are still used today, make non-Europeans wish for a right to name themselves as a selfing enterprise. The colour black has become a marked identity among African scholars and those theorising and fighting coloniality because of its links with slavery. Slavery is an evil with a White face and Black victims, and this has led many theorists to opt for African instead of Black. Mazrui (1986) notes that African slaves in the northern hemisphere were commanded to forget they were African and to remember they were Black as a way of ridding their memories of their African origins and identity. Black, therefore, as a race category also carries the stigma and violence of slavery. This stigma is the expressive force of the ethnonym Black, which is realised in its other synonyms, Ethiopian and Negro. Negro has been classified as an ethnophaulism and is under prohibition; this is why African is a preferred euphemism.

The colonial and imperial stigmas associated with the 'Black' race have also affected the name Africa; it, too, is linked to western ethnophaulism for describing the opposite of Caucasian. Africa is a historically tainted category due to prejudice which has been colonially collocated with the name. In European and North American media, the image of Africa is associated with AIDS, hunger, civil war, corruption, authoritarianism and all things that Europe and America are not (Adesanmi, 2008; Matsinhe, 2011). Africa is pejorated morally, and it is even physically pejorated to appear smaller than Europe in cartography (Morlin-Yron, 2017). While some descriptive names, such as Chinaman and Indian-American, have been disqualified as slurs in America, African-American is classed as a descriptive ethnonym (Croom, 2014). Africa is pejorated to reference a country in American compound race terminology. Africa is usually not given the privilege of being identified by its individual states but is totalised as a uniform entity. Monmonier (2006) identifies Japanese-Americans, Chinese-Americans, Italian-Americans and Indian-Americans, but no African country is specified. While identifying Americans using foreign lands is ethnophaulism, the name African-American is a double phaulism in that among the racial slurs where some are othered by country, Africa is pejorated to the level of countries.

Names are not just referential or symbolic semiotics; according to Hertzler (1965), they are a type of magic whereby the name goes beyond the word-reality symbolism to index quantities and qualities of concepts and space. The word can reference good and evil in a concept or part of the world, and such indices create othered nominative categories. The pejoration of Africa is testimony that colonial race relations developed names that othered not only racial groups but their spaces, too; this phenomenon derives ethnophaulic toponyms. The concept of ethnophaulism has also been researched in toponyms and proven to have the same derogatory force as in ethnonyms (Brown et al., 2015; Nick, 2018). In apartheid South Africa, under the Group Areas Act of 1950, which forcefully moved non-Whites for living in the 'wrong areas', Africans were separated from Europeans, and their places were named in ethnophaulic toponyms, 'Bantustans' and 'Homelands' (Evans, 2019). The two toponyms carry the meaning of racial segregation, and they other African spaces within their own continent. Affluent suburbs in South Africa's urban centres are called *Emakhishini*, 'at the kitchens' (Ngwenya, 2014), a reminder that Africans worked and continue to work there as domestic workers to the so-called Caucasians. The use of the name insults Africans and is a reminder of those evil memories of apartheid and its inequalities.

Names given to Europeans by Africans on their initial encounters represent instances of sophisticated othering. These can be analysed as descriptive content, with no accompanying social inequalities. The Nguni of Southern Africa called them *Abangelamadolo*, 'those without knees', describing the trousers that covered their knees. Such names are descriptive, as the Africans were describing an aspect of social culture which is not biological. Human taxonomies are influenced by cultural differences, and as such, people can move from one taxonomy into another; all they need to do is assimilate that culture through language, dress and other social markers of human groups. Racism is amplified when people look at difference using biological descriptors, because these cannot be changed once marked. There are some names for White people in Africa which derive from biological classification, such as *amaKhiwa* from the colour of ripe figs; *oMpumulonde*, 'people with long nose'; and *oNdlebe zikhanya ilanga*, 'people with transparent ears'. Such names go beyond just description to express not only difference but contempt as well.

Realising that colour is used by Europeans to savage Africans, African cultures created their own anti-racist racisms in naming Europeans using colour as race marking. The name *amaKhiwa* for White people has racial connotations, as it references skin colour. *AmaKhiwa*, like its counterparts, *abeLungu, abeLumbi, vaR-umbi, waZungu, Aboforo* and *Oburoni*, has had its fair share of racial controversy. Wilson (1998) narrates her encounter with the racialised name *Oburoni* while teaching in Ghana. Sibanda (2016) argues that *iKhiwa* is an inoffensive descriptive name for a White person in Ndebele. He states that when locals encountered White people for the first time, they referred to them as *amaKhiwa*, which is plural for *umkhiwa* (fig tree). The Tswana in Botswana and South Africa refer to White people as *Makgoa*, which is a (dialectical) variation of the Nguni *amaKhiwa* and follows the same fig tree etymology. There is a colour similarity between a ripened fig and European skin. However, Rödlach (2006) identifies the name *amaKhiwa* as derogatory; he says *abeLungu* is respectful, and if one wants to be less respectful, they use *amaKhiwa*, which is related to the fruit of the fig tree. Suffice it to say that Nguni people also associate ripened figs with the colour red, as evidenced by the Ndebele proverb *ikhiwane elibomvu libolile*, 'a red (ripened) fig is rotten'. An editorial of *News 24* from July 24 2013 captures anti-racist ethnophaulisms for Boers and all so-called Caucasians in South Africa:

> An antonym for *uMlungu* is '*Bhulu*' (Xhosa) or '*Bhunu*' (Zulu). It is literally taken from 'Boer' which the Afrikaner proudly called/calls himself to denote pride in his race/culture, his undefeatable strength and superiority. Blacks associated *Bhunu* or *Bhulu* with aggressiveness, ruthlessness, racism against Blacks and unjust government. What Blacks had done was take a name that Afrikaners used to proudly/positively call themselves and attributed it with their negative encounters with Whites. They have used a White man's weapon against him. A White man is called *uMlungu* because of his perceived social status and superiority; however, when that White man ill-treats a Black person, he is called a *Bhunu/Bhulu*.

Names such as *Mlungu, Khiwa, Bhunu* and *Bhulu* have been associated with negative expression of anti-racist anticolonialism, and they are ethnophaulic. Africans have gone as far as trying to attribute negativity to the name Caucasian or White and inversely attribute its glory to Africa and being Black. Black Zimbabwean languages express and emphasise the racial difference between Black and White Africans (Rödlach, 2006; Comaroff & Comaroff, 1993). There is a clear distinction between White people and Black people, and the distinction is extended to culture and world view. African culture is imagined as authentic, while European culture is labelled as artificial (White, 2007).

The construction of Black moral superiority and calling it *ubuntu*, as opposed to *isikhiwa/isilungu*, others western civilisation as immoral and barbaric. This construction of African glory presupposes that being good comes naturally with being an African autochthon and being bad mannered is inherently western. Such categorisation is too general and cannot hold for human subjects; however, at the level of decoloniality, this racial othering may serve as ego boosting for the racialised or simple decolonial revenge nomenclature. Postcolonial theories also have problems of reactionary totalising against global trends and identities. Some theories emphasise history and tradition anachronistically, to exclude Africans and other colonials from participating in hybridising global cultures and systems of power. While cultural renaissance and revolution are important for the recreation of the self in Africa, over-romanticisation of African cultural authenticity takes Africa far back in time and diminishes its global relevance.

In Africa, racialised ethnophaulisms are not restricted to Europeans and Africans only; there are some ethnophaulisms Africans aim at other groups. People of Indian origin have been doing business in Africa for centuries now, and most own shops. The group is usually referred to as *Amakula* (Nguni) or *Makula* (Shona), and it includes Indian, Arab, Chinese and Pakistani nationals, although the ethnophaulism has now generally narrowed to target Indians. The *Dictionary of South African English* (2020) defines the word *Amakula/maCoola/Mkulas* as the plural of a derogatory name among Zulu speakers, an insulting name for people of Indian origin. On the etymology of the name Kula/Coolie, the *Encyclopaedia Britannica* (2011) states that:

> Coolie (from Hindi *Kuli,* an aboriginal tribal name, or from Tamil *kuli,* 'wages'), in usually pejorative European usage, an unskilled labourer or porter usually in or from the Far East hired for low or subsistence wages. The so-called coolie trade began in the late 1840s as a response to the labour shortage brought on by the worldwide movement to abolish slavery.

The coolie wage labourers were 'hired' from Aden, and they included Indian, Chinese and Pakistani nationals in the majority (Walker, 2014). The name is an ethnophaulism from racialised imperial labour, just as 'Negro' implies slavery. It is an ethnophaulism imported from Europe-Asia race inequalities into Africa, and most Africans are oblivious to this etymology.

Indians are called *Amwenye* in Malawi and Zambia, a name they share with the Lemba and other Asians in the country. The *Word Sense Online Dictionary* (2021) points out that *mwenye* in Chichewa language is from Kiswahili, meaning 'owner', most likely a reference to 'the shop owner'. It then became a name for people of Indian descent. *Amwenye*'s etymology leads to precolonial feudal systems, whereby Africans were othered by Asian traders. Bruder (2008, p. 122) alludes to a 'red skinned race of traders, known as *Amwenye*. . . . *Mwenye* evokes feudal lord or master.' The use of the name *Amwenye* to reference Indians amounts to self othering by Malawians and Zambians. The name evokes times when Africans were subjects of Indian feudal lords, and this is an instance of the Asian/eastern coloniality of money and power in Africa. The Chinese are now excluded from the *Mkula*, meaning, at least in Zimbabwe, they are not called *Amwenye* either but are derided for their cheap and fragile goods that do not last. The ethnophaulism *Zhingzhong*, from the common sounds in Mandarin, is used by Zimbabweans to reference Chinese nationals in the country; *Amazhingzhong* and *Mazhingzhong* in Ndebele and Shona, respectively.

## 4.2 Names as exhibits of ethnic tensions

There are some ethnophaulisms that do not cross the race line but are used within it, and they affect Africans. These ethnophaulisms exhibit ingroup loyalties and express animosity to other Africans. Fishman (1971, p. 1) posits that:

> language is a referent for loyalties and animosities, and indicator of social statuses and personal relationships, and a marker of situations and topics, as

well as of societal goals and the large-scale value-laden arenas of interaction that typify every speech community.

Ndlovu (2011) has argued that when retronyms are used to differentiate ethnicities, the ingroup usually uses foul language about the outgroup to differentiate it. The foul language used reflects more the attitudes of the namers than it describes the target. Hall (1991, p. 2) observes that 'Ethnic stereotypes, ancient and modern, though revealing almost nothing about the groups they are intended to define, say a great deal about the community which produces them.' Precolonial, colonial and postcolonial tensions have motivated Africans to use ethnophaulisms on each other. Language forms part of a people's identity (Argenter, 2000). Ndlovu and Mangena (2014) observe that the name of a language (lingonym) is usually the name for the ethnicity (ethnonym). The language-ethnicity nexus has seen people create some derogatory names for others based on how they speak.

At a global level, Black people are ranked to create images of superiority in others. There are many people in the West and the East who see Africa as one small country where everyone knows all people in the country. Living in Europe, I realised Blacks are almost always identified as Americans if found in places of the high life such as expensive restaurants and beaches. Such ranking of Blacks creates African(ness) problems for African-Americans. While visiting Iran in 2015, many people were fascinated seeing Black people on the very 'white' walkways, and they sought to know whether we were '*Amerikana*', to which we truthfully answered in the negative. They then asked whether we were from India or Africa. This grading of blackness by region depicts Black hierarchies whereby the name Black is gradable by vicinity to White spaces. A 'Black-American' is above all Black and can be followed by a Black-Indian, and the least of the Blacks is the Black-African. These hierarchies create ethnophaulisms out of the ethnonyms Black-Indian and Black-African, and African-Americans are the de facto Black-English.

Another glorified African ethnicity is Lemba. Indians are called *Mwenye* in Malawi and Zambia because they are sellers, and they come from a history of being feudal lords (Bruder, 2008). The Lemba people found in most Southern African countries are also called *Amwenye* or *Vashava*. The name *Amwenye* suggests that, like Indians and Arabs, they too came from Asia and hence were foreign to Africa, and this others them and excludes them from African autochthony. Bruder (2008) argues that the name *Vashava* comes from *Musavi* (*sava*), which is Bantu meaning to trade; to call them traders links them to foreign identities, yet, at the same time, it may elevate their ethnic status to a level higher than that of other African ethnicities. The Lemba are called and proudly call themselves Black Jews (Tamarkin, 2020), a name which scores them superiority in a continent which glorifies Abrahamic religions. They are usually seen as better cultured and held in high esteem, as evidenced by the way they are revered for their dietary choices. In public gatherings in Zimbabwe, they do not eat any flesh which was not slaughtered by one of their own. The Midlands area of Mberengwa in Zimbabwe has a high concentration of the Lemba, and being non-Lemba, you can be ridiculed as the uncircumcised. The Lemba have been genetically linked to Jews. While the Lemba are identified as *Amwenye* in Zimbabwe, the term originates in the Chichewa language of Malawi referencing Indians. The Chichewa nomen designation for the ethnic other, though appellative, is a perfect instance of othering, as it includes the word 'other' in the expression *Anthu a mitundu yina*, 'people of other ethnicities'. Africans other and rank each other, creating localised colonialities of power.

The Ndebele state organised present-day Zimbabwe into a conglomeration of ethnicities under one king. The Ndebele state has been characterised as having had a caste system which othered non-Nguni ethnicities; this othering was and still is expressed in ethnophaulisms. Makoni (2011, p. 441) posits:

> The Ndebele society is heterogeneous and, therefore, divided along caste lines into *abeZansi, abeNhla*, and *amaHole*. The aristocracy, *abeZansi*, often identified itself with the Nguni clan and the Zulu language, while the commoners were a heterogeneous group that had been drawn from the Sotho and the Tswana and were often referred to as *amaHole* (commoners). This act of naming other group members using derogatory names reflects the tension between Zulu aristocrats and the Ndebele commoners.

The *abeZansi*, 'the Southerners', are the aristocrats; the *abeNhla*, 'the Northerners', consisting of the Sotho-Tswana group, are the intermediate group; and the Shona, Kalanga, Tonga and Venda are the lowest class of *amaHole* (Ndlovu, 2015). Ndlovu-Gatsheni (2009) opines that the name *Amahole* is a shortened version of *Amaholingubo*, 'those with long clothes', apparently from the long garments they got from Arab traders. This makes the name a descriptive ethnonym. However, the name is an ethnophaulism because of its reference to the lowest caste in the Ndebele state. The Tonga, who were part of the *Amahole* caste, are also further othered as *Mazambezi*. Alexander and Alexander (1997) identify the name *amaZambezi* (Zambezi River people) as used negatively on the Tonga people. They trace the negativity to the earlier Ndebele state, which captured them along the Zambezi River and made them slaves. The name has become derogatory today partly due to its links to this slave history. They quote one Tonga interviewee as saying Zambezi is a river, not people; the Tonga do not call people by rivers. Otherwise, that would have them call the Ndebele, for example, the Shangani people after the Shangani River, which traverses the Ndebele environs in Zimbabwe.

The coming of colonialism and earlier contact with Europeans and Arabs brought into Africa 'modern' lifestyles in terms of clothing, tools and machinery, and this created a rift between those who experienced this transformation earlier than others. There are ethnic slurs which were created on the modernity-primitive dichotomy. In the early years of colonialism in Zimbabwe, for example, Alexander and Alexander (1997, p. 194) state that 'to originate in the South, to have been at the heart of the Ndebele state, was to be modern; to originate in the remote North, land of tobacco, hunting, raiding, and taking of captives, was to be primitive.' One prominent ethnic slur which references or is at least associated with being primitive is *Shankwe*. Alexander and Alexander (1997) describe the name *Shankwe* as referencing a poor tobacco or snuff seller from the northern parts of Zimbabwe during the time of the advent of colonialism. The *Shankwe* (*Sankwe*) people were looked down upon as poor primitive nomads who had nothing but the tobacco they travelled around selling.

The Shona and Ndebele of Zimbabwe further employ derogatory pronunciation of names to create ethnophaulisms. Ethnonyms, anthroponyms and toponyms carry in them people's identities (Ndlovu, 2017), and their flagrant violation is derogatory. Ndlovu further observes that there are some phonemes that are foreign either to Ndebele or Shona phonology, and their violation is understandable as genuine transphonologies. However, he states that some phonemes which make up the phonological stock of these languages are violated intentionally to spite the ethnic other. This is common with toponyms and ethnonyms; for example, he states that the Ndebele flagrantly replace **[r]** with **[l]** and **[ʧ]** with **[s]** in some Shona names to derive expressive derogatory content. The Shona, on the other hand, flagrantly replace **[l]** with **[r]** in some Ndebele names. These flagrant transphonologies are exemplified in Table 4.1.

The flagrant transphonologies amount to antilocutions. Ndlovu (2017, p. 121) observes that both the Ndebele and the Shona are offended by these transphonologies. He quotes Shona interviewees as saying, 'Why are they able to say "read", yet when it is Shona, they say "Lusape", it is just meant to insult the Shona; how come in the case of "potato chips" they do not say potato *sips*?'

*Table 4.1* Flagrant ethnophaulic transphonologies between the Ndebele and the Shona of Zimbabwe

| | |
|---|---|
| **Shona flagrant replacement of [l] with [r] to derive derogatory Ndebele names** | |
| **Ndebele name** | **Flagrant Shona transphonology** |
| Lobhengula (anthroponym/ toponym) [lobeŋʊla] | Robhengura [robeŋgʊra] |
| Ndebele (ethnonym) [ndɛβelɛ] | Ndeere [ndéere] |
| Lahleka (toponym) [laɬeɣa] | Rahleka [raɬeka] |
| **Ndebele flagrant replacement of [r] with [l] to derive derogatory Shona names** | |
| **Shona name** | **Flagrant Ndebele transphonology** |
| Mberengwa (toponym) [mbéreŋgwa] | Mbelengwa [mbéleŋwa] |
| Zezuru (ethnonym) [zezʊru] | Zezulu [zezʊlu] |
| Rusape (toponym) [rʊsape] | Lusape [lʊsape] |
| **Ndebele flagrant replacement of [ʧ] with [s] to derive derogatory Shona names** | |
| **Shona name** | **Flagrant Ndebele transphonology** |
| Chitungwiza (toponym) [ʧitʊŋgwiza] | Situngwiza [sitʊŋgwiza] |
| Chipinge (toponym) [ʧipiŋge] | Sipinge [sipiŋge] |
| Chikaranga (ethnonym) [ʧikaraŋga] | Sikaranga[sikaraŋga] |

He further quotes one Ndebele man in an interview as saying that 'Shona people are very unfair in that, they come and stay with us in our areas and expect us to speak to them in Shona, it is not the case that they cannot pronounce the **[l]** sound but, it is intentional to show us that they do not want to learn Ndebele.'

There are some ethnophaulic transcriptions of some names in Zimbabwe that have caused outcries. The Tsonga people in Zimbabwe have lived under Shona hegemony for a long time, and some graphemes they deem Shona have offended them. This has caused controversy, especially regarding the spelling of their ethnonym Shangani. The Great Zimbabwe University had problems when it introduced Shangani; the community rejected the name and orthography linguists had used. The community noted that the orthography 'Shangani' is Shona. Theirs is written as 'Xangana'. They understood the **/-sh-/** grapheme for **[ʃ]** as a continuation of Shona hegemony. They opted for **/-x-/**, the grapheme which was already in use in the South African Tsonga writing system. The Kalanga, who have lived under Ndebele and Shona hegemony, also have problems with the spelling of some of their toponyms, such as Tsholotsho **[tʃolotʃo]** instead of the Kalanga orthography *Tjolotjolo*. To them, the Ndebele spelling is an ethnophaulism. There was a Kalanga outcry when the name of the river *Tjankwa* was written using Shona orthography on a public road sign: it was written as *Chankwa*. The road sign was defaced, and the proper Kalanga orthography, *Tjankwa*, was used in the graffiti, which prompted authorities to change the name to the Kalanga orthography.

## 4.3 Foreignising and nationalising nomenclature

The power of names and naming is demonstrated by Hall (1991), who looks at the influences of the Greek-Barbarian dichotomy in how the name Barbarians, which means 'not speaking Greek', was used to other Persians and mobilise support against them. Hall and Rose (2006, p. 25) argue that 'cultural identity is fomented by sustaining cultural boundaries and boundedness.' To belong in this way is to create ingroup identity by excluding identities seen as alien and foreign. Names can be used as an arsenal by outgroups, and the recipients can use them to define the nature of the situation confronting them; from the name, they can assess their chances of survival (Khong, 1992). Hall and Rose (2006, p. 25) opine that 'the "Other" is always and continuously a threat to the security and integrity of those who share a common home.' There are some ethnophaulisms that clearly mark the other as not belonging. The content and meaning of these ethnophaulisms aggravate xenophobic hostilities.

Mukhopadhyay (2008, p. 15) states that Europeans came to America as immigrants and refugees, and most came after slavery had brought Africans to America. America already had native Americans when this happened. 'Yet the term Caucasian, because it now lacks any geographic connotation, masks this group's foreign ancestry while other labels, such as Asian American or African American, highlight those groups' foreign roots.' Even the autochthons are named with a qualifying appendage, native-American, yet Europeans are not. Mukhopadhyay (2008, p. 15) states that:

> The word Caucasian also reinforces the tendency to equate 'American' with people of European descent because, of a one-word designation, Caucasian reinforces the 'hyphenated' status of other American groups. Linguistically, adding a modifier to a generic term for example, adding Asian or African to American generally signifies that the modified form is less 'normal.' The more fundamental, typical, 'normal' form is left unmarked. (For example, we add the gender modifier 'male' to mark the unusual, abnormal category of 'male' nurses. 'Nurse' refers to the typical, taken-for-granted. 'normal' nurse, who is female.)

While scholarship prohibits the use of the ethnonym Black American as derogatory, its euphemism, African American, is foreignising. What African American means is that they are aliens, yet European Americans are just called Caucasian. Aliens are othered and made to lack belonging in both their country and the host country; in the host, they are excluded by policy and policing, yet in theirs, they are already excluded by distance. Kearney (1998, p. 128) suggests that 'the ambiguity of the alien results from policy and policing which inscribe both these identities.' Monmonier (2006) identifies the designation Chinaman as a Chinese ethnophaulism in America, and this ethnophaulism has the same descriptive, foreignising content as African American. The description African is usually associated with being Black. Reducing Africa to the colour black is tantamount to excluding a significant percentage of Africans, especially in Arab North Africa. Racialising identity makes it difficult for non-Blacks to be African and non-Whites to be European or American.

In Chichewa, Malawians call foreign nationals *Anthu akunja* (people from outside), and this refers to Africans from other African countries, yet White people (*Azungu*), who are in most cases tourists or working for nongovernmental organisations, are called *Anthu obwela* (visitors). In Tswana, foreign nationals are excluded by name as coming from elsewhere or far through the name *Batswakwa* (meaning come from elsewhere or far); such a name speaks to one's lack of belonging with the people. In Baoule language in the Ivory Coast, foreign nationals are called *Aofue* (stranger). The delegation of the word stranger to name one from outside your borders is motivated by othering, since it is not strange to see a Black person from Ghana, for example, in the Ivory Coast. White people were named strangers by Africans who encountered them for the first time; this was understandable since they had not seen a White person before, hence strange. However, Africans who usually blame their divisions on colonialism used and still use ethnophaulisms depicting other Africans as strangers and foreigners. Adesanmi (2008) identifies how Africans in South Africa invent their own 'Kaffirs' in other Africans who immigrate into that country:

> *Makwerekwere* is the derogatory term used by Black South Africans to describe non-South African Blacks. It reminds one of how the ancient Greeks referred to foreigners whose language they did not understand as the *Barbaroi*. To the Black South African, *makwerekwere* refers to Black immigrants from the rest of Africa, especially Nigerians. I was confounded by the fact that Black South Africa had begun to manufacture its own *kaffirs* so soon after apartheid.

Globalised diversities, especially in African cosmopolitan spaces, should be able to create fluid cosmopolitanism where people can go against origins and be trans- or international, capable of living at the crossing of boundaries (Kristeva, 1993). However, onomastic realities point to the opposite happening in African cosmopolitan urban spaces; people still mark others as foreign to the metropolis. Mbembé (2004), critiquing African metropolitan urbanism, describes it as a site of excesses, of hysteria and exclusions. Clifford (1997, p. 7) opines that 'the making and remaking of identities takes place in the contact zones, along the policed and transgressive intercultural frontiers of nations, peoples, locales.' Mamabolo (2015, p. 144) says that 'African immigrants in South Africa are labelled by derogatory names such as "Makwerekwere", "makhalangas" or "magrigambas", while in other parts of the country they are characterised as "Mekgaritswana", "Makula", "Mapafo" and "Makgaretein".' He further states that these names are offensive; some reference foreign nationals as a nuisance in their homes; for example, Mekgaritswana, Mapafo and Makgaretein ('curtains') describe the goods sold door to door by these foreign nationals. This expresses the feeling of being annoyed by foreign nationals and hence calling them *Mapoti*. *Mapoti* derives from the acronym MAPOTI (Most Annoying Person on the Internet) coined by Ryan Higa (*Urban Dictionary*, 2013).

South African metropoles such as Johannesburg have seen a redefinition of identities, especially of foreign nationals, who are othered as not belonging. The otherness of Zimbabweans in South Africa is alluded to by Ryan (2010, p. 16), who notes that 'Zimbabweans who have settled legally and illegally are regarded as foreigners or *Makwerekwere*.' Matsinhe (2011, p. 5) posits that:

> *Makwerekwere* refers to the outsiders, those who speak unintelligible languages. *Kwere-kwere* is supposedly the sound of unintelligible languages. It also means the outsiders speak the language of the insiders unintelligibly. However, in the context of South African anti-migrants, the *Makwerekwere* has negative valences akin to those of nigger or kaffir. This assessment applies to *Magrigamba* and *Mapoti*, despite the fact many of those who are thus categorised come from countries whose languages are also spoken in

> South Africa, e.g., Tswana in Botswana, Tsonga in Mozambique, Ndebele in Zimbabwe, Sotho in Lesotho, Swati in Swaziland.

*Kwere kwere* is idiophonic of non-human sounds; it is a form of animalisation and justification to exclude. The names are crafted to emphasise foreignness. In cases of cross-border identities, non-cross border labels are used; for example, the Tsonga people, found in South Africa, Zimbabwe, Mozambique and Eswatini, are called Shangani, not Tsonga, if they immigrate into South Africa to mark them as foreign. Zimbabweans are also known as *Amakhalanga*, a name which tries to separate Zulu from Zimbabwean Ndebele.

Describing the Othered and precarious condition of Zimbabweans in both xenophobic South Africa and in their own country, Ryan (2010, p. 15) notes that:

> cast adrift on waves of xenophobia, Zimbabwean refugees and migrants are the great unwanted; rejected, policed and constantly threatened with imprisonment and expatriation. Once home, they immediately turn around and return, for there is nothing to stay for, no food, no work, no money. Their only hope is South Africa.

Zimbabweans ironically experience a rare kind of xenophobia, whereby, if they come back home from South Africa, they are detested as having 'South African immorality'. Names such as *iNjiva*, *Majonijoni* (one from Johannesburg), *Mtshifana* and *Ngoli* (one from Goli/Johannesburg) have become ethnophaulisms for Zimbabwean migrant workers in South Africa when they come back home, usually during the December holidays (Ndlovu, 2020). They are othered as belonging to Johannesburg, yet in South Africa, they are othered as foreigners, creating aliens in them through naming.

There is a common thread of fouling foreign nationals, whereby they are referred to using non-human noun classes, thereby making them animals of sorts. In Botswana, a Zimbabwean is called *leZimbabwean* instead of *moZimbabwe*. Kgari-Masondo and Masondo (2019, p. 93) concur that:

> this is indicated in the language of the Batswana. For example, classification of people in Setswana falls under *Mo-Ba*, (*motho-batho*), while they are classified as *le-ma* if deemed less than human. For example, a Nigerian might fall under this category with objects *leNigeria-maNigeria* because she/he is regarded as an outsider since she/he is not from South Africa.

The classification implies animal parasites; foreign nationals have been labelled as *Amazeze*, "blood sucking parasites" (Mamabolo, 2015). The ethnophaulism *Amagrigamba* has parasitic connotations. Tafira (2011) posits that a *grigamba* is one who comes with nothing except the clothes they are wearing, but when they leave, they leave with wealth. This has seen South Africans view immigrants as worse than witches. Kgari-Masondo and Masondo (2019, p. 96) observed that:

> A Nigerian is termed as *iNigerian-amaNigerian* 'Nigerian-Nigerians', *iZimbabwean amaZimbabwean* 'Zimbabwean-Zimbabweans', that is not a category of people. A human being falls under **umu-aba = *umuntu-abantu*** 'person-people', *umthakathi-abathakathi* 'wizard-wizards'. The African immigrants are worse than witches from the way they are categorised.

Those from Malawi are also called *MaNyasa*, which morphologically means animals from Malawi (Nyasaland). Malawians are also called 'aliens' in Zimbabwe and referenced in the animal class as coming from Nyasaland, *MaNyasarandi/AmaNyasarandi*. Their national identity cards indicate 'alien' under the category village of origin.

European colonisers were identified as foreigners meddling in the domestic affairs of Africans in Zimbabwe. The Shona named the native commissioner and his office with the foreignising name *Mudzviti*, and the office was and is still called *kwaMudzviti*. The Ndebele also named the native commissioner to express that he/she was an interfering outsider, *uNdabazabantu* (people's issues). This name, in the context of Ndebele cultural expressions, denotes one who does not belong, involving himself or herself in issues that do not concern them. The names *Mudzviti* and *Ndabazantu* other the colonial White as one who is not welcome and is forcing himself or herself on people. The Shona earlier on used the name *Mudziti* to refer to Ndebele people, and this ethnophaulism remains in use even today. MacGonagle (2008, p. 37) traces the name *Dzviti* to the Ndau people of Eastern Zimbabwe, who used it to describe the Gaza Nguni who invaded their land under Soshangane. He states that '*bziti* means invading warrior.' The name is now a Shona ethnophaulism for the Nguni in Zimbabwe. Ndlovu and Mangena (2014, p. 81) posit that 'The word *dzviti* is a Shona word that means invader, and is the same term that Shona groups use to refer to the Ndebele as a reminder that they also are invaders who do not belong in Zimbabwe.'

The colonial administration in Zimbabwe embarked on land reforms whereby Africans were evicted from their homes to make way for White commercial farmers. This programme saw many ethnicities mix through evictions and resettlements. Evictees and their host ethnicities were involved in ethnic labelling and counter-labelling (Nyambara, 2002; Worby, 1994). This labelling and counter-labelling are exemplified in the Gokwe resettlement areas in Zimbabwe. Worby (1994, p. 389) observes that 'the earlier inhabitants of Gokwe called the evictees *Madheruka*, an onomatopoetic word intended to evoke the sound of the lorry engines that brought them, the evictees in turn referred to their hosts as *Shangwe*, which had connotations of backwardness.' Nyambara (2002) opines that the name *Dheruka* **[deruka]** is onomatopoeia evoking the sounds of lorry revs **[druuuuuu]**. He further links the name to lorries by suggesting that the *Shankwe* people of Gokwe named the arriving evictees 'those who descended from lorries.' He argues *Dheruka* is a derivative form *deluka*, Ndebele or Kalanga for descend. While *deluka* is not Ndebele for descend, it is close to the Ndebele word *dilika*, which means descend or come down. It can still mean the same in Shona and Kalanga; in Nyai, a descent or slope is *(ma)teru*, and *deruka* can be easily traced to *teru*.

Robins (1994) also identifies the name *amaDeluka* as used by the Sotho people in Zimbabwe referencing people of other ethnicities, especially the Ndebele who were evicted by colonial land tenure policies and resettled among the Sotho. He argues that in the Sotho context, the name means people who were ferried onto their land on government lorries, and he concludes that this was a very bad word. Alexander et al. (2000) also look at ethnic tensions caused by colonial evictions and resettlements in Zimbabwe's Shangani area, and they conclude that naming played a big role in power politics between the 'progressive' evictees, labelled *amaFilabusi*, *amabhunu* or *amadeluka*, and the earlier inhabitants of Shangani, who were thought to be primitive. Musoni (2014) studies the effects of colonial evictions on Zimbabwean ethnic relations in the Buhera area, which is a predominantly Shona area in which Ndebele people under Chief Gwebu were resettled. He observes that to the present day, the two groups live in suspicion of each other, and ethnic relations are tense and characterised by labelling and stereotypes.

## 4.4 Conclusion

Africa and Africans are affected by antilocutions globally and locally. Language that is crafted to express contempt is used by ingroups to exclude outgroups in a crude and cruel way. Ethnophaulisms are the names that people use to insult other identities, usually based on stereotypes. The names are used to express racist, ethnic and foreignising feelings by ingroups. Africans have been named by Europe and North America as undesired breeds through names stemming from racist theorising such as eugenics and evolution of species. The names other African skin as black and indicative of degeneration from the White standard. The racialised ethnophaulisms create selves in White people and animals in Black people. They also create sickly beings in Asians. The use of physical features such as skin colour to designate identity is designed in most cases to compare and dehumanise. Human skin colouration has been misnamed to create pure White ones and impure Black ones. While Black has been prohibited and its euphemism African used in naming people, the term 'African' itself others and alienates African Americans from American autochthony. Africans have created their own anti-racist racism in naming Europeans by using skin colour and other physical features and through authenticating African culture through theory and philosophies. Africans also use ethnophaulisms against each other to ridicule social classes and perceived under-development. Ethnophaulisms are abundant in migration discourses in Africa both within and without borders.

Africans use names that indicate the other to be alien in their spaces, and such names have progressed to xenophobic attacks in South Africa.

## References


Adesanmi, P. (2008). *Makwerekwere: Black South Africa's instant-mix Kaffirs*. www.pambazuka.org/en/category/panafrican/45870

Agar, N. (1998). Liberal eugenics. *Public Affairs Quarterly*, *12*(2), 137–155.

Alexander, J., & Alexander, J. (1997). Modernity and ethnicity in a frontier society: Understanding difference in Northwestern Zimbabwe. *Journal of Southern African Studies*, *23*(2), 187–201.

Alexander, J., McGregor, J., & Ranger, T. O. (2000). *Violence and memory: One hundred years in the "dark forests" of Matabeleland*. James Currey.

Allen, I. L. (1983). *The language of ethnic conflict: Social organization and lexical culture*. Columbia University Press.

Allport, G. W. (1954). *The nature of prejudice*. Addison-Wesley.

Anderson, L., & Lepore, E. (2013). What did you call me? Slurs as prohibited words setting things up. *Analytic Philosophy*, *54*(3), 350–363.

Argenter, J. A. (2000). Cultural identity and heteroglossia. *Sociolinguistic Studies*, 27–39.

Baum, B. (2006). *The rise and fall of the Caucasian race: A political history of racial identity*. New York University Press.

Bekerie, A. (2004). Ethiopica: Some historical reflections on the origin of the word ethiopia. *International Journal of Ethiopian Studies*, *1*(2), 110–121. www.jstor.org/stable/27828841

Bhopal, R. (2007). The beautiful skull and Blumenbach's errors: The birth of the scientific concept of race. *BMJ: British Medical Journal*, *335*(7633), 1308–1309.

Bianchi, C. (2014). Slurs and appropriation: An echoic account. *Journal of Pragmatics*, *66*, 35–44.

Bilewicz, M., & Soral, W. (2020). Hate speech epidemic: The dynamic effects of derogatory language on intergroup relations and political radicalization. *Political Psychology*, *41*, 3–33.

Bosmajian, H. A. (1974). *The language of oppression*. Public Affairs Press.

Britannica, T. (2011, November 22). Editors of encyclopaedia. *Coolie*. www.britannica.com/topic/coolie-Asian-labourer

Brown, J., Reznik, T., & Matan, G. (2015, October 29). Racial slurs are woven deep into the American landscape. *Vocativ*. www.vocativ.com/news/244179/racial-slurs-are-woven-deep-into-the-american-landscape/index.html

Bruder, E. (2008). *The Black Jews of Africa: History, religion, identity*. Oxford University Press.

Cahoone, L. E. (2003). *From modernism to postmodernism: An anthology* (2nd ed.). Blackwell.

Clifford, J. (1997). *Routes: Travel and translation in the late twentieth century*. Harvard University Press.

Comaroff, J., & Comaroff, J. (1993). Introduction. In J. Comaroff & J. Comaroff (Eds.), *Modernity and its malcontents: Ritual and power in postcolonial Africa* (xi–xxxvii). University of Chicago Press.

Crang, M. (1998). *Cultural geography*. Routledge.

Croom, A. M. (2013). How to do things with slurs: Studies in the way of derogatory words. *Language & Communication*, *33*(3), 177–204.

Croom, A. M. (2014). Remarks on "the semantics of racial slurs". *Linguistic and Philosophical Investigations*, *13*, 11–32.

Dictionary of South African English. (2020). *"Amakula", pl. n. dictionary unit for South African English*. Retrieved March 4, 2021, from https://dsae.co.za/entry/amakula/e00251

Dominguez, V. R. (1994). A taste for "the other": Intellectual complicity in racializing practices. *Current Anthropology, 35*(4), 333–348.

Ericson, E. E. (1939). Ecthronyms: Derisive names for various peoples. *Words, 5*, 100–103.

Etymonline Dictionary. (2021, March 3). Hottentot. www.etymonline.com/word/hottentot

Evans, L. (2019). Contextualising apartheid at the end of empire: Repression, "development" and the Bantustans. *The Journal of Imperial and Commonwealth History, 47*(2), 372–411.

Fairclough, N. (2012). Critical discourse analysis. *International Scientific Researchers (ISR), 7*, 452–487.

Fishman, J. A. (1971). *Sociolinguistics: A brief introduction*. Newbury House Publishers.

Galton, F. (1904). Eugenics: Its definition, scope, and aims. *American Journal of Sociology, 10*(1), 1–25.

Gelber, K. (2002). *Speaking back: The free speech versus hate speech debate*. John Benjamins. https://doi.org/10.1075/dapsac.1

Gilroy, P. (2004). *Between camps-nations, cultures and the allure of race*. Routledge.

Hall, C., & Rose, S. O. (2006). Introduction: Being at home with the empire. In C. Hall & S. O. Rose (Eds.), *At home with the empire: Metropolitan culture and the imperial world* (pp. 1–31). Cambridge University Press.

Hall, E. (1991). *Inventing the barbarian: Greek self-definition through tragedy*. Clarendon Press.

Hedger, J. (2012). The semantics of racial slurs: Using Kaplan's framework to provide a theory of the meaning of derogatory epithets. *Linguistic and Philosophical Investigations, 11*, 74–84.

Hedger, J. (2013). Meaning and racial slurs: Derogatory epithets and the semantics/pragmatics interface. *Language and Communication, 33*, 205–213. http://doi.org/10.1016/j.langcom.2013.04.004

Hertzler, J. (1965). *A sociology of language*. Random House.

Hickling-Hudson, A. (2009). Southern theory and its dynamics for postcolonial education. *Counterpoints*, 365–375.

Kaplan, D. (1999). *The meaning of ouch and oops: Explorations in the theory of meaning as use* [Unpublished MA, University of California].

Kearney, M. (1998). Transnationalism in California and Mexico at the end of an empire. In T. M. Wilson & D. Hastings (Eds.), *Border identities – nation state at international frontiers* (pp. 117–141). Cambridge University Press.

Kgari-Masondo, M. C., & Masondo, S. (2019). For peace sake. *Journal of African Foreign Affairs, 6*(3), 87–102.

Khong, Y. F. (1992). *Analogies at war: Korea, Munich, Dien Bien Phu and the Vietnam decisions of 1965*. Princeton University Press.

Kövecses, Z. (2017). Conceptual metaphor theory. In E. Semino & Z. Demjen (Eds.), *The Routledge handbook of metaphor and language* (pp. 13–27). Routledge.

Kristeva, J. (1993). *Nations without nationalism*. Columbia University Press.

Lindfors, B. (2001). Hottentot, Bushman, Kaffir: The making of racist stereotypes in 19th-century Britain. In *Encounter images in the meetings between Africa and Europe* (pp. 54–75). https://citeseerx.ist.psu.edu/viewdoc/download?doi=10.1.1.439.8325&rep=rep1&type=pdf#page=54

Maart, R. (2014). Philosophy born of massacres. Marikana, the theatre of cruelty: The killing of the "kaffir". *Acta Academica, 46*(4), 1–28.

MacGonagle, E. (2008). Living with a tyrant: Ndau memories and identities in the shadow of Ngungunyana. *The International Journal of African Historical Studies, 41*(1), 29–53.

Madsen, S. O., & Vallentin, S. (2018, July). The processes of othering in public organization. *Academy of Management Proceedings*, *1*, 17597. https://doi.org/10.5465/AMBPP.2018.17597abstract

Makoni, S. (2011). A critical analysis of the historical and contemporary status of minority languages in Zimbabwe. *Current Issues in Language Planning*, *12*(4), 437–455.

Mamabolo, M. A. (2015). Drivers of community xenophobic attacks in South Africa: Poverty and unemployment. *TD: The Journal for Transdisciplinary Research in Southern Africa*, *11*(4), 143–150.

Martinot, S. (2011). *The coloniality of power: Notes toward de-colonization*. San Francisco State University. www.ocf.berkeley.edu/~marto/coloniality.htm#:~:text=The%20%22coloniality%20of%20power%22%20is,the%20Americas%20to%20the%20present

Matsinhe, D. M. (2011). *Apartheid vertigo: The rise in discrimination against Africans in South Africa*. Ashgate Publishing.

Mazrui, A. A. (1986). *The Africans: A triple heritage*. BBC Publications.

Mbembé, J. A. (2004). Aesthetics of superfluity: Johannesburg the elusive metropolis. *Public Culture*, *16*(3), 373–405.

Miller, R. W. (1963). Down's syndrome (mongolism), other congenital malformations and cancers among the sibs of leukemic children. *New England Journal of Medicine*, *268*(8), 393–401.

Monmonier, M. (2006). *From squaw tit to whorehouse meadow: How maps name, claim, and inflame*. University of Chicago Press.

Moore, R. B. (1992). *The name "Negro": Its origin and evil use*. Black Classic Press.

Morlin-Yron, S. (2017). *What's the real size of Africa? How western states used maps to downplay size of continent*. www.osundefender.com/wp-content/uploads/2018/02/Africa-vs-Canada-Map.pdf

Mukhopadhyay, C. C. (2008). Getting rid of the word Caucasian. In M. Pollock (Ed.), *Everyday anti-racism* (pp. 12–16). www.sjsu.edu/people/carol.mukhopadhyay/race/Mukhopadhyay-Caucasian-article.pdf

Mullen, B. (2001). Ethnophaulisms for ethnic immigrant groups. *Journal of Social Issues*, *57*(3), 457–475.

Musoni, F. (2014). Forced resettlement, ethnicity, and the (un) making of the Ndebele identity in Buhera District, Zimbabwe. *African Studies Review*, *57*(3), 79–100.

Ndlovu, E. (2015). Mother-tongue education in Venda: An ethnolinguistic vitality critique. *Language Matters*, *46*(3), 364–388.

Ndlovu, S. (2011). Colonial legacy in the Ndebele ethnocentric retronym. *Monash University Linguistics Papers*, 7(2), 59–67.

Ndlovu, S. (2017). Transphonologisation as ethnophaulism between the Ndebele and the Shona of Zimbabwe in selected toponyms and ethnonyms. *Nomina Africana: Journal of African Onomastics*, *31*(2), 117–125.

Ndlovu, S. (2020). Juxtaposing Zulu and Zimbabwean Ndebele lexico-semantic differences: An etymological and shibboleth analysis. *African Identities*, 1–14.

Ndlovu, S., & Mangena, T. (2014). Articulations of "othering" through ethnic names and naming: Selected Zimbabwean cases. *Nomina Africana: Journal of African Onomastics*, *28*(2), 75–86.

Ndlovu-Gatsheni, S. J. (2009). *Do 'Zimbabweans' exist?: Trajectories of nationalism, national identity formation and crisis in a postcolonial state* (Vol. 3). Peter Lang.

News 24. (2013, July 24). *Umlungu the accepted racist word*. www.news24.com/MyNews24/Umlungu-the-accepted-racist-word-20130724

Ngwenya, T. N. (2014). The fifty rand note. *Imbizo*, *5*(1), 118–132.

Nick, I. M. (2018). A note on the 2017 landmark US ruling on the constitutionality of prohibiting the trademarking of potentially disparaging names. *Names, 66*(4), 256–262.

Nuessel, F. (2019). Ethnophaulic toponyms in the United States. In O. Felecan (Ed.), *Onomastics between sacred and profane* (pp. 185–196). Vernon Press.

Nyambara, P. S. (2002). Madheruka and Shangwe: Ethnic identities and the culture of modernity in Gokwe, Northwestern Zimbabwe, 1963–79. *Journal of African History*, 287–306.

Palmore, E. B. (1962). Ethnophaulisms and ethnocentrism. *American Journal of Sociology, 67*, 442–445.

Pankiw, B., & Bienvenue, R. M. (1990). Parental responses to ethnic name-calling: A sociological inquiry. *Canadian Ethnic Studies, 22*, 78–98.

Paradies, Y. (2005). Anti-racism and indigenous Australians. *Analyses of Social Issues and Public Policy, 5*(1), 1–28.

Parker, G. W. (1918). *The children of the sun*. Black Classic.

Perry, T. (2016, March 5). *The racist origins of the word Caucasian*. www.good.is/articles/the-last-country-to-still-use-the-term-caucasian

Rahman, J. (2012). The N word: Its history and use in the African American community. *Journal of English Linguistics, 40*(2), 137–171.

Rice, D. R., Abrams, D., Badea, C., Bohner, G., Carnaghi, A., Dementi, L. I., & Trzebinski, J. (2010). What did you just call me? European and American ratings of the valence of ethnophaulisms. *Journal of Language and Social Psychology, 29*(1), 117–131.

Roback, A. A. (1944). *A dictionary of international slurs*. Sci-Art.

Robins, S. L. (1994). Contesting the social geometry of state power: A case study of land-use planning in Matabeleland, Zimbabwe. *Social Dynamics, 20*(2), 91–118.

Rödlach, A. (2006). *Witches, westerners, and HIV: AIDS and cultures of blame in Africa*. Left Coast Press.

Ryan, P. (2010). Giving up on given: The making of identity in the contact zone or "she do identity in different voices". *Scrutiny2: Issues in English Studies in Southern Africa, 15*(1), 8–19.

Schmahmann, B. (2020). Senzeni Marasela's reworking of women's histories in *Beyond Booty: Covering Sarah Baartman and Other Tales*. *Textile*, 1–27.

Scott, J. W. (1995). Multiculturalism and the politics of identity. In J. Rajchman (Ed.), *The identity in question* (pp. 3–14). Routledge.

Searle, J. R. (1975). Indirect speech acts. *Speech Acts*, 59–82.

Sedler, R. (1992). The unconstitutionality of campus bans on "racist speech": The view from without and within. *University of Pittsburgh Law Review, 53*, 631–683.

Sibanda, M. (2016). *Carrying the vision: Eelin and her missionary friends*. Andrews United Kingdom Limited.

Tafira, K. (2011). Is xenophobia racism? *Anthropology Southern Africa, 34*(3–4), 114–121.

Tajfel, H. (1974). Social identity and intergroup behaviour. *Social Science Information, 13*, 65–93.

Tamarkin, N. (2020). *Genetic afterlives: Black Jewish indigeneity in South Africa*. Duke University Press.

Teo, T. (2009). Psychology without caucasians. *Canadian Psychology/Psychologie Canadienne, 50*(2), 91–97.

Tilly, C. (1999). *Durable inequality*. University of California Press.

Urban Dictionary. (2013). *MAPOTI*. Retrieved October 12, 2021, from www.urbandictionary.com/define.php?term=MAPOTI

Walker, J. (2014). *Aden insurgency: The savage war in Yemen 1962–67*. Pen and Sword.

White, C. M. (2007). More authentic than thou: Authenticity and othering in Fiji tourism discourse. *Tourist Studies*, 7(1), 25–49.

Wijaya, R., Andersan, G., Santoso, S. P., & Irawaty, W. (2020). Green reduction of graphene oxide using kaffir lime peel extract (*Citrus hystrix*) and its application as adsorbent for methylene blue. *Scientific Reports*, *10*(1), 1–9.

Wilson, A. H. (1998). Oburoni outside the whale: Reflections on an experience in Ghana. *Theory & Research in Social Education*, *26*(3), 410–429.

Worby, E. (1994). Maps, names, and ethnic games: The epistemology and iconography of colonial power in Northwestern Zimbabwe. *Journal of Southern African Studies*, *20*(3), 371–392.

WordSense Online Dictionary. (2021, March 4). *Amwenye*. www.wordsense.eu/Amwenye/

## Section Two

# Selfing and othering in colonial and de-colonial onomastics in Africa

# 5 *UMlungu/Mzungu/Oborofo* decoloniality and coloniality nuances

## 5.0 Introduction

The rhetorical value of names is similar to that of narratives, images, euphemisms and analogies. They are all reactions to information, and they seek to order, interpret and simplify it (Bhatia, 2005). Adler (1978, p. 12) argues that 'to name is to identify an object, remove it from the unknown, and then assign to it a set of characteristics, motives, values and behaviours.' Naming White people across Africa is based on certain characteristics and behaviours, and the names underscore the naming motives of ethnophaulism and xenophobia which culminate in the creation of decolonial rhetoric in these names. The colonial experiences and ideologies of social Darwinism embedded White racial supremacy in these otherwise semantically and historically othering names to create ameliorated value. This turned the tables against Africans and their initial motives in giving the names in the first place.

Names and naming of White people in Africa have always been associated with power matrixes. This has created and continues to create contradictions. The first White people to come to African societies are usually the subjects of the various descriptive names given to White people across the continent. Most early White people in Africa were slave traders, explorers, missionaries, colonialists and colonial aiders. These processes, in the majority, involved violence and inhuman treatment of Africans, resulting in negative names so designed to capture the bad memories of Africa's early White encounters. Likaka (2009) opines that naming Whites in the Congo, for example, was a way of recording early forms of colonial oppression, harsh punishments and indignities. These negative descriptors of White people later shifted in meaning due to their reference to the ruling colonial class of White people. The negative names came to refer to White colonial opulence and power and were even extended to include Black people who fit into the capitalist opulence which was previously identified with colonial race hierarchies. In West Africa, for example, the name *Oburoni* for White people now references wealth and power, a deviation from its original racialised anti-colonial reference. Ochonu (2019, p. 26) alludes to this meaning shift as he notes that 'Oburoni's racial etymology and provenance are somewhat ambiguous, since the term is also used to denote "stranger" or

DOI: 10.4324/9781003170761-7

"foreigner" in a non-racial register.' The various names for White people in Africa appear to have been formed as resistance rhetoric and later, due to their association with power, they became endearing. However the racial indices are coming back to the meaning scope of these names, and they have been cause for concern in racially sensitive countries such as South Africa.

This chapter is motivated by the controversy and ambivalence surrounding nomen delegations for White people or Europeans in Africa. The term *uMlungu*, for example, denoting White person, has been making headlines as 'a now racist ethnophaulism' in post-apartheid South Africa. The question is how the name can be aligned to pejorative inferences yet, generally be embellished with ameliorated nuances? Loewe (2016), writing for *The Dispatch Live*, tells the story of an East London (South Africa) White man who used the 'K' word on a Black man he accused of calling him *Mlungu*. Both parties are reported to have laid charges of *crimen injuria*. The White man is quoted as claiming that if he is *uMlungu*, then the Black man is a k★★★★r. He further quotes Kaschula as saying, 'context is crucial. *UMlungu* could be used in a pejorative way.' A South African blogger on *Reddit.com* (2018) indicates that his White boss overheard him referring to him as *uMlungu wami* (my *Mlungu*), and 'he was furious, saying the word "*Mlungu*" has racial connotations and is as offensive as the dreaded "k" word.' The blog attracted a lot of interest, with divided opinions and feelings on the name. The *Oxford Dictionary Online* (2020) also defines *Mlungu* as offensive, stating that it is now somewhat offensive, especially as a form of address. It traces the name to the mid-19th century from Xhosa and Zulu *uMlungu*.

This chapter identifies names for White people in Africa and investigates the etymologies and motives for the names. It further analyses the names using ideologies of coloniality and decoloniality so as to unearth the controversies and contradictions in these names. The chapter discusses names for White people on four thematic levels as nuanced by etymologies from the data. These are, first, the foreignising etymologies which exclude Europeans from African spaces; second, racial slurs formed to fight colonialism; third, the amelioration of these names to reference White opulence and power due to colonial power matrices; and fourth, the elevated White supremacy in the names which equates White people to deities. The study was motivated by the fact that these names, across Africa, seem to be synonyms, an indication that they reference similar conditions of encountering White people. The objectives of the study were to identify the names and trace their origins and nuance the semiotics that makes them both good and bad names. Data analysis is done thematically according to the meanings and etymologies of the names to answer the question of why some White people are (now) offended by these names, while Black people consider the names endearing.

The study is a socio-historical approach to anthroponomastics. It deploys qualitative approaches of etymological analysis, document analysis and thematic analysis. Etymological analysis is a key method in discovering the history of words and concepts. Schadeberg (1989) states that etymological analysis depends on plausible environments in the linguistic and cultural heritages of the people, and this makes etymologies testimonies and hypotheses about the past. Etymological analysis focuses on the origins of concepts, their historical formations and their meaning (Hosseini et al., 2012). Unstructured interviews were done with lexicologists and culture scholars in Southern, East and West Africa to collect the names and their meanings and etymologies. The researcher is a linguist in Southern Africa and has intuitive knowledge of most names for White people in South Africa, Zimbabwe, Botswana, Eswatini and Lesotho. The study also deploys document analysis as a qualitative method to analyse texts on these names across Africa. Theories of coloniality, decoloniality, social Darwinism and ethnophaulism aid the analysis, which is a critical discourse analysis of the names employing semiotic strategies of iconicity to map the metaphoric references of these names. The various mappings are guided by etymological data, and they are analysed as conceptual metaphors. The names reveal colonial and decolonial otherness and self.

## 5.1 *Mzungu* as de-colonial xenophobia

*Mzungu* is a Bantu-language term used in Kenya, Tanzania, Malawi, Rwanda, Burundi, Uganda, Democratic Republic of Congo, Comoros, Mayotte and Zambia referring to people of European descent. The *Urban Dictionary* (2008) refers to *mzungu* as a Swahili word which means someone who wanders without purpose, someone constantly on the move. It came to be applied to all White people in East Africa, as most were encountered as traders, visiting colonial officials or tourists. Schadeberg (1989) identifies one of the early uses of the word *mzungu* for White people in the Swahili naming of playing cards in East Africa. The king is *mzungu wa nne* (fourth White person), the jack *mzungu wa tatu* (third White person) and the queen *mzungu wa pili* (second White person). *Mzungu*'s reference to one who wanders aimlessly implies that the name givers described the named as foreign to the land, and the reference denotes xenophobic motivations. One presumably White blogger on *muzungublogu-ganda* (2020) states that the name *Muzungu* comes from Kiswahili, where *zungu* is the word for spinning around on the same spot. 'That dizzy lost look was perfected by the first White people arriving in East Africa, or so the story goes, and Ugandans have not stopped laughing at us yet!' Extricating the etymology of *Mzungu* in KiSwahili, Mamdani (1998, p. 6) notes that '*Mzungu*, however, does not literally mean a White person. It simply means a restless person, a person who will not stay in one place, a person full of anxieties.'

The etymology of the name *Muzungu* linking its meaning to lost, dizzy people confirms that Africans resisted early colonial manoeuvres, and the name suggests that. The compound word *muzunguzungu* is Kiswahili for a dizzy person; when dizzy, you do not know your way. Hence, the lost image foreignises White people in Africa. Spitzer (2014, p. 1) defines *muzungu* as:

> A common term for a European or 'White' person in East Africa (plural *wazungu*). This term can have many connotations. Linguistically, it derives

> from the Kiswahili term *kuzungua* which means 'to go around'; hence, etymology tells us that the idiom is associated with people who are on the move. Historically, it became a synonym for light-skinned foreigners who seem to have the common feature of travelling a lot.

It is clear from the etymology and meaning analysis of the term *muzungu* that the motives for naming were to make sure White people were labelled as not belonging but passing foreigners, who are in Africa because they do not know their way back home. Colonialism is mapped onto dizziness and being lost, an indication that White people are not at home in Africa, which, in fact, is xenophobic othering of White people in Africa based on the 'dizziness' of occupying other peoples' space. White and European shenanigans throughout colonialism typify efforts of dizzy people, because they were in unfamiliar territory which they sought to change so that it fit into their dizziness. Interview data from Chichewa in Malawi and Nyanja in Zambia also has *Azungu* and *Bazungu* for White people, respectively, with the same etymology of dizziness and wandering. The Shona of Zimbabwe call them *vaZungu* and the Ndau *vaYungu*, and dizziness in Shona is *dzungu*. The root *zungu* is a proto-Bantu root describing the feelings dizzy and lost; in Nguni, for example, spinning around is *isizingelezane*, which causes *isiyezi* (dizziness). The Nguni word for loneliness is also a derivative from Bantu *zungu*, as loneliness is called *isizungu*, White people's stranger realities in the name *Muzungu* are expressed in the Nguni word *isizungu* (loneliness).

Moving from *Muzungu* dizziness in East Africa to Southern Africa, one encounters another name for White people with similar connotations. The Nguni word *uMlungu*, which has caused controversy in South Africa, has xenophobic othering of White people as part of its meaning etymology. One folk etymology for the origins of the term *AbeLungu*, plural for *uMlungu* for White people, is the sea-foam thesis. *Ubulungu* is the white foam that forms on sea beaches, the drifting ashore and the colour of the form both map onto Europeans coming to Pondoland in South Africa from the sea, more so those who were shipwrecked. Kirby (1954) identifies the Abelungu clan in Eastern South Africa as descendants of foreign European ancestors shipwrecked on the Pondoland coast. Hayward (2020) opines that the shipwreck thesis may be folk etymology aimed at diffusing the volition and force of colonisation by reducing the first Whites to desperate victims who encountered Africans by chance. The etymology emphasises the humanity of the Africans in accommodating Whites as compared to other discourses of defeat and conquest. Such an etymology concurs with the lost and dizzy etymology of *Muzungu* in East Africa. However, the image of white sea foam is striking imagery for foreignising White people.

The *Urban Dictionary* (2008) describes the word *uMlungu* as a Zulu word used in South Africa meaning 'White person'; originally it comes from the white foam that collects along the shore of the beach.

Commenting on *MyNews24* online (2013), one presumably White commentator protests:

> How can South Africa ever become a truly rainbow nation when we still accept certain racist words? I was eating at a restaurant recently and what was more common in the restaurant than food, was the word *uMlungu*. This word literally means white scum and is a very racist way to describe a White individual.

Another White South African responding to a *Quora.com* (2017) blog survey on African names for White people wrote:

> There are several explanations for this term, but the one I like most came from a Xhosa friend. According to him it means the white foam that forms on a beach due to the actions of the waves. As our ancestors came with ships, I can see the connection and find it rather appropriate.

The reference to ocean scum appears to be the etymology White people in South Africa loathe. Table 5.1 maps the images in the etymology of *abeLungu*.

The name *abeLungu* is evidence that White people do not belong in Africa, and this evidence others them as foreigners who have their home elsewhere. The othering uses image and process to imagine White people as aliens; the colour and the floating are images of xenophobic naming so created to remind generations that Whites came: they are not autochthones. The rainbow nation rhetoric in South Africa seeks to make everyone, regardless of their race, a political autochthon, and it is this unity rhetoric that White people use to challenge the name.

White people are also named to be perpetual strangers in West Africa, too. *Oburoni*, for example, is a Ghanaian term for White person but originally denotes a stranger or foreigner in a non-racial register. However, Ochonu

*Table 5.1 AbeLungu* relational frame metaphor analysis

| | |
|---|---|
| Metaphor: White people are ocean scum | |
| **Source domain** – Maritime pollution | **Target domain** – Race relations (descriptions) |
| Vehicle – Scum of the ocean | Tenor – White people |
| **Mappings** | |
| White colour of scum | White colour of colonisers |
| Floating to shore | Sailing of White people to African shores |
| Pollution | Colonial effects on Africa |
| ***Tertium comparationis*** | |
| The metaphor is both an image and experience mapping. The primary ontological correlation is the colour white. The experience of scum drifting towards the coast is mapped onto the sailing done by Whites to the coasts of Africa. Colonialism is mapped onto the pollution caused by the scum on the shoreline. | |

(2019, p. 26) states that 'foreigner and stranger in the Ghanaian context can coincide with a reference to racial otherness.' Matson (1956) states that, along the West African coast incorporating Ghana, White people are called *Oburoni*. He identifies the following dialectical variations of the term: Nzima – *Blofole*, Ga – *Blofonyo*, Ada and Krobo – *Blefono*. He further argues that the root *boro-* is linked to the concept of the horizon; hence, Europe is called *Aborokyiri*. The root *-kyiri* means behind, back of or far away, and *Aborokyini* therefore means people from beyond the horizon or from far away from it. To come from beyond the horizon is to be the extreme of foreigners, and this name also others a White person in Africa and is xenophobic exclusion. While *Oburoni* is now a class endearment due to semantic extensions from colonial race relations, Ochonu (2019, p. 26) posits that:

> In its original form, *Oburoni* or *Oburuni* (singular, or plural, *Abrofo*) was a designation for Europeans without regard to nationality and status. Although this racial etymology included a transition from a mildly negative usage to a positive one of admiration and endearment as Europeans came to symbolise wealth and status rather than the destitution of earlier European missionary visitors, the racial element remained at its semiotic heart.

The theme of destitution in the early White visitors to Africa is carried in the shipwreck, dizziness, sea foam and wandering etymologies, and this creates a historically othered and foreignised White in Africa. The names for White people in this thematic category are metaphors for foreigners who are othered for coming from distant horizons (*Aborokyiri*), who came by sea (*abeLungu*) and found themselves as strangers (*Oburoni*) in Africa, and the strange land confused them (*waZungu*). These names were given by Africans most likely to traders, explorers and missionaries. They appear to be sophisticated othering of Europeans as foreign to Africa. However, the advent of violent contacts with White people such as slavery and colonialism inflated and heightened the xenophobia in the names and naming, creating not only foreignising but also loaded decolonial slurs in the names.

## 5.2 *Aborofo* as de-colonial ethnophaulism

Ethnophaulism is a term for inter-group slurs, be they racial or ethnic. Ndlovu (2017) states that ethnophaulisms are disparaging references to the outgroup other created to fight, exclude or undermine. In an effort to fight and rid Africa of colonising and enslaving White people, and after seeing the ills of slavery and colonialism, Africans used names to indicate their distaste of White imperialism. Unlike the foreignising names given to missionaries and other seemingly peaceable White pioneers, colonialists and slave traders were named with the motive to insult. Ethnophaulisms are fighting words aimed at approximating physical harm using words (Ndlovu, 2015). Names given to White people by Africans are rich in colonial memory and images of early encounters of Africans with exploring and colonising Europeans. Likaka (2009, p. 52) supports this claim in his study of Congolese names for White people. He states that 'In naming the colonisers, Congolese villagers prompted naming conventions that became a creating mnemonic method of recording colonial situations.' Colonisers were named not only to exclude them but also to fight them. This is evidenced by the etymologies of names for White people that have clear links to slavery and colonial violence to Africans. The gun and its deathly sound scared Africans, and they associated it with the practice of witchcraft, which indeed it was. Kuper (1965) argues that to Africans, pointing a stick from a distance and killing people was an act of witchcraft, and the killers were called wizards. Darwish (2010, p. 191) reasons that 'Indeed, names during military conflicts have connotations which reach far beyond their literal meanings.' The names are not only referential to Europeans but express African thoughts and feelings about slavery and colonialism in ways that other White colonialists as unwelcome trouble causers in Africa (wizards). Some of the ethnophaulisms are loaded with anger and insult towards the White people.

In West Africa, there are two schools of thought about the etymology of the name *Aburoni* for White people. Bosiwah et al. (2015) concur with Matson (1956)'s 'beyond the horizon' etymology but allude to a second etymology which identifies White people as wicked. The variant of *aburoni*, *aborofo*, can be linguistically analysed to give the two theories:

**a-boro-fo**; **a-** (inflectional affix for number) ***-boro-*** (root meaning horizon) and ***-fo*** (derivational affix indicating an origin).

However, they also argue that in Akan, *aborofo* references wickedness, as schematised in the following:

***Aboro-fo***: ***aboro-*** (*root* meaning wicked) ***-fo*** (inflectional affix for plural).

The Akan etymology and linguistic analysis give the meaning 'wicked people' to the name *Aborofo*. Botchway (2008, p. 190) confirms the wicked etymology and says in Akan, Fante, Twi and Asante, *Aborofo* yields two words: ***aboro-***, which connotes wickedness, malevolence, envy and danger, and ***-fo***, a word that means a group of people. Bosiwah et al. (2015) also concur and note that ***aboro-*** means venom. It also connotes mean, selfish and distractive, and these qualities could have been what the Africans perceived of the western capitalist life as opposed to their communalism. The range of vices associated with the meaning scope of *Aboforo* in Akan give an image of the violence associated with slavery and colonial conquest in Africa. The crude othering of White people as wicked people or otherwise evil spirits in African theology was motivated by their own violence against Africans, which is confirmed by history. The names are creative mnemonics for these unfortunate periods, and they serve as decolonial slurs. Martinot (2011, p. 5) refers to White violence on Africans:

> But in defining Africans as subhuman slave labour, Whites also defined them as a threat, against which White society had to unite in solidarity, for the preservation of which any violence was permissible apriori as defensive violence. Thus, whiteness emerges as a structure of paranoia, social consensus, and violence, each of which generates the others.

The wickedness of White people in the name *Aboforo* is linked to their violence. Bosiwah et al. (2015) quote a Ghanaian respondent confirming that the name means wicked people because of the association of White people with slave trade and creating divisions and hatred among Black people. A violent and divisive person is a witch or wizard in Africa; that is what White people did, and their actions typified those of witches. Kuper (1965, p. 298) posits that in Nguni culture, 'the *abatsakatsi* (wizards/witches) were the agents of harm and misfortune whose final weapon was death.' White supremacy created theologies to support its race attitude; this is confirmed by Rödlach (2006), who quotes some Black Zimbabweans arguing that White people had to make themselves believe that Black people are not human but animals (baboons) so that they did not get a bad conscience for mistreating them. It is like treating animals.

Referencing White people as wicked witches and wizards is not only a West African phenomenon; Southern Africa, which experienced less slavery compared to West and East Africa, also references White people as wicked witches and wizards. In Nguni and Nyai varieties, the names *uMlungu* and *Murungu* have the variants *uMlumbi* and *Murumbi*, respectively. These are variant names for White people, and they do not reference white ocean scum, which is a metaphor for White people arriving on ships. They reference evil and magical wickedness. In Nguni, for example, the word *-lumba* is a root meaning wicked magical tricks, as exemplified in the following:

Verb: *lumba*; **lumb-** (verb root meaning magical tricking) **-a** (final verb vowel).

General noun: *ilumbo*; **i-** (singular noun class) **-lumb-** (root meaning magical trick) **-o** (final vowel general noun derivational affix from verb).

Agent noun: *um(u)lumbi*; **um(u)-** (singular human noun class) **-lumb-** (root meaning magical trick) **-i** (final vowel deriving agent noun).

According to Doke and Vilakazi (1948, p. 468), *kulumba* is a Nguni/Zulu verb which means '(1) do wonders; perform conjuring tricks, make inventions; (2) indulge in occult practices; practice witchcraft; (3) concoct, fabricate, invent stories; tell lies.'

The evil magical tricks in the name *abeLumbi* refer to their war machines and deviant culture from the known, especially the lack of respect for African gods, kings and people. In Nguni folk etymology, the name *abeLumbi* is credited to Nguni Kings Shaka of the Zulu and Somhlolo of the Swati, who are said to have christened the intruders *abeLumbi* or magicians/wizards, so named for their firepower at war and the paraphernalia of western gadgets they had which were new to the people. Zulu folk etymology traces the name *abeLumbi* to King Shaka, who is said to have called White people by the Zulu word *mlumbi/melumbi*, the one who deceives/tricks people. He is said to have named them this after they used guns on his soldiers, and he saw that as a trick, *ukwelumba*. The reference to wizards is also linked to their evil and mass killings, obviously due to superior arsenal. Kuper (1965, p. 300) gathers the name originated from a dream had by King Sobhuza 1, Somhlolo, on the coming of White people to colonise Africa. He ruled the Swati people from 1815–1839. In the dream, the ancestors showed him '*abelumbi* (animals, wizards) entering his country; their skin was like red corn.' They brought amazing inventions (*amalumbo*) and had magic weapons which killed from a distance with the noise of lightning.

One interviewee from Zimbabwe noted that the Shona of Zimbabwe have a folk song which laments the arrival of Whites in their communities: '*pasi pamera Madhunamutuna*' (apparitions have grown from the ground). White people are therefore named *Madhunamituna* or *Madzimudzangara* (apparitions) from Shona folk etymology. This links their identity to witchcraft and evil. Their growing from the ground references them as strangers; the Shona, being landlocked, could not see them coming on ships like the coastal communities could. The light complexion of the White people could have made the Shona perceive them as ghosts, as folk etymology in Africa talks of shiny ghosts. The Karanga of Zimbabwe also use the name *vaRumbi* for White people, and it is linked to their evils associated with colonialism. While the author's thesis is that missionaries were good Whites and the evil names applied only after imperialists, one interviewee in Zimbabwe indicated that missionaries were also *varumbi* (wizards). He gives an example of Jesuits at Chishawasha mission who wanted to kill all males 14 years and older in an attempt to end polygamy. In Shona, the name *vaRumbi* is associated with witchcraft. It derives from the verb root *-romba*, whereby *kuromba* is the act of witchcraft or using witchcraft, just as the case of the Nguni verb *ukulumba*. It is very common in Zimbabwe to hear people suspecting rich or powerful people of using evil occult powers, and they say *akaromba* (he/she used witchcraft to be rich or powerful).

Witchcraft and the occult in Africa are associated with certain animals. Kuper (1965, p. 298) asserts that *abatsakatsi* (witches and wizards) in Swati culture used certain animals, and they themselves were referred to as animals, as they used animals, sent animals on evil errands and put the spirit of animals in their victims. The animal-wizard analogy in the mapping of White identity in early colonial years in Southern Africa has interesting *primum* and *secundum comparatum* represented in Table 5.2.

The evil connotations in the names *Aboforo*, *abeLumbi* and *Madzimudzangara* are based on colonial violence both physical, mental and social. It is such a violation of Africans which led them to seek independence through the

*Table 5.2 Aboforo/abeLumbi/vaRumbi* metaphor mappings

| | |
|---|---|
| Metaphor: White people are evil wizards/witches | |
| **Source domain** – religion and belief system | **Target domain** – race relations |
| Vehicle – wizards/witches and animals | Tenor – White people |
| **Mappings** | |
| Witches send animals to kill people and take their possessions | Empire sent colonialists to kill and colonise Africans |
| Witches use thunder and lightning to kill from a distance | Colonialists used blazing gunfire to kill from a distance |
| Witches put animal spirits in people | Colonialism inculcated white culture in Africans |
| ***Tertium comparationis*** | |
| The names are social practice mappings linking the evils of spiritual vice in the occult to the physical and mental violence and death which were brought to Africa through slavery and colonisation. | |

violent means of war. The violence that was created through colonialism creates an image of death in White colonisers, hence witches. Imagining Whites as witches did not end with colonial encounters of injustice and slavery, but recent research indicate that Africans still suspect White people to be up to witchcraft to eliminate Black people. Africans have associated HIV and AIDS with Euro-American intentions to wipe out Black people from Africa so that they can repossess it. The race conspiracy theory on HIV and AIDS in Africa, for example, has been recorded in Zimbabwe (Feldskov & Frederiksen, 2000; Rödlach, 2006) and in Nigeria (Anwuluorah, 2017).

White people are not only othered as wizards and witches through names, but they are regarded as pollutants in certain etymologies. The image of Whites polluting Africa is also captured in some names given to White colonialists in the Congo. Likaka (2009, p. 54) alludes to Congolese people having named Mr Bosani, the Belgian prison supervisor in colonial Congo, who built Kasongo prison in the 1900s, *Yamba Yamba*. To *yamba* is to defecate, and the repetition emphasises intensity or frequency. The name was given to the prison supervisor because he subjected prisoners to inhuman conditions whereby, they were not allowed latrines but had to defecate in the prison cells. This evil practice associated the prison supervisor with faeces. The name *Yamba Yamba* gives the image of pollution, just like the pollution of beaches by white ocean foam. The term *mzungu* used in East Africa as a name for White people also has semantic extensions and connotations on 'whitish dirt'. The *Urban Dictionary* (2008) defines *mzungu* as 'any disgusting whitish substance that gradually accretes at an office as a consequence of an unhygienic person working there for way too long.' It gives the example; 'my co-worker borrowed my phone and now it is slathered in *mzungu*.' The etymology linking the name *Muzungu* to dirt indicates a loathing of colonialists and colonialism by Africans; the name others colonialists and colonialism as dirt that pollutes Africa. Another ethnophaulic etymology of the name *Mlungu* is proffered by Rödlach (2006) from his study of race relations in Zimbabwe. He discovered that the term originally referred to a puppy, most likely due to the Whites' inability to function maturely in an indigenous society, much like a puppy clumsily relates to other dogs. Referring to White people as puppies is a sign of rejecting colonialism and equating coloniality with animal behaviour.

## 5.3 *UMlungu* as White economic and decorum self

Despite the xenophobic and ethnophaulic etymologies and semantics of the names *Aboruni, Aboforo, Muzungu, abeLungu, vaRungu, Azungu* and *vaRumbi*, the names were ameliorated by colonial structures. The names now mean master, one of superior social status, the enlightened one and an academic more than they refer to their original meanings. The names are associated more with racialised opulence created by colonial capitalism. To Africans, being White became synonymous with being at the top of all social hierarchies. The social hierarchies were created through systematic racism which othered other races and elevated White people; this elevation affected the names that Africans had given to White people. Massey and Denton (1993) argue that racism operates to restrict socioeconomic attainment for the racial other, and it does this by determining access to educational and employment opportunities. Segregation has been a key mechanism by which racial inequality has been created and reinforced.

Most Africans, through colonial education and mis-education, have internalised racist ideologies and tend to believe in White supremacy. Lake (2003, p. xii) argues that this has led some 'Africans to reject their own image and attempt to replicate European standards. This process has been manifested by de-kinking African hair and adulating light skin.' The process of believing in foreign images as beauty and forgetting your own is what Mazrui (1986, p. 109) calls 'engineered or contrived amnesia.' Colonialism succeeded in creating an aspiration for 'cultural Europeanisation' in Africans (Quijano, 2007, p. 169). Ndlovu-Gatsheni (2014, p. 194) alludes to epistemological colonisation, which amounts to colonisation of the mind, and it affected African thinking and knowledge processes. Bosiwah et al. (2015) indicate that *aburoni* now expresses some qualities of virtue and social elevation within Black communities in Ghana. Qualities such as beauty, education, good manners and grooming, and even love are expressed as qualifiers to the *oburoni* social class. They note that Akan lovers use *oburoni* to express adoration to their partners; *me buroni*, which means 'my European', expresses adoration to a loved one. Pierre (2013) notes that tropes of whiteness continue to define female beauty and desirability in Ghanaian society.

In South Africa, after the legal controversies around the name *Mlungu*, the spokesman for the Provincial Department of Sport, Recreation, Arts and Culture in the Eastern Cape Province is quoted by Loewe (2016) as saying:

> *uMlungu* has no offensive or derogatory meaning whatsoever. There are Black people who refer to other Black people as '*uMlungu*', a reference

> most often made in recognition to social standing and affluence. Today '*ama-BEE*' and '*uMlungu*' are terms used interchangeably by people in townships and from rural areas to describe a Black or White boss with power and money.

Association of the name *Mlungu* with power and money is evidence of the racial othering of Africans in colonial Africa. Amelioration of historically pejorative African nomen for White people accounts for what Ochonu (2019, p. 26) terms 'the afterlife of colonial race work.' Paradies (2005, p. 3) asserts, 'Thus racism, as a type of racialisation, operates by increasing power differentials through either disadvantaging subordinate racial groups and/or by advantaging dominant racial groups.' Colonialism socially re-constructed the meanings of names for White people in Africa and created a superior White race in the semantic scope of these names. This White superiority became envy for Africans, and the names now include Black people who are rich or who behave like White people. Some even go a step further and try to change their skin tones and hair textures so as to be *Aboforo*. Ochonu (2019, p. 26) states that, 'Like *Oyinbo* and *Oburoni, Mzungu* confers actual or honorary whiteness and all that it connotes or references. Once conferred, the conferee becomes an unwitting beneficiary of the subconscious, deeply rooted psychology of race.' This coloniality of the mind expressed through rich Africans using names designated for White people is found all across Africa as an afterlife of colonialism. The paradox of the coloniality of power is that Black Africans are aspiring to be called by the very names they created to other colonialists as foreign wanderers and wizards who came to pollute Africa.

The tendency to associate White supremacy with the ethnophaulic names *abeLungu, vaRungu, Aburoni, Wazungu* (foreigners) and *abeLumbi, vaRumbi, Aboforo* (witches) is dying down. Kuper (1965, p. 299) identifies the names *abeLungu* and *abeLumbi* as both referring to White people in Swati and notes, 'I came to realise that they were not synonymous and that *abeLumbi* was used more frequently by old, illiterate Swazi. Educated Swazi, at least in my presence, used only the term *abeLungu*.' The older generation had memories of colonial violence and understood the manoeuvres of witches, yet the educated people now metaphorically have 'the spirit of animals'. It is clear, then, that through Christianity and western culture, White people became symbols of good in the eyes of the people who went through their education system. This process saw the reverse othering in the names for White people whereby the othered wizards now became righteous role models to be envied by the now othered Africans who are now 'animals' outside White civilisation and righteousness.

### *5.3.1* **Mulungu** ***innuendoes***

The name *Mulungu* is the name for God, the supreme deity in some East and Southern African languages. There are etymologies which link the names *Mlungu* and *Murungu* for White people to the name for God, *Mulungu*. *Mulungu* refers to the Christian or Islamic God. The Swahili name for God, *Mungu*, is a contraction of the original form *Mulungu*, which still appears in early Swahili manuscripts. The name *Mulungu* is used to reference God in the following African countries: Kenya, Uganda, Ruanda, Democratic Republic of the Congo, Malawi, Tanzania, Mozambique and Zambia. The provenance now associated with names for White people now contradicts their meanings among Black people in Africa. The association of Whites with provision of employment links them to the concept of providing livelihoods for people; this dependence can be easily misconstrued as worship. The transition of Whites from strangers and witches to endeared beings resembles the proverbial 'Stockholm syndrome'. The high esteem with which Whites and whiteness are regarded in Africa confirms the effects of White supremacist theologies.

The racial trajectory ladder appears to start with Black people at the bottom, and as you go up towards God, colour shades become lighter. Ferris (1913, p. 296) confirms the hierarchaisation of races towards God when he says, 'After the Negrosaxon has been made over into the likeness of the White man he can hope to be made over into the image of God.' Africans could have been mesmerised by the magic of the *baLumbi* and thought them to possess supernatural powers, or Whites themselves through racialised theologies created gods in their identity as opposed to African identity. The names for White people elevate them and demean Africans, and Africans see whiteness as a virtue and being Black as some form of curse. Ochonu (2019, p. 26) states that:

> The light skin or the straight hair or a combination of the two can and does supplant class as the supreme signifier of status and respectability in contemporary Africa. In Ghana and Nigeria, the popular appellative words *Oburoni* and *Oyinbo* are descriptive constructs for a range of generic physical whiteness and for people who are deemed to embody a certain understanding of behavioural and cultural whiteness.

There is evidence from Southern Africa that it is in fact White people who named themselves *abeLungu*/*abaLungu* as a way of onomastic erasure of the name *abeLumbi* and its occult nuances. Kuper (1965, p. 299) notes that there is oral evidence in Eswatini that White missionaries could not live with the name *abeLumbi* because it meant they were the very wizards they preached against. The etymology states that these missionaries changed the name 'from *beLumbi* to *beLungu* from the root ***-kulunga***, which has several meanings, including: (1) to get into order, fit, correct; (2) be morally good.'

The Mail and Guardian (2006) quotes journalist Khaba Mkhize, who suggests that the term *Mlungu* derives from *lunga* (Nguni for goodness/righteousness). He cites Beyers Naudé and Bishop John Colenso as examples of White men who deserve the *Mlungu* label. Harrison (2004) espouses how the two

Bishops fought against apartheid in South Africa. Such an analysis and belief in White benevolence and goodness elevate them to a spiritual level higher than Africans, a subtle suggestion at deification. Responding to a Tweet on the etymology of the Nguni name for White person, *Mlungu*, one respondent wrote:

> *uMlungu* comes from the Bantu word *murungu* meaning God. When the colonisers came, African people mistook them for children of the almighty, I do not know why really! But even today in countries such as Zambia and Malawi they refer to God as *Murungu* or *uMlungu*!

Systematic racism and social Darwinism affected African images of White people and transformed negative images in naming them to aristocratic ones. Now we see even divine images applied to name White people. The White man is socially created through colonial racism to be a god to Africans; this is expressed by the etymology of the names *Murungu* and *Mlungu* in Shona and Nguni respectively, for White people argued to derive from *Mulungu*, the word for God in Swahili.

The race hierarchies created to propel White people up towards God use other races as a ladder, with Black people at the base of the ladder. Williams (1999, p. 176) observed this with US racism and notes that:

> Historically, racial categorisation has been rooted in racism, and racial classification schemes have had an implicit or explicit relative ranking of various racial groups. Within the U.S. context, whites have always been at the top, Blacks at the bottom, and other groups in between.

The fact that God is the antithesis of the devil implies that those at the base of this ideological ladder are closer to or with the devil, if not the devils themselves. The names *vaRungu* and *abeLungu* link whiteness to righteousness. Efforts at character building and civility are seen as trying to be white; in this way, Africans are othered as ungodly people who can only be closer to God by trying to be White physically, economically and culturally. Figure 5.1 illustrates the divine race implications in the etymologies of names of white people traced to the name *Mulungu*, 'God'.

The colour spectrum is linked not only to being fit, as in social Darwinism but also to God and heaven. Darker people are associated with the antithesis of God and heaven, and they can be saved by aspiring to be white (Ferris, 1913). A good example of the deification of White people in Africa through naming is found in the Baoule language in Ivory Coast, where I established through interviews that White people are called *Blofue*. The name is derived from blending ***blolo-*** (meaning heaven) + ***-fue*** (meaning inhabitant). The name therefore means inhabitants of heaven, creating demigods in White people and inversely 'satanising' Africans as inhabitants of hell, since they are not of heaven.

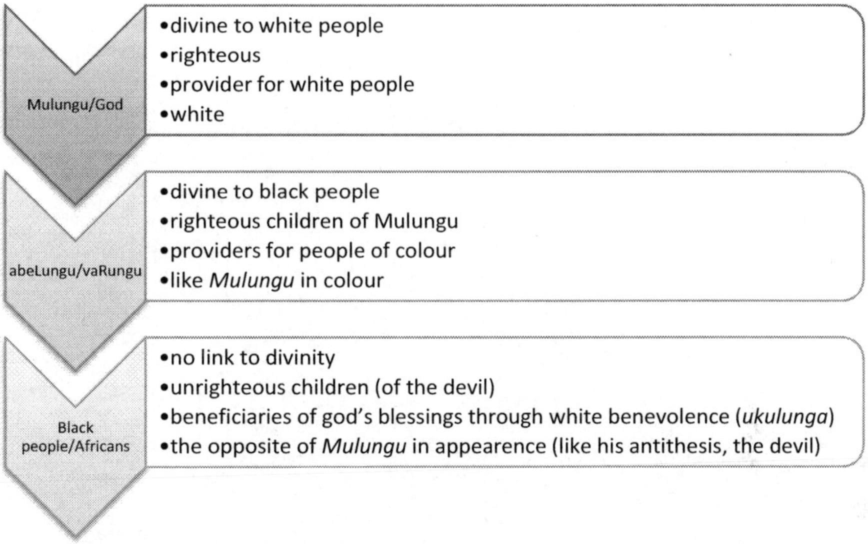


*Figure 5.1* Implications of divine race hierarchies in naming White people in Africa

## 5.4 Conclusion

Names given to White people in African languages and cultures are a window through which colonialities of power and culture can be explored. The names throughout West, Central, East and Southern Africa are creative mnemonics of all types of early contacts between White people and Africa. The early explorers and missionaries were a strange sight to Africans, who named them as such. The names *Mzungu*, *Mlungu* and *Aburoni* indicate African sophisticated othering of White people who were seen as desperate strangers who had come from faraway lands and needed help. The coming of slavery and colonialism later saw the coining of names to achieve crude nomen othering of White people, indicating the distaste Africans had of colonialism and slavery. Racial slur etymologies characterise African motives for naming Whites as agents of violence and corruption of African ethos. In this category, names such as *Mulumbi, Murumbi, Aboforo* were coined to name whites as evil. *Mzungu* and *Mlungu* also carry ethnophaulic references which portray colonialism as pollution in Africa. Through colonial racism and White supremacy created through imperial institutions, White people came to be at the top of social hierarchies, and Black people envied them, and these names underwent semantic amelioration to reference White opulence and decorum. The elevation of Whites up the social strata ended up associating them with deities. Figure 5.2 illustrates the genesis and evolution of African names for White people.

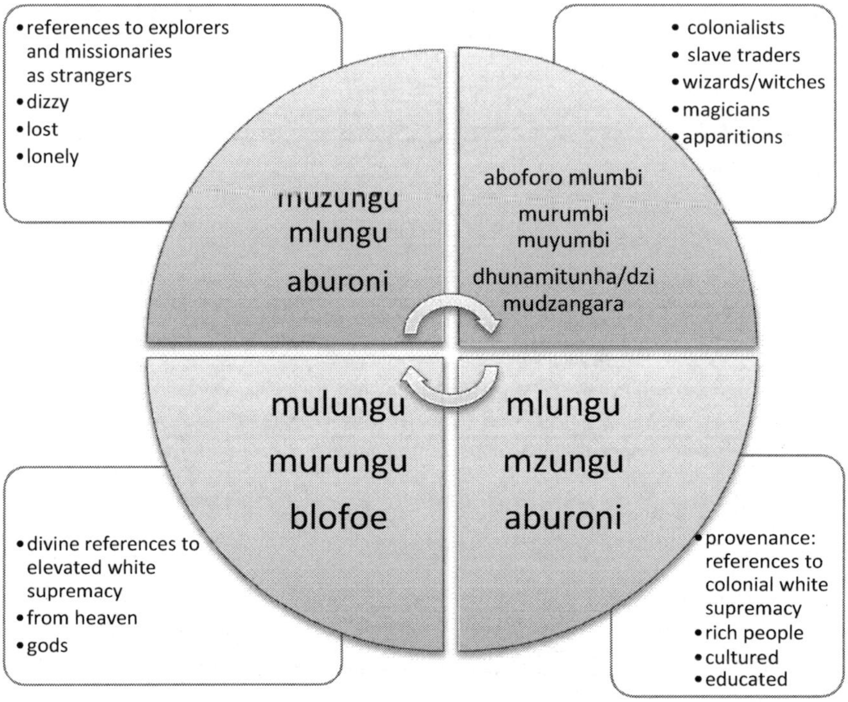


*Figure 5.2* Amelioration of names of White people in Africa

The etymologies start from stranger references which other Whites as foreigners in Africa and move on to evil references which other Whites for the evils of slavery and colonialism. Amelioration was a transformation created by Whites; however, the trend is proving to be a cycle, as we now have White people, especially in South Africa, now complaining of these names and linking them back to stranger and foreignising etymologies.

## References

Adler, M. K. (1978). *Naming and addressing: A sociolinguistic study*. Helmut Buske.

Anwuluorah, O. P. (2017). The prevalence of HIV/AIDS epidemic in Anambra State, Nigeria: Exploring gender, cultural and socio-religious perspectives. *AFRREV IJAH: An International Journal of Arts and Humanities*, *6*(1), 39–53.

Bhatia, M. V. (2005). Fighting words: Naming terrorists, bandits, rebels and other violent actors. *Third World Quarterly*, *26*(1), 5–22.

Bosiwah, L., Abrefa, K. B., & Asenso, C. O. (2015). An etymological study of the word *"aborɔfo"* (Europeans) and its impact on Akan language. *International Journal of Applied Linguistics and Translation*, *1*(1), 1–7.

Botchway, De-Valera N. Y. M. (2008). When the people decide: Colonialism, social and emergence of modern nationalism in the Gold Coast. *Drumspeak, International Journal of Humanities*, *1*(2), 168–217.

Darwish, I. (2010). Pre-peace and post-peace referring in Jordanian journalistic Arabic. *Names*, *58*(4), 191–196.

Doke, C. M., & Vilakazi, B. W. (1948). *English-Zulu dictionary*. Witwatersrand University Press.

Feldskov, T., & Frederiksen, A. M. (2000). *Survey on the knowledge on HIV: Madala-, Jongwe-, Siyamuninga-, and Nemadziva Villages, Gokwe North District, Midlands Province, Zimbabwe*. University of Zimbabwe Publications.

Ferris, W. H. (1913). *The African abroad: Or, his evolution in western civilization, tracing his development under Caucasian milieu* (Vol. 2). Johnson Reprint Corporation.

Harrison, P. (2004). *South Africa's top sites: Spiritual*. New Africa Books.

Hayward, J. (2020). Orality in the digital age. In R. H. Kaschula & H. E. Wolff (Eds.), *The transformative power of language: From postcolonial to knowledge societies in Africa* (pp. 277–303). Cambridge University Press.

Hosseini, E., Sarfallah, S., Bakhshipour, F., & Dolatabadi, H. R. (2012). The impact of using etymological analysis on teaching vocabulary to EFL university students. *Theory & Practice in Language Studies*, *2*(9), 1868–1876. https://doi.org/10.4304/tpls.2.9.1868-1876.

Kirby, P. R. (1954). Gquma, Mdepa and the Amatshomane clan: A by-way of miscegenation in South Africa. *African Studies*, *13*(1), 1–24.

Kuper, H. (1965). Colour, categories and colonialism: The Swazi case 1. In V. W. Turner (Ed.), *Colonialism in Africa 1870–1960* (pp. 286–307). Cambridge University Press.

Lake, O. (2003). *Blue veins and kinky hair: Naming and color consciousness in African America*. Greenwood Publishing Group.

Likaka, O. (2009). *Naming colonialism: History and collective memory in the Congo, 1870–1960*. University of Wisconsin Press.

Loewe, M. (2016, November 21). Experts say Umlungu is not negative in meaning [correspondent]. *Dispatch Live*. www.dispatchlive.co.za/news/2016-11-21-experts-say-umlungu-is-not-negative-in-meaning/

Mail and Guardian. (2006, June 30). *Mlungus ubuntu and abantu*. https://mg.co.za/article/2006-06-30-mlungus-ubuntu-and-abantu/

Mamdani, M. (1998, May 13). *When does a settler become a native?* Reflections on the Colonial Roots of Citizenship in Equatorial and South Africa, Text of an Inaugural Lecture as AC Jordan Professor of African Studies, University of Cape Town, New Series 208.

Massey, D. S., & Denton, N. A. (1993). *American apartheid: Segregation and the making of the underclass*. Harvard University Press.

Martinot, S. (2011). *The coloniality of power: Notes toward de-colonization*. San Francisco State University. www.ocf.berkeley.edu/~marto/coloniality.htm#:~:text=The%20%22coloniality%20of%20power%22%20is,the%20Americas%20to%20the%20present

Matson, J. N. (1956). History in Akan words. *Transactions of the Gold Coast & Togoland Historical Society*, *2*(2), 63–70.

Mazrui, A. A. (1986). *The Africans: A triple heritage*. British Broadcasting Corporation Publications.

Muzungu Blog Uganda. (2020, October 4). *About the muzungu definition*. http://muzungubloguganda.com/about-the-muzungu/muzungu-definition/#.W5pphPlTLIU

Ndlovu, S. (2015). Thematic characterisation of Ndebele *izichothozo*. *South African Journal of African Languages*, *35*(1), 113–121.

Ndlovu, S. (2017). Transphonologisation as ethnophaulism between the Ndebele and the Shona of Zimbabwe in selected toponyms and ethnonyms. *Nomina Africana: Journal of African Onomastics, 31*(2), 117–125.

Ndlovu-Gatsheni, S. J. (2014). Global coloniality and the challenges of creating African futures. *Strategic Review for Southern Africa, 36*(2), 181–202.

News 24. (2013, July 24). *Umlungu the accepted racist word.* www.news24.com/MyNews24/Umlungu-the-accepted-racist-word-20130724

Ochonu, M. E. (2019). Looking for race: Pigmented pasts and colonial mentality in "non racial" Africa. In P. Essed, K. Farquharson, K. Pillay, & E. White (Eds.), *Relating worlds of racism* (pp. 3–37). Palgrave Macmillan. https://doi.org/10.1007/978-3-319-78990-3_1

The Oxford Dictionary Online. (2020, October 6). *Umlungu.* https://en.oxforddictionaries.com/definition/umlungu

Paradies, Y. (2005). Anti-racism and indigenous Australians. *Analyses of Social Issues and Public Policy, 5*(1), 1–28.

Pierre, J. (2013). *The predicament of blackness: Postcolonial Ghana and the politics of race.* University of Chicago Press.

Quijano, A (2007). Coloniality and modernity/rationality. *Cultural Studies, 21*(2–3), 168–178.

Quora.com. (2017, October 4). *What do they call White people in Africa?* www.quora.com/What-do-they-call-white-people-in-Africa

Reddit.com. (2018, December 11). *Is it considered racist to refer to a White person as umlungu?* www.reddit.com/r/southafrica/comments/a58lp8/is_it_considered_racist_to_refer_to_a_white/

Rödlach, A. (2006). *Witches, westerners, and HIV: AIDS and cultures of blame in Africa.* Left Coast Press.

Schadeberg, T. C. (1989, November 7–8). *Historical inferences from Swahili etymologies.* Unwritten Testimonies of the Past, Proceedings of the International Symposium, Ojrzanów n. Warsaw. www.afrykanistyka.uw.edu.pl/pliki/files/publikacje/12_schadeberg.pdf

Spitzer, H. (2014). *Mzungu, how are you? Reflections on the human element of North-South partnerships.* https://appear.at/fileadmin/Dokumente/appear.at/implementation_and_reporting/Gender/article_HelmutSpitzer_2014.pdf

Urban Dictionary. (2008, December 23). *Mzungu* www.urbandictionary.com/define.php?term=mzungu, Umlungu; www.urbandictionary.com/define.php?term=Umlungu

Williams, D. R. (1999). Race, socioeconomic status, and health: The added effects of racism and discrimination. *Annals of New York Academic Science, 896*, 173–188. https://deepblue.lib.umich.edu/bitstream/handle/2027.42/71908/j.1749-6632.1999.tb08114.x.pdf?sequence=1

# 6 Onomastic attestations of coloniality in Africa

## 6.0 Introduction

The toponymic landscape is a reflection of power, linguistic, economic and cultural dynamics of an area. It has been established that the authority to name is premised on even greater authority; the position of namers is established at the apex of society through currencies of power such as might and money. Names are part of the language and symbols of power. Richardson (1991, p. 1) posits that 'from Charlemagne to the Tsars, from British imperialism to Italian fascism, the language and symbols of the Roman republic and the Roman emperors have been essential elements in the self-expression of imperial powers.' Naming establishes ownership and can be used to delimit space and objects, to mark them as belonging to the namer. Naming, especially space, marks ownership and jurisdiction. Ndlovu (2018) notes that naming space is part of identifying with it and owning it, while Bruns (1984, p. 29) posits that 'Certainly it has always been understood that the world belongs to the one who names it.' This chapter explores how names are deployed in colonial and decolonial power matrices as agents of de-historisisation. The central argument is that names are key aspect of racist and anti-racist political, cultural and economic struggles in Africa. European colonialism renamed Africa to affirm its othered non-sovereignty. Nimako and Willemsen (2011, p. 20) postulate that 'for the "outside world," the importance of the Peace of Westphalia lay not in the reciprocal recognition of the sovereignty of the signatories, but rather in the non-recognition of the sovereignty of others.' Research has established that names do express coloniality (Mapara & Nyota, 2016; Pongweni, 2017) and represent power dynamics (Neethling, 2010). Naming space is dependent on political power. The Democratic Republic of Congo (DRC), for example, has changed names seven times since 1885 (Leahy, 2018), all depending on who had political power at the times of the name changes. The changed names, especially toponyms, usually become part of the language used in public signage. This is called the linguistic landscape.

The concept LL derives from geographical landscapes. Gorter (2006) states that landscape is a noun which references the literal expanse of land or its pictorial representation. The description of a language situation in an area

DOI: 10.4324/9781003170761-8

corresponds to the physical expanse reference, while the pictorial representation corresponds to the symbolic representations of public language usage. Kallen (2010) extends the concept of LL to cover public signage, and he calls this the semiotic landscape. Ndlovu (2016, p. 23) states that there is a clear nexus between onomastics and LL:

> The study of onomastics overlaps with another area of applied linguistics called the linguistic landscape. Linguistic landscape is the language as it is used in public spaces such as in notices and billboards. Toponyms are part of language use in the public space as they characterise the environment.

Some names may not be written physically, but they are the primary mental language describing the area. Landry and Bourhis (1997, p. 25) define linguistic landscape as:

> The language of public road signs, advertising billboard, street names, place names, commercial shop signs, and public signs on government buildings combines to form the linguistic landscape of a given territory, region, or urban agglomeration.

The domain of LL has been largely researched as a multilingual phenomenon using quantitative methods in multilingual urban metropoles (Coupland & Garrett, 2010; Blommaert, 2013). However, Blommaert and Maly (2016) argue for a qualitative and semiotic approach to LL, ethnographic LL analysis. They opine that, while LL offers an insight into the sociolinguistic regimes of an area, it also reflects on social and political indices. Ethnographic LL analysis goes beyond the indicative catalogues of areal multilingualism into power matrices and hierarchies. Blommaert and Maly (2016, pp. 2–3) further argue for qualitative LL because:

> Public spaces are social arenas, circumscriptions on which control, discipline, belonging and membership operate and in which they are being played out. Furthermore, public space is also an instrument of power, discipline and regulation: it organises the social dynamics deployed in that space. . . . Communication in the public space, consequently, is communication in a field of power. The question thus becomes: how does space organise semiotic regimes?

Visible public language is not randomly inscribed; it is a product of a proleptic exercise designed to affect the minds of addressees (Scollon & Scollon, 2003). The addresser navigates the past, the present and the future to effectively manipulate the addressees. Naming place and key heritage concepts such as money relates to power dynamics. Berg and Kearns (1996, p. 99) point out that:

> The naming of places is a key component in the relationship between place and the politics of identity in contemporary societies. In this sense, naming

is a form of norming. Names are part of both a symbolic and a material order that provides normality and legitimacy to those who dominate the politics of (place) representation.

This chapter engages the theories of othering, postcolonial and coloniality in analysing the toponymic landscape of Africa to reveal political, economic and religio-cultural imperialism. The idea of the 'other' originates with Hegel's (1807) master-slave dialectic, where he argues for creation of identity by distancing one's self from the encountered other. The notion of the other was later popularised by De Beauvoir (1949), who argues that the notion of the other opposes and helps create the self. Jensen (2011) states that othering is a sub-theory in postcolonial theory, and this reflects on how the colonisers used othering to foster an imaginary coloniser superior identity as opposed to the inferior colonised identity. Rukundwa and Aarde (2007, p. 1190) state that 'postcolonial theory does not declare war on the past but challenges the consequences of the past that are exploitative.' Benyera (2020) opines that African problems stem from coloniality; policies in Africa are modelled around those of the same states which enslaved, looted and colonised Africa. Present African governmentality is an extension of coloniality. This is also attested by key national onomastics such as the names of countries, currencies, streets, churches and water bodies. Nhemachena (2016) says that colonialism goes beyond othering to incorporate other vices such as dispossession, assimilation and incorporation. Chigozie (2018, p. 3) argues that 'Imperialism is seen as the establishment of economic and political dominance over other nations. The major forms of imperialism include; Economic imperialism, Political imperialism and Socio-cultural imperialism.'

The names analysed in the chapter were collected through intuition, unstructured interviews, participant observations and literature (journals, maps, atlas, news sites), and they are analysed conceptually to expose their colonial implications and meanings. The data consist of names of countries and names of streets in Dakar, Lagos, Nairobi, Bulawayo and Johannesburg so as to give a balanced picture of French, British and apartheid colonialities in Africa. It also includes names of lakes and waterfalls, names of chartered colonial companies, multinational companies, African currencies, Christian denominations in Africa and colonially misnamed toponyms in Zimbabwe. The study employs Altheide's (1987) ethnographic content analysis and ethnographic LL analysis (Blommaert & Maly, 2016) to deduce meanings and symbolisms. Emphasis is on describing and conceptualising data. In outlining a methodology for ECA, Altheide and Schneider (2013) note that researchers need to learn about the production process and context of texts and understand formatting and patterns of the texts and imagery. They further argue that ECA is conceptually oriented rather than categorically. ECA does not use data to tell stories but rather to expose meaning and effects texts have through grounding them in the social world and social processes.

## 6.1 The imperial self in African toponymy

This section examines political and territorial designations of African spaces by colonialism. In this category, the focus is on names of countries and streets in colonial urban Africa, hydronyms and transphonologisation of African toponyms. The main argument is that Europeans used names to designate Africa as an extension of their empires and that in so doing, the original names of African spaces were ostracised and othered out of the linguistic landscape in imperial fashion. Said (1994, p. 4) defines imperialism as 'any system of domination and subordination organised with an imperial centre and a periphery.' African names were pushed to the peripheries of history and power. Young (2015, p. 54) posits that 'imperialism operates from the centre, is a state policy and is developed for ideological as well as financial reasons.' The European character was imagined on Africa through naming; as Uluocha (2015, p. 182) argues, 'a place name imparts a certain character on a place.' According to Borkfelt (2011, p. 116):

> In the example of Columbus and San Salvador, not only does his act of naming signify his taking possession of the island on behalf of his God and the Spanish Monarchy, it also signifies that he thinks himself righteous in doing so, despite the fact that it has a native population, who have already named it, as he well knows.

Columbus accorded himself the divine authority to change names. Greenblatt (2017, p. 82) quotes him as saying 'the Indians call it Guanahani, he writes, thus cancelling native nomenclature to assert his power.' The same cancellations were applied on African toponyms to other Africans and imagine Europeans as the authentic owners of the continent.

### *6.1.1 Naming colonised states in Africa*

African states were named after colonial powers, creating compound naming in some cases. The name of the colonial power was used to prefix Africa, and a cartographical point was usually affixed in between the two, as in German-West-Africa and Portuguese-East-Africa. The names created the imperial link with the overlord country. Chigozie (2018, p. 3) views political imperialism as 'a situation where a country may have had its own government but it operates as the imperialist country told it to.' The colonies were directly controlled from Europe. Never mind the theories on the different colonial policies; the idea was to create a colony that was emblematic of the colonising power, and names of public spaces are good examples of this emblematic resemblance. Ben-Rafael et al. (2006, p. 8) reason thus:

> LL, indeed, constitutes the very scene-made of streets, corners, circuses, parks, buildings – where society's public life takes place. As such, this scene

> carries crucial sociosymbolic importance as it actually identifies – and thus serves as the emblem of societies, communities and regions. Representations of Paris' scenery, including its LL, can be viewed as nothing less than emblematic of France, and the same is true, of course, of other major cities.

The names given to colonised African countries served as landmarks of different colonial jurisdictions. Berg and Kearns (1996) opine that naming has the power to normalise abnormalities and inequalities in race, gender and politics. The scramble for Africa after the Berlin conference of 1878 was partly normalised through naming the annexed territories. The imperial possession of Africa was normalised as legitimate extensions of empires through naming African spaces as part of or belonging to Europe. Africa was partitioned among western countries and othered as European possession. The possession was emphasised through names which clearly stated that parts of Africa belonged to Europeans. The names were possessive compound names with the European country name as the possessive root. The names used cartography, African names and names of rivers and deserts to mark the delimitations of the colonial expanse. The compound toponyms normalised Africa as belonging to Europe and normalised coloniality of space, power, people and culture. Table 6.1 gives examples of names that normalised possession of Africa by Europe through naming it in compound possessive names.

While these designations were colonial nomenclature expected to be obsolete in a 'free' Africa, they are still used to classify Africa in literature. Africa is still divided into European zones depending on which colonial language is

*Table 6.1* Colonial toponyms indicating ownership of Africa by European countries

| *Colonising possessive* | *Delimitation of African space* | *Current countries which were within the delimitation* |
|---|---|---|
| French | Congo | Gabon, Republic of Congo (RC) |
| | Equatorial Africa | Chad, Central Africa Republic, Gabon, RC |
| | Sudan | Mali |
| | West Africa | Mauritania, Senegal, Mali, Guinea, Cote d'Ivoire, Niger, Burkina Faso, Benin |
| | Somaliland | Djibouti |
| British | Somaliland | Somalia |
| | East Africa | Kenya, Uganda |
| Germany | East Africa | Tanzania, Zanzibar, Rwanda, Burundi |
| | South West Africa | Namibia |
| Portuguese | Guinea | Guinea Bissau |
| | East Africa | Mozambique |
| Spanish | Guinea | Equatorial Guinea |
| | Sahara | Western Sahara |
| Belgian | Congo | Democratic Republic of the Congo |

the official language or lingua franca in the country. The dominant language speaks of colonial language policies and their hegemonic after-effects on the African linguistic landscape. This after-life of colonial linguistics is still used to delegate toponyms. The English, French and Portuguese still partition Africa from a linguistic landscaping point whereby there is still English, French and Portuguese Africa. The countries are grouped into Anglophone, Francophone and Lusophone Africa; such naming is akin to the partitioning of Africa in the Berlin conference.

The decolonisation agenda incorporated mental processes of ridding African mindsets of colonial mentality. One such process was the renaming of independent African states. Moll (2009, p. 305) argues that:

> Africa had to be freed from the odour of its colonial past and what better place to start than reclaiming the African names of countries? The traces of colonialism had to be removed and the suppressed Africans healed by rethinking and repossessing the names of their countries.

However, years after the end of colonial occupation of Africa, the continent is still named to indicate possession by western cultures and languages. Africa is still physically and mentally divided into colonial powers, and naming exposes these colonialities. There is a continued coloniality of power, culture and language in Africa, as it is still divided among the colonial powers. Today the continent is divided into English, French, Portuguese, Spanish and German, just as was the plan at the Berlin conference. While it can be argued that the divisions are based on language, it is clear that the divisions other African languages, and this othering affects African identities too. After political independences in Africa, Feuser (1997) characterises African cultures and countries as Anglo, Franco, Luso and Germanophone, while Fombad and Steytler (2020) divide Africa into Franco, Anglo, Luso, Arabo and Hispanophone. All these names attest to African coloniality and how Europe continues to possess Africa and Africans. Europe is the self while Africa and its people are othered possessions. The colonial divisions also affect individual African countries such as Cameroon, where there is a divide between Anglo and Francophone.

The majority of colonial African country names were European language lexis or morphemes. Campbell (2019) argues that 'How African countries received their names is intrinsically interesting, but that Europeans named so many is also a salutary reminder of the origins of these countries.' Some of the colonial names remain up to the present day; for example, he notes that the name Cameroon was derived from Portuguese *Rio dos Camaroes*, which means 'river of shrimp.' Uluocha (2015, p. 184) observes that 'The cultural and language contact between Africans on one hand and the Arabs and Europeans on the other, is reflected in the place names of the African countries.' Some African countries have normalised surviving as Europe's others; they even continued with European colonial names after political independence. The majority adopted European naming traditions and used them to derive their own new names. This is another expression of coloniality, an indication that Europe still names Africa and defines it because of its power advantages. The Latinate locative suffix for land toponyms **-ia**, for example, was used to derive new names for the following countries: Tanzania, Zambia, Namibia, Algeria, Tunisia, Nigeria, Somalia, Eretria, Ethiopia and Liberia. The **-ia** is colonial morphology which still characterises many African country names after renaming.

Some countries adopted European language cartography on their names, such as South Africa, South Sudan and Western Sahara. The majority also incorporate western-language political descriptors such as republic, democratic and people's republic. These appended adjectives make the LL of the names European. While the name South Africa, for example, is English and by all LL purposes colonial, it is in the same category with names that use European languages in their content, such as the suffix **-ia**. It could have been better to change the name from an English script to an African one, such as *Zansi* Africa or Afrika *Borwa*, as it is sometimes called, which are Nguni and Sotho for South, respectively.

The British used the suffix **-land** in some toponyms to mark them as British territories. This of course derives from their own toponym, *English-land*, which derives the name England. In Africa, they extended this appellation to their colonies, such as Somali-land, Swazi-land and Nyasa-land. Swaziland remained with this colonial appendage far longer than other affected countries; however, they have also rid their name of it. Leahy (2018) points out that 'King Mswati III had long complained that people outside of Africa confused his country with Switzerland.' The country name was changed to a Nguni locative, eSwatini, which still translates to 'the land of the Swati.' ESwatini joins the few African countries with purely indigenous noncolonial names, and these are Botswana, Uganda, Rwanda, Kenya, Zimbabwe, Angola, Mali and Ghana. Ethnic power struggles within countries help maintain some colonial names and lexis on African country names, African countries such as the DRC and Benin have had manifold name changes. Moll (2009, p. 305) posits, 'It appears that personal craving for power, ethnic conflict and political faction differences became the driving force for manifold name changes.' These ethnic tensions usually find common ground in colonial nomenclature.

### *6.1.2 Hodonyms and hydronyms as evidence of the colonial self in Africa*

Hodonyms are the taxonomy of onomastics that deals with names of streets under toponymy, while hydronyms are the names of water bodies. The colonial governments built urban centres in Africa, and they named the streets to mark colonial ownership as well. Lakes, waterfalls and at times rivers were renamed using European names and heritage. These names were spatial metaphors of the colonial power and disempowerment processes. According to Kallen (2010, p. 42), 'This spatial metaphor ascribes position within a social hierarchy to the originators of signs, and focuses on the landscape as a reflex of social and linguistic hierarchies.' Those who took part in colonial battles against African kingdoms were mostly honoured by having their names on the LL. Azaryahu (2011, p. 31) observes this 'in street names in Abidjan, the capital of the former French colony of Côte d'Ivoire, which were named after French colonial heroes.' This section uses hodonyms from French West Africa – Dakar (Senegal) is the case in point – and Nairobi (Kenya) hodonyms for British East Africa, Bulawayo (Zimbabwe) for British Southern Africa and Johannesburg (SA) for apartheid hodonyms. Some examples are drawn from Lagos, Nigeria. Hydronyms are taken from Africa's great lakes region and Zimbabwe.

Colonialism was never easy in most if not all African countries; it cost the coloniser lives. Most of the people who died in colonising battles were honoured through having their names on urban toponymy. Colonising battles were key national events in Europe. Light (2004, p. 154) states that 'Those names which commemorate key events or personalities from a country's history are a manifestation of political order, and can be significant expressions of national identity with a powerful symbolic importance.' The French, the British and apartheid South Africa also honoured their monarchs and politicians back in Europe by naming African streets after them. Table 6.2 gives some African streets that were named in commemoration of colonising figures.

The urban landscape was marked as European. Africans were sidelined in the naming process until some changes were done after political independence. However, some of these names remain in postcolonial Africa. Ndlovu (2013, p. 296) states that 'There are some Ndebele toponyms that are a remnant from the colonial era in Zimbabwe. These toponyms came into being due to the colonial experience in Zimbabwe that saw the British rule the country for years.' The French went further to celebrate French cultural icons on Senegalese streets. Njoh (2017, p. 1178) says:

> Occasionally, streets and places were named to commemorate the achievement of French cultural icons. Two streets, namely rue Victor Hugo and rue Emile Zola stand out in this regard. The former was in honour of Victor Marie Hugo (1802–1885), a French poet, novelist and dramatist of the Romantic Movement. The second was in honour of Emile-Edouard-Charles-Antoine Zola (1840–1902), a prominent French novelist and political activist.

The celebration of European culture on African urban LL was extended to include European institutions of power and civilisations. Some streets were named to reference colonial institutions of mental slavery such as churches and exploitative institutions such as oil mills, markets and ports. Table 6.3 shows some streets named to identify colonial institutions in Africa.

Colonial institutions which overpowered Africa into colonialism are also commemorated in colonial street toponymy. The French imperial prowess was glorified through the Dakar street name *rue Imperiale*, which means 'Imperial road'; here, the imperialism is glaring and the othering of African power is

*Table 6.2* Colonial figures in African hodonymy

| *Town and country* | *Colonial street name* | *Commemorated colonial figure* |
|---|---|---|
| Dakar – Senegal | Boulevard Pinet-Laprade | Jean-Marie Emile Pinet Laprade: French architect who drew the city plan. |
| | Avenue William-Ponty | William Ponty: Governor general of AOF 1908–1915. |
| | Rue Vincens | Vincens: Colonial French army engineer in West Africa, killed in battle. |
| | Avenue Roume | Ernest Nester Roume: Second governor general of AOF. |
| | Rue Dagorne | Dagorne: Surname of a French soldier killed in the battle to colonise Senegal. |
| Nairobi – Kenya | Herdinge Street | Sir Arthur Henry Herdinge: First colonial administrator of Kenya. |
| | Eliot Street | Sir Charles Eliot: Colonial commissioner in Kenya 1900–1904. |
| | Whitehouse Road | George Whitehouse: British colonial railway engineer in East Africa. |
| | Salisbury Way | Lord Salisbury: British prime minister during the colonisation period (Victorian era). |
| | Victoria Street | Queen Victoria: British matriarch during the colonisation period. |
| Bulawayo – Zimbabwe | Barrow Street | Barrow: Pioneer column army officer during the colonisation of Zimbabwe. |
| | Wilson Street | Major Allan Wilson: British army commander slain during the Anglo-Ndebele war of 1893. |
| | Grey Street | Earl Grey: Member of the board of directors for the BSAC. |
| | Jameson Street | Dr. Leander Starr Jameson: Rhodes' most trusted aide, who started the Anglo-Ndebele war of 1893. |
| | Selbourne Avenue | Lord Selbourne: British high commissioner to South Africa, who visited Bulawayo in 1906. |
| Johannesburg – South Africa | Hendrik Verwoerd Drive | Hendrik Verwoerd: Former South African prime minister and architect of apartheid. |
| | DF Malan Drive | Daniel Francois Malan: former South African prime minister, 1948–1954. Apartheid started during his tenure. |
| | Hans Strijdom Drive | Johannes Gerhardus Strijdom: apartheid SA prime minister 1954–1958. |

explicit. The colonial institutions of power such as duke, king, queen, commissioner, president, coronation and consul were all used to name urban streets across colonial Africa to affirm the new categories of power governing the continent. The indigenous power structures and names were othered and sidelined to indicate the power shifts. Where African languages were used to name streets, the intention was to emphasise colonial conquest of the area or

*Table 6.3* Hodonyms glorifying colonial institutions in Africa

| *City and country* | *Colonial street name* | *Commemorated imperial site or institution* |
|---|---|---|
| Dakar – Senegal | Avenue du Barachois | Barrage Avenue, referencing the coastal barrage in the port. |
| Dakar – Senegal | Rue du Cimetiere | Cemetery Road – road marking the old European cemetery. |
| Dakar – Senegal | Rue de l'Administration | Administration Road – leading to the colonial administration building. |
| Dakar – Senegal | Rue de l'Hospital | Hospital Road – leading to the hospital. |
| Lagos – Nigeria | Oil Mill Street | Leading to the oil mill. |
| Lagos – Nigeria | Palm Church Street | Street of the palm church. |
| Joburg and Lagos – (SA and Nigeria) | Market Street | Leading to the market. |
| Joburg – SA | Kerk Street | Church street – street of the Anglican church. |
| Bulawayo – Zimbabwe | Fort Street | Site of the BSAC military fort. |

a translation of colonial power structures, such as in *Ajele* Street in Lagos; the name is just a Yoruba translation of 'consul'.

The colonial ownership of African space through renaming was extended to natural water bodies. Lakes, rivers, pools and waterfalls formed part of African livelihoods, culture and religion, and they were named before Europeans 'discovered' them. Njoh (2017, p. 1175) postulates:

> In 1858, the British explorer, John Hanning Speke, stumbled onto a gargantuan lake in East Africa. He proceeded to christen this body of water, which he ironically claimed to have discovered, Lake Victoria. This is despite the fact that indigenous groups of the region, including Kinyarwanda, Lou and Luganda speaking people had known the lake for millennia as Nyanza, Nam Lolwe, and Nalubaale, respectively.

These pseudo-discoveries, some of which were sponsored by the British royal family through the Royal Geographical Society, sought to glorify their benefactors and rulers by naming African lakes and waterfalls after the royal family. Table 6.4 gives colonial renaming and erasure of African names for lakes and waterfalls.

While street names can be argued to have been applied to urban spaces created by colonialism in Africa, the renaming of water bodies 'discovered' by Europeans in Africa is an act of erasing African names and history in favour of colonial hegemony. Africa's great lakes were named to be private property of the British royal family by European explorers. The Queen and her family members characterised the colonial *hydronymscape* and, in the process, African names were gradually eroded. The naming grew even worse with dams built by colonial administrations; these were almost entirely named in honour

*Table 6.4* Colonial renaming of African water bodies

| *Colonial hydronym* | *Etymology* | *Erased African hydronym* | *Etymology* |
|---|---|---|---|
| Lake Albert – Uganda and DRC | Renamed by British explorer Samuel Baker after Prince Albert, husband to British Queen Victoria. | Mwitanzige | Banyoro and Batooro languages meaning locust killer; the people believed locusts died trying to cross the lake. |
| Lake Victoria | After Queen Victoria. | Nyanza | Kinyarwanda/Luganda meaning large mass of water. |
| Lake George | Renamed by British explorer Henry Stanley after King George of England, son to Albert and Victoria. | Dweru or Katongo | It is on the Katongo river. |
| Ripon Falls | Renamed by John Hanning Speke after George Robinson, 1st Marquess of Ripon, undersecretary of colonial India. | Jinja | From Luganda *mayinja* which means 'stones'. |
| Victoria Falls | Renamed by Scottish explorer David Livingstone after Queen Victoria. | Mosi oa Tunya | Tonga language for 'smoke that thunders'. |

of colonial engineers, funders, architects and politicians. Some African water bodies have been changed back to the original names. According to Moll (2009, p. 305), 'Black states wished to redeem their self-respect through reinstating the original names given by the inhabitants to African areas and countries.' However, some of the colonial names are still in use today.

### *6.1.3 Colonial transphonologies and erasure of some Zimbabwean toponyms*

Colonial othering of African toponyms included the altering of some names in a process called transphonologisation. The process can create both meaningless and meaningful changes. Ndlovu (2017) posits that transphonologisation also derives ethnophaulisms. Neethling (2005, p. 136) concurs when he points out that in transphonologisations, 'There is sound play on the one hand which could be considered as light-hearted and friendly, but at times also reflecting phonetic liberties, suggesting a lack of effort to get it right.' The lack of effort by the British to get some indigenous toponyms right resulted in meaningless phonemes and graphemes, while in some cases, the new transphonologies had different inferential meaning through their sound resemblance to other terms or concepts. Table 6.5 gives some transphonologised indigenous toponyms which are rendered meaningless through transphonologisation.

The toponyms Bulawayo and Emeveni perpetuate Ndebele royal and military histories, and they are part of the country's heritage. The name Bulawayo was pronounced by the colonising English as [buluwejo], although the orthography remained correct. The name Bulawayo is the passive form of the Ndebele verb *bulala*, 'kill', meaning the one being killed. Ransford (1967) asserts that the name was first used by Shaka king of the Zulu to name his capital in recognition of his childhood struggles. He further points out that, in 1870, Lobengula became king of the Matabele in what is now present-day Zimbabwe, and he established a new capital which he named Bulawayo after his struggles to the throne. The transphonology loses all the imbedded history, as the name becomes meaningless. Emeveni is also an element of Ndebele military history: Lobengula's *Ameva* regiment was stationed in the area now occupied by Amaveni township in Kwekwe. *Emeveni* is the correct Ndebele locative for the place of the *Ameva* regiment, yet the transphonology distorts the locative by removing the locative prefix **e-** yet maintaining the locative suffix **-eni**, creating a meaningless word and in the process obliterating Ndebele military history.

There are some Shona toponyms that were distorted, the resultant renditions rendered meaningless and the history carried by the toponyms has been lost to transphonology. The toponyms Chipuriro, Uhera and Zvishavane carry elements of Shona material culture, ethnicity and geography. However, the transphonologies erode this connection, leaving names that are just used for referential purposes. Chipuriro is a corn thrashing area, an indication that the place was a good farming area, and the farming history of the Shona is erased by the transphonology Spolilo. The Shona locative *uhera*, used as a toponym, demarcates the land of the Hera people, yet the transphonology creates a meaningless term from the toponym, symbolically robbing the Hera people of their

*Table 6.5* Meaningless English transphonologies of indigenous Zimbabwean toponyms

| *Indigenous toponym* | *Etymology* | *Meaningless English transphonology* |
|---|---|---|
| Bulawayo [βulawajo] | Ndebele: one being killed from Zulu and Ndebele royal histories | Buluweyo [buluwejo] |
| Emeveni [emeveni] | Ndebele: at the *ameva* (thorns) regiment where Lobengula's regiment was stationed | Amaveni [amaveni] |
| Chipuriro/Guruve [ʧʰip'uriro] | Shona: grain thrashing area | Sipolilo [sip'olilo] |
| Uhera [uhera] | Shona: locative/*nyika yevahera* (land of the *vaHeras*) | Buhera [buhera] |
| Zvishavane [ʐiʃaʋanɛ] | Shona: reddish mountains | Shabani [ʃabani] |

land. Some toponyms are used to describe the terrain and mark it, such as Zvishavane, which describes the radish mountains in the area. The English distorted the name to a meaningless rendition, Shabani, and by so doing, the Shona cannot describe the land in their language; this way, it ceases to be theirs.

There are some indigenous toponyms that were transphonologised by the English, and the resultant transphonologies created new meaning inferences that are different from the original ones, effectively distorting the history imbedded in the toponyms. Table 6.6 gives some indigenous toponyms that have been distorted away from their original meanings to some strange meaning inferences.

Toponyms are at times used by people descriptively to describe elements of their ecological culture. The names *Qweqwe* (crust) and *Mbalabala* (of different colours) are Ndebele describing environmental realities of the Qweqwe river and the topography of the *Mbalabala* area, respectively. The *Qweqwe* river flows through red clay soils, and the silt that remains after a flood is muddy. When it dries up, it forms a crust, *uqweqwe* in Ndebele. This element of Ndebele hydrological heritage is eroded by the transphonology Kwekwe, which is closer in form and meaning to the Ndebele word for a skin disease, *isikhwekhwe*. The heritage and association with the river are reduced to sickness, an instance of fouling the ethnic other. The topography of Mbalabala has many colours, and this is captured in the name *umbala*, 'colour' in Ndebele; repeating the stem creates the concept colourful. The transphonology now means a kudu, which has no significant history and association to the place.

Shona military and ethnic history is also preserved in some Zimbabwean toponyms. However, English transphonologies of some of these Shona names align them to different and at times fouling semantic fields. The toponyms Chirinda and Chinemukutu, for example, carry Shona history and heritage, which are

*Table 6.6* Weird semantic inferences in some English transphonologies of Zimbabwean toponyms

| *Indigenous toponym* | *Etymology* | *English transphonology* | *New meaning inference* |
|---|---|---|---|
| Qweqwe [!$^{w}$ɛ!$^{w}$ɛ] | Ndebele: crust which forms on the river bed | Queque [k$^{w}$ɛ k$^{w}$ɛ] | Ndebele: *isikhwekhwe* is a skin disease |
| Mbalabala [mbalaβala] | Ndebele: different colours (of the soils) | Balabala [balabala] | Ndebele: kudu |
| Chirinda [ʧ$^{h}$irinda] | Shona: Chirinda/ tower for military lookout | Silinda [silinda] | Cylinder |
| Chinemukutu [ʧ$^{h}$inemukut'u] | Shona: name of Mbwazhe founder of Gutu dynasty. He was a hunter, and *mukutu* is a bunch of arrows | Gutu [gut'u] | Shona: bad and choking smell |

lost in their English transphonologies. Chirinda derives from the mountain which was used by Shona soldiers as a tower to look out for approaching armies. The military history defines the Shona, and the toponym is a record of their past military heroics. However, the military heroics are watered down to mean a cylinder in the transphonology, suggesting that the mountain is cylindrical, which it is not. Chinemukutu is more insulting in its transphonological rendition than other transphonologies, particularly because it derives from an ethnic leader but was diverted to mean disgusting smell. The meaning inference of a disgusting smell speaks of what Ndlovu (2018) describes as colonial arrogance in the colonies. Chinemukutu, so named after his *mukutu* arrow bag (the bag with the arrows), was a great hunter, and, most importantly, he was the founder of the Gumbo dynasty. The name was transphonologised to Gutu and used to refer to his area; *gutu* is Shona for a pungent choking smell. The name can be construed as a racial slur referring to the area as a smelly place or smelly people.

## 6.2 African economic colonialities in names

According to Chigozie (2018, p. 3), 'Economic imperialism is a type of imperialism that allows the area to operate as its own nation, but the imperialist nations control its trade and other business and resources.' The urban-rural dichotomy and its origins in colonialism, in the majority of African contexts, has been named to reveal the colonial othering of Africans from the economy. Urban centres, which became drivers of colonial economies and continue to be economic hubs, are named to belong to the White people in many African languages and cultures. In Ndebele, for example, a town is also known as *esikhiweni*, 'White people's place'. The fact that Africans associate wealth with whiteness or being European is also expressed in the naming of other Black Africans as Whites when they get rich. The names given to African currencies are testimony to the economic coloniality of Africa. The continent was first named to indicate exploitation of resources, and the colonisation was implemented by chartered companies which were named to reveal the colonial sponsor. The exploiting companies persist today under the guise of global business. The naming of money and business confirms that Europeans own the economies in Africa and Africans were and are still the economic others.

### *6.2.1 The colonial names of money in Africa*

African economic coloniality can be read in the very currencies named and used by independent African states. Currencies were and are still a powerful conquering tool for empire; they are also part of the LL and the sign landscape, as they bear names and other aspects of heritage and power printed or pictured on them. Snodgrass (2019, p. 9) explains that 'throughout the 20th century, African colonies tended to trade in the coin of the European overlord or in local coinage that imitated the mottoes and motifs of the parent country.'

He further notes that currencies were used by liberated African countries to depict their heritage and struggle against colonialism. The names of currencies were imperial seals on the economic coloniality of Africa, and they symbolised dependence on the colonial overlords. Africa was othered as having no economy or money of its own. Several colonial currency names were used on the African colonies, and these names originate within the imperial empire.

One of the currency names which was introduced in Africa through colonialism and imperialism was the dinar. The name derives from Roman silver coins around 1570, and it is from Latin *denarius*, which means 'containing ten.' Other African countries were introduced to the dollar currency, another European name and heritage. Taskinsoy (2019) avows that the name dollar, is from German *taler*, later *thaler*, an abbreviation of *Joachimstaler*. It originates from the silver coin minted in mines near the town Joachimstal, northwest of Bohemia. France introduced its currency, the franc, to its colonies; the name carries with it a rich history of France. Kemp (1971) traces the name to the early French coins which were inscribed *Francorum Rex*, which means, 'king of the Franks'. The name franc for currency is a symbol of the king of France and his dominion; it is a symbol of coloniality and French authority. The British introduced the pound and shilling as names and currencies in Africa. Parker (2016) states that 'The British pound has its origins in continental Europe under the Roman era. Its name derives from the Latin word *poundus* meaning "weight".' As a unit of money in Old English, it referred to a pound of silver (Schmidt, 1940). Other British colonials used the shilling. Nierfeld (2012) posits that shilling is from Old English *scilling*, a coin consisting of a varying number of pence. He notes that the name was used in many European languages, creating variants such as Old German *skilling*, German *Schilling*, Old Norse *skillingr*, Dutch *schelling* and Gothic *skilliggs*. The Portuguese also forced the escudo on their colonies, a heritage from their scutum shield.

The currencies dinar, dollar, franc, pound, shilling, and escudo were colonial forms of economic and cultural coloniality, as they spread European history, heritage and culture to the colonies. These names came in to displace African names and forms of money. Snodgrass (2019) states that Black Africa produced a range of folk currencies before the arrival of foreign money in 300 BCE. He identifies, cattle, copper bracelets, salt, cotton, bar ingots, beads, tobacco and gold dust as early African currencies. Snodgrass (2019, p. 8) also argues that 'in 330CE, the African Kingdom of Aksum, produced the first indigenous African coinage, . . . traders carried the coins as far east as Yemen.' These forms of money obviously bore African names which were developed into names of currencies. The imposition of European currencies othered these African currencies to extinction. Upon gaining political independence, African countries changed currencies and images on them. However, with all the rich history of African money and its names, most African countries still bear colonial currency names, as indicated in Table 6.7.

The majority of African countries still use European names to name their currencies even though they are no longer linked to the colonial overlord

*Table 6.7* Coloniality of African currencies

| *Colonial name for currency* | *African countries still using the name* | *Total count* |
|---|---|---|
| Franc | Burundi, Cameroon, CAR, Chad, Republic of the Congo, Equatorial Guinea, Gabon, Benin, Burkina Faso, guinea Bissau, Ivory Coast, Mali, Niger, Senegal, Togo, Comoros, DRC, Djibouti, Guinea, Rwanda | 20 |
| Shilling | Kenya, Tanzania, Uganda, Somalia | 4 |
| Pound | Egypt, Sudan, South Sudan | 3 |
| Dollar/dalasi | Namibia, Liberia, Zimbabwe, Gambia | 4 |
| Dinar/dirham-drachma | Algeria, Libya, Tunisia, Morocco | 4 |
| Escudo/dobra | Cape Verde, Sao Tome and Principe | 2 |
| **Total** | | **37/54** |

central banks. Most African currencies are weak, and there is no monetary value in keeping the colonial names at the expense of African ones. The rupee and the rand are also linked to Indian and Afrikaner imperialism in Africa. Snodgrass (2019) alludes to the fact that currencies were used by liberated African countries to depict their heritage and struggle against colonialism. The irony is that these currencies are engraved with African heritage and history but still carry the colonial name they seek to negate. However, some African countries did rename their currencies using African names, as shown in Table 6.8.

These African countries explored their histories and heritages to find names for their currencies as a way of shedding the colonial ones. The names draw from the history of African forms of money which were othered and ostracised by imperial names and currencies.

### *6.2.2 Colonial naming of African spaces for resource extraction*

Names were used to normalise African economic coloniality, which was part of colonial governmentality. Ndlovu-Gatsheni (2020, p. 46) describes the economic otherness of Africa in the global economies, 'The political economy of Africa is fundamentally a tale of how the continent and its people were dragged into the evolving and unfolding global coloniality through such processes as enslavement, mercantilism and colonialism.' Amin (1976) advises that economic coloniality divided Africa into three macro regions: West Africa was the *economie de traite*; East, Central and Southern Africa became labour reserves; and concessionary companies fronted the coloniality of resource looting across the continent. In the *economie de traite* coloniality, Africans were forced to abandon propagation of their cultural food crops for western cash crops to supply colonising states through exports. This coloniality was normalised through agrarian export-inclined nomenclature for African countries, such as the Grain Coast and Pepper Coast. African states were also named to normalise slavery and exportation of African labour through names such as the Slave Coast.

*Table 6.8* Indigenous African names of currency

| *African name for currency* | *Countries* | *Etymology* |
|---|---|---|
| Kwacha | Zambia, Malawi | Nyanja, Bemba, Tonga: meaning dawn |
| Kwanza | Angola | Swahili: for first fruits |
| Pula | Botswana | Tswana: meaning rainfall |
| Loti | Lesotho | Sotho: for mountain |
| Lilangeni | Eswatini | Swati: for sun |
| Cedi | Ghana | Akan: cowry shell used as currency before colonial dollar |
| Naira | Nigeria | Alteration of Nigeria or Arabic: for shining star |
| Metical | Mozambique | Arabic: mithqal meaning weight |
| Birr | Ethiopia | Amharic: meaning silver |

*Table 6.9* Names attesting to African resource coloniality

| *Name normalising resource externalisation* | *Externalised resource* | *Current country name* |
|---|---|---|
| Gold Coast | Gold | Ghana |
| Ivory Coast | Ivory | Cote d'Ivoire |
| Slave Coast | Slaves/labour | Benin |
| Grain Coast | Grain | Liberia |
| Pepper Coast | Paper | Liberia |

Concessionary company coloniality was after African resources, and those parts of Africa which had natural resources were named to normalise them as looting spots through names such as the Gold Coast and the Ivory Coast. Table 6.9 illustrates how Africa was named for resource extraction.

The areas were conveniently named as coasts to emphasise their links to shipping the resources out of Africa to the West.

The partitioning of Africa among European countries was facilitated by chartered companies that secured colonies on behalf of their governments in Europe. These companies, just like the colonial administrative territories, used European country names to identify African spaces for colonialism. Chigozie (2018) states that the British East Africa Company (BEAC) was used to occupy British colonies in East Africa, the British South Africa Company (BSAC) enabled the colonisation of the Rhodesias and the Royal Niger Company secured West Africa for British imperialism. The country names, such as British West Africa, are directly linked to the names of chartered companies which colonised these areas on behalf of the imperial centre. Vail (1976) identifies similar companies which operated to occupy Mozambique for the Portuguese; these were the *Companhia do Niassa* and the *Companhia de Mocambique*. These companies, according to Chigozie (2018, p. 3), 'plundered and exploited the native peoples for their minerals and other resources.' African resources were looted in the scramble for the continent, and this led to the underdevelopment of Africa and the development of Europe (Bush, 2008). The inequality created African otherness. The chattered company names bore explicit and at times implied links to the country which contracted them to exploit colonials.

The phenomenon of chartered companies continues to this day in the guise of multinational companies (MNCs). Akong (2020) states that externalisation of African minerals persists in postcolonial Africa. Chigozie (2018, p. 5) notes that MNCs in Africa 'establish alliances between international capitalists and domestic capitalist elite.' Ayelazuno and Mawuko-Yevugah (2020) also concur that African resources continue to be looted in the 21st century with the complicity of many African leaders. Chigozie (2018) traces MNCs back to the imperial and colonising chartered companies. The Market Screener (2021) identifies Anglo-American as a multinational company in the mining sector, mining diamonds, copper, iron ore, platinum, palladium, manganese, nickel, rhodium and other minerals. The company is dominant in African mining and also incorporates other imperial MNCs such as Standard Chartered Bank and Standard Bank and Total Petroleum. The company retains the name Anglo-American, and it has its head office in London. It operates just like the chartered colonial companies which delivered African resources to the imperial centres. The African mining linguistic landscape is also dominated by other European names such as BHP and Rio Tinto. Reuters on May 9, 2007, identified BHP (Broken Hill Proprietary) as an Anglo-Australian mining company, the biggest in the world. Its name was derived from its Broken Hill mining venture in New South Wales, Australia. Wales is in the United Kingdom, and the naming of Australian environs as New South Wales is itself colonial nomenclature. From this coloniality of Australia comes African economic coloniality through BHP. The second-largest mining company globally is Rio Tinto, which is Spanish for River Tinto. The company was so named after its initial mining venture in Huelva Spain on the River Tinto. The name Rio Tinto is very common in African mining today, symbolising the Europeanness of African mining in the post colonies.

The domination of Anglo-American names is also prevalent in the energy sector. Petroleum companies still brandish colonial nomenclature and continue exploiting African oil and gas. French, British, American, Dutch, Italian and Belgian companies still carry the mandate of serving colonial centres by exploiting African oil. The Encyclopaedia Britannica (2012) identifies Total Petroleum as a French MNC initiated by the French government, now incorporating Belgian Petroleum Conglomerate. The many Total garages and oil rigs in Africa attest to French and Belgian economic coloniality in the continent. The British empire persists in the name British Petroleum (BP). Tharoor (2010), writing for *TIME Magazine*, traces the name BP from Anglo-Persian Petroleum during the British imperial exploration of oil in Iran. The name was changed to BP, and today the name British in the company name is a commemoration of the continuation of global coloniality of African recourses. The British partnered with the Dutch to form the Royal Dutch Shell, a British-Dutch multinational oil and gas company. Imperial MNCs dominate the African energy business. Turner (1976) identifies the MNCs dominating Nigerian oil exploration as Shell, PB, Mobil (United States) and Agrip (Italy). Chigozie (2018) argues that these MNCs monopolise markets through patents – Adidas (shoes), Siemens (electricals) and Microsoft (software), and Africans are at the mercy of these Euro-American companies.

## 6.3 Onomastic conflations of imperial state and church in Africa

Imperialism was extended to other African culture and religion. Chigozie (2018, p. 3) identifies socio-cultural imperialism as when 'the dominating country deliberately tried to change customs, religious, lifestyles and languages in some of the countries. Generally, the imperialist countries assumed their cultures to be superior, and often saw themselves as bringing improvements in the society.' Christianity was hailed as bringing light to Africa; however, the naming of churches was linked to the colonial centres in Europe.

There are some church names that bear glaring reference to colonial powers in Europe, and these conflate the church and colonial agenda. Such names create political problems for churches in Africa. Maxwell (2006, p. 164) observes that 'missionaries acted as unwitting agents of colonialism which used Christianity as a tool for western domination of Africa.' Sundkler (1961) argues that the colour bar that operated to separate and oppress Blacks in South Africa was also operational in churches, and this separation led Africans to form protest churches. Mbiti (1986) states that western missions dominated the African church to the extent that the church lacked independence to develop African models, and this led to religious protest advocating African models for the African church. Using western toponyms to name churches in Africa created ownership and control problems from the onset.

The problem of colonial toponyms in church names created and continues to create tensions within churches with Africans seeking more African names and missionary direction. Walls (1979, p. 49) identifies the problem of terminology in naming African churches: 'firstly, what is an independent church? Nowadays most African churches are independent in the sense that their leadership is African, their ministry overwhelmingly African, and missionary direction minimal.' Missionary direction is imperial control from the overlord country. Some churches are named to attest political coloniality. Table 6.10 gives some church names in Zimbabwe that indicate possession by colonial centres.

The use of European toponyms in naming churches in Africa and Zimbabwe in particular is colonial arrogance and an affirmation that the church is not for Africans but belongs to Westerners, who also are the colonisers. The African is psychologically alienated from these churches, and this creates identity crisis and tensions, whereby those who do not come from the descriptor countries cannot fully belong to a church using the name of an alien country. The names create an expected tension in nomenclature whereby colonial names are to be

*Table 6.10* Imperial toponymy in some Zimbabwean church names

| *Church name* | *Imperial toponym in the name* |
|---|---|
| Roman Catholic (universal) | Rome/Italy |
| Anglican (of England) | England |
| Dutch Reformed | Netherlands |
| Free Presbyterian church of Scotland | Scotland |
| London Missionary Society | London |
| Greek Orthodox (traditional) | Greece |

removed for African ones, as is the case with the names of countries, cities and streets after political independence. The meanings of the sentences that make up the names of the churches are clear possessive statements indicating that the churches are owned by the colonial powers (Ndlovu, 2019).

The colonial names established religious dependence on the West. Chitando (2005, p. 90) argues, 'the fixation with European missionaries in the establishment of the dominant denominations threatens to efface the role of Black evangelists.' Some African reverends in these churches fought anti-colonial wars within the churches to liberate the African church from colonial names. Daneel (1971) observes that Rev Zvobgo broke away from the Dutch Reformed Church in Masvingo Zimbabwe to form the African Reformed Church after being inspired by Rev Moyana, one of the leaders of the Ethiopian church in South Africa. The name of the church that Rev Zvobgo formed as a breakaway remains evidence of colonial tensions in Zimbabwean churches. African church founders and leaders also incorporated liberation politics in naming their churches so as to liberate both church and state. Daneel (2004, p. 31) identifies Bishop Mutendi as doing this:

> Mutendi's appeal for tribal leaders in Zimbabwe derived largely from his courageous resistance to colonial rule in the educational religious spheres for which he was arrested and detained on several occasions. His Zion city symbolised not only the Christian kingdom but also the Rozvi dynasty of centuries ago, which evoked the bygone glory of Shona nationhood.

Agitation to transform African Christendom was motivated in part by the flagrant association of some churches with colonising countries. As Africans were fighting to change the character and names imposed on their spaces by colonial masters, names of churches were also affected, as many pro-African retronyms were derived from the names of "mainline" European churches.

## 6.4 Conclusion

Names have been used as symbols of colonial authority in Africa. Political, economic and socio-religious imperialism can be attested in the names

European colonisers assigned to African spaces, currencies and churches they founded in the continent. The Berlin conference, which partitioned Africa among European countries, can be read in the regional names of parts of the continent. The designations Anglophone, Francophone, Hispanophone, Germanophone and Lusophone identify Africa as belonging to the different European countries, leaving Africans without space. The names are used to politically other Africa as a non-sovereign. While these were colonial delimitations, they persist to the present day. The colonial administrations established urban areas; with these came the phenomena of hodonyms. Streets were named to commemorate colonial victories over the vanquished Africans; some of the hodonyms glorified colonial monarchs, philosophy, culture and art. The glorification and selfing of European power in Africa were extended to water bodies. The African names were erased as insignificant, and new European names were used instead. While colonisers did not change all names, they altered some, creating meaningless forms, and at times, the altered forms changed the meanings. This was a form of onomastic othering and erasure. Africa was also named as a source for European resources: there are names given to African spaces that betray looting of African resources such as labour, gold and ivory. Names given to African currencies were one glaring example of economic imperialism; however, most of these names are still in use today. The companies that fronted colonialism in Africa were named to indicate the colonial country sponsoring them. These chartered companies continue exploiting Africa under the guise of MNCs, which are still named to expose the colonial forces behind them. The colonial religion did not want to be associated with Africa, and the names of Christian denominations betray their colonial agenda. Names have been used and continue to be used as emblems of African coloniality.

## References


Akong, C. (2020). Reframing matter: Towards a material-discursive framework for Africa's minerals. *The Extractive Industries and Society*, 7(2), 461–469.

Altheide, D. L. (1987). Ethnographic content analysis. *Qualitative Sociology*, *10*, 65–77.

Altheide, D. L., & Schneider, C. J. (2013). *Qualitative media analysis* (2nd ed.). Sage.

Amin, S. (1976). *Unequal development: An essay on the social formations of peripheral capitalism*. Harvester.

Ayelazuno, J. A., & Mawuko-Yevugah, L. (2020). Kwame Nkrumah's political economy of Africa. In *The Palgrave handbook of African political economy* (pp. 171–192). Palgrave Macmillan.

Azaryahu, M. (2011). The critical turn and beyond: The case of commemorative street naming. *ACME: An International Journal for Critical Geographies*, *10*(1), 28–33.

Ben-Rafael, E., Shohamy, E., Hasan Amara, M., & Trumper-Hecht, N. (2006). Linguistic landscape as symbolic construction of the public space: The case of Israel. *International Journal of Multilingualism*, *3*(1), 7–30.

Benyera, E. (2020). The colonial state is the problem in Africa. In *Reimagining justice, human rights and leadership in Africa* (pp. 21–35). Springer.

Berg, L. D., & Kearns, R. A. (1996). Naming as norming: "Race", gender, and the identity politics of places in Aotearoa/New Zealand. *Environment and Planning*, *14*(1), 99–122.

Blommaert, J. (2013). *Ethnography, superdiversity and linguistic landscapes: Chronicles of complexity*. Multilingual Matters.

Blommaert, J., & Maly, I. (2016). Ethnographic linguistic landscape analysis and social change. *Language and Superdiversity*, *191*, 211.

Borkfelt, S. (2011). What's in a name? Consequences of naming non-human animals. *Animals*, *1*(1), 116–125. http://doi.org/10.3390/ani1010116

Britannica, T. (Eds.). (2012). *Total SA*. Retrieved March 17, 2021, from www.britannica.com/topic/Total-SA

Bruns, G. L. (1984). Language and power. *Chicago Review*, *34*(2), 27–43.

Bush, R. (2008). Scrambling to the bottom? Mining, resources & underdevelopment. *Review of African Political Economy*, *35*(117), 361–366.

Campbell, J. (2019, October 9). *The origins of African states, and their names*. www.cfr.org/blog/origins-african-states-and-their-names

Chigozie, N. P. (2018). Multinationals as agents of imperialism: A case study of third world countries. *Equatorial Journal of Communication Technology*, *2*, 1–8.

Chitando, E. (2005). Naming the phenomena: The challenge of African independent churches. *Studia Historiae Ecclesiasticae*, *31*(1), 85–110.

Coupland, N., & Garrett, P. (2010). Linguistic landscapes, discursive frames and metacultural performance: The case of Welsh Patagonia. *International Journal of the Sociology of Language*, *205*, 7–36.

Daneel, M. L. (1971). *Old and new in Southern Shona independent churches: Background and rise of the major movements*. Mouton.

Daneel, M. L. (2004). African initiated churches in Southern Africa: Protest movements or mission churches? In D. M. Lewis (Ed.), *Christianity reborn: The global expansion of evangelicalism in the twentieth century* (pp. 1–67). Eerdmans.

De Beauvoir, S. (1949). *Le deuxième sexe*. Gallimard.

Feuser, W. (1997). Literary representations of childhood and youth in anglophone, francophone, lusophone and germanophone African literature. *Présence Africaine*, 100–122.

Fombad, C. M., & Steytler, N. (Eds.). (2020). *Corruption and constitutionalism in Africa*. Oxford University Press.

Gorter, D. (2006). Introduction: The study of the linguistic landscape as a new approach to multilingualism. *International Journal of Multilingualism*, *3*(1), 1–6.

Greenblatt, S. (2017). *Marvelous possessions: The wonder of the new world*. University of Chicago Press.

Hegel, G. W. F. (1807). *Phänomenologie des Geistes*. Suhrkamp.

Jensen, S. Q. (2011). Othering, identity formation and agency. *Quantitative Studies*, *2*(2), 63–78.

Kallen, J. L. (2010). Changing landscapes: Language, space and policy in the Dublin linguistic landscape. In A. Jaworski & C. Thurlow (Eds.), *Semiotic landscapes: Language, image, space* (pp. 41–58). Continuum.

Kemp, T. (1971). *Economic forces in French history*. Dennis Dobson.

Landry, R., & Bourhis, R. Y. (1997). Linguistic landscape and ethnolinguistic vitality: An empirical study. *Journal of Language and Social Psychology*, *16*(1), 23–49.

Leahy, S. (2018, October 4). These countries changed their names, here is how it worked out. *National Geographic*. www.nationalgeographic.co.uk/history-and-civilisation/2018/10/these-countries-changed-their-names-heres-how-it-worked-out

Light, D. (2004). Street names in Bucharest, 1990–1997: Exploring the modern historical geographies of post-socialist change. *Journal of Historical Geography, 30*(1), 154–172.

Mapara, J., & Nyota, S. (2016). Suburban blight: Perpetuating colonial memory through naming in Mutare, Zimbabwe. In O. Nyambi, T. Mangena, & C. Pfukwa (Eds.), *The post-colonial conditions of names and naming practices in Southern Africa* (pp. 289–306). Cambridge Scholars Publishing.

Market Screener. (2021, March 17). *Anglo-American PLC*. www.marketscreener.com/quote/stock/ANGLO-AMERICAN-PLC-4007113/company/dollar. www.etymonline.com/word/dollar

Maxwell, D. (2006). *African gifts of the spirit: Pentecostalism and the rise of a Zimbabwean transformational religious movement*. Weaver Press.

Mbiti, J. S. (1986). *Bible and theology in African Christianity*. Oxford University Press.

Moll, J. (2009). Colonial names of countries in Africa before and after uhuru. *Tydskrif vir Geesteswetenskappe, 49*(2), 305–320.

Ndlovu, S. (2013). Historicity of some Ndebele toponyms in Zimbabwe. *Greener Journal of Social Sciences, 3*(5), 292–298.

Ndlovu, S. (2016). The Bulawayo linguistic landscape as linguistic heritage: Hodonyms and oikonyms. *Igama Journal of African Onomastics Studies, 1*(2), 22–34.

Ndlovu, S. (2017). Transphonologisation as ethnophaulism between the Ndebele and the Shona of Zimbabwe in selected toponyms and ethnonyms. *Nomina Africana: Journal of African Onomastics, 31*(2), 117–125.

Ndlovu, S. (2018). An Afrocentric analysis of some Zimbabwean proverbs and sayings. *Journal of Pan African Studies, 12*(3), 126–140.

Ndlovu, S. (2019). Colonial and brand tensions in some Zimbabwean religious nomenclature. In E. G. Konyana & D. Oguntola-Laguda (Eds.), *Religious violence and conflict management in Africa: Phenomenological and epistemological engagements* (pp. 117–133). Africa Institute for Culture, Peace, Dialogue and Tolerance Studies.

Ndlovu-Gatsheni, S. J. (2020). Four journeys of capital and their consequences for Africa. In *The Palgrave handbook of African political economy* (pp. 45–61). Palgrave Macmillan.

Neethling, B. (2005). *Naming among the Xhosa of South Africa*. Edwin Mellen Press.

Neethling, B. (2010). Shifting economic power and a shifting onomastic landscape in post-1994 South Africa. *South African Journal of African Languages, 30*(1), 79–87.

Nhemachena, A. (2016). Animism, coloniality and humanism: Reversing the empire's framing of Africa. In M. Mawere & A. Nhemachena (Eds.), *Theory, knowledge and politics: What role for the academy in the sustainability of Africa* (pp. 13–54). Langaa RPCIG.

Nierfeld, T. V. G. (2012). A note on the etymology of Germanic +skellingaz "shilling": With an appendix on Latin siliqua "a small coin". *Germania Semitica, 259*, 485–496.

Nimako, K., & Willemsen, G. (2011). *The Dutch Atlantic: Slavery, abolition and emancipation*. Polity Press.

Njoh, A. J. (2017). Toponymic inscription as an instrument of power in Africa: The case of colonial and post-colonial Dakar and Nairobi. *Journal of Asian and African Studies, 52*(8), 1174–1192.

Parker, C. (2016, June 27). *A short history of the British pound*. www.weforum.org/agenda/2016/06/a-short-history-of-the-british-pound

Pongweni, A. (2017). The impact of English on the naming practices of the Shona people of Zimbabwe. *Nomina Africana, 31*(2), 101–116.

Ransford, O. N. (1967). An historical sketch of Bulawayo. *Rhodesiana, 16*, 56–65. www.rhodesia.nl/rhodesiana/volume16.pdf

Reuters, (2007, May 9). *Factbox: BHP Billiton and Rio Tinto, the world's largest miners*. www.reuters.com/article/us-rio-bhpbillton1-idUSKUA93179620070509

Richardson, J. S. (1991). Imperium Romanum: Empire and the language of power. *The Journal of Roman Studies*, *81*, 1–9.

Rukundwa, L. S., & Aarde, A. G. (2007). The formation of postcolonial theory. *Theological Studies*, *63*(3), 1171–1194.

Said, E. (1994). *Culture and imperialism*. Vantage Publishers.

Schmidt, G. (1940). The Latin element in the English currency system. *Journal of the Warburg and Courtauld Institutes*, *3*(3–4), 251–254.

Scollon, R., & Scollon, S. W. (2003). *Discourses in place: Language in the material world*. Routledge.

Snodgrass, M. E. (2019). *Coins and currency: An historical encyclopedia*. McFarland.

Sundkler, B. G. M. (1961). *Bantu prophets in South Africa*. Oxford University Press.

Taskinsoy, J. (2019, March 6). *The transition from barter trade to impediments of the dollar system: One nation, one currency, one monopoly*. www.researchgate.net/profile/John_Taskinsoy3/publication/331559802

Tharoor, I. (2010, June 2). A brief history of BP. *TIME Magazine*. http://content.time.com/time/magazine/article/0,9171,1993882,00.html

Turner, T. (1976). Multinational corporations and the instability of the Nigerian state. *Review of African Political Economy*, *3*(5), 63–79.

Uluocha, N. O. (2015). Decolonizing place-names: Strategic imperative for preserving indigenous cartography in post-colonial Africa. *African Journal of History and Culture*, 7(9), 180–192.

Vail, L. (1976). Mozambique's chartered companies: The rule of the feeble. *Journal of African History*, *17*(3), 389–416. https://doi.org/10.1017/S0021853700000505

Walls, A. F. (1979). The anabaptists of Africa? The challenge of the African independent churches. *Occasional Bulletin of Missionary Research*, *3*(2), 48–52.

Young, R. (2015). *Empire, colony, pot colony*. Wiley Publishers.

# 7 Colonial othering of African anthroponymy

## 7.0 Introduction

While language is culture and identity, names are the part of language which expresses identity more succinctly. The prominent British actor Thandie Newton's name has been known as Thandie, a spelling convention that disconnected her from her African links. She decided to revert to the original name Thandiwe, 'Beloved' in Nguni, by bringing back the **-w-**, which was colonially deleted to imagine English identity. Okello (2020, p. 78) postulates that 'a name is one of the most explicit pointers of identity.' One's name is part of their identity. Mbiti (1969) argues that an African cannot be separated from their name; the name and the being are one. Koopman (2002) further states that in Zulu culture, wizards can use one's name to bewitch someone because the name and being are one. Names make an individual: they are recollections of memory and experience (Likaka, 2009). Herbert (1999) opines that, in Africa, personal names are repositories of history and part of a people's heritage. African names are not arbitrarily appropriated to people; they reference sociocultural symbolism (Suzman, 1994). Igboin (2014, p. 30) posits that 'To compromise the African name seems to mean to lose one's identity or individualism . . . The abandonment of traditional names is a sign of cultural disintegration, which requires drastic measures for prevention.' According to Ngubane (2000), African names are a window into the traditions of a people.

Naming newborns is a function of religion in African cultures, much as it is in other global regions. Mbiti (1969) states that the process of naming newborns in Africa creates and recreates family and community identities. He further argues that, in an African name, there is convergence of the living and the living-dead; the name is both identity and worship. The spirituality of naming people in Africa is confirmed in the Akan, Ewe and Ga naming of newborns, whereby a newborn is believed to be a visiting spirit who can only decide to stay in the world as a human after seven days. It is with this background that their newborns are named after seven days, and this is true of many African cultures (Anim, 1993). Krige (1936) identifies a similar trend among the Zulu where the fathers and grandfathers are the namers for newborns. They do this within a few weeks of birth, after consulting other family members.

DOI: 10.4324/9781003170761-9

The physical, mental and social environments are key considerations in naming children in Africa. Agyekum (2006) states that the Akan of West Africa consider, gender, material possessions and place in coming up with names for newborns. Krige (1936) states that names are historically relevant to the family; they recall events, or they are in memory of a departed ancestor. Names are not only a record of history, but they serve pragmatic purposes. Igboin (2014) argues that African names are historical and cultural, and they also serve as a template for family and societal behaviours. Negative and positive names both serve the purpose of offering society an example to learn from. Echekwube (2005) concurs that African names are both intrinsically and extrinsically meaningful. They are symbolic to both the namer and the named. Stewart (1996) studied naming conventions across Africa: Baganda in Uganda, Hausa in Nigeria, Kikuyu in Kenya and the Sotho of Southern Africa, and concluded that African names are culturally imagined, and they are historical and practically active in shaping the life of the bearer. Contact with Europe changed African naming; Igboin (2014) states that colonialists and Christianity bluntly refused to recognise African names and their import.

It goes without say that the indigenous African names were in African languages and that the European names came as a result of the processes of slavery, colonialism, urbanisation, globalisation and Christianity. A western name and a Christian name are viewed as the same (Ayantayo, 2010). Igboin (2014, p. 30) observes that 'for many Africans, as a consequence of the influences of slave trade, mission and colonialism, western names are not distinguished from Christian ones, even though they have radically different motives.' The coercive power of slavery, colonialism and Christianity was responsible for the many European names and naming traditions we see in Africa today (Moyo, 2012; Dube et al., 2007; Neethling, 2003). Thomas (1997, p. 396) quotes a slave trader as saying:

> we marked the slaves [whom] we had bought, on the breast or shoulder with a hot iron, having the ship's name on it, the place being before anointed with a little palm oil, which caused but little pain, the mark being usually well in four or five days.

This is an example of the violence that characterised the change from African to colonial names. According to Heller (1975, p. v), 'the psychological impact was intended to reduce one to the level of a stereotype of nonperson.'

According to Okello and Nyakwaka (2016), African naming systems changed because of colonial religion, education and urbanisation. They further opine that missionaries required conversion before one could be enrolled in formal education. Suzman (1994, p. 255) says, 'Western acculturation, religion, and economic pressures have altered traditional social institutions and attitudes. The extended family is no longer the only social source of names.' Colonialism introduced non-family namers in the mould of nurses, teachers and priests. These were not grounded in African culture; in fact, they continued with their European culture and imposed it on African naming conventions. Dube et al. (2007) add colonial employers to the list of name givers, as they argue that these renamed Black Africans indiscriminately with European names. The change in the naming practices and othering of African languages and culture resulted in alienated naming of Africans, creating identity crises. The changes affected both African first names and surnames, effectively altering key identity pointers. Bearers of colonial names carry with them coloniality of being, while colonial surnames evidence colonial legacy and heritage, passed from generation to generation, creating a legacy of coloniality.

The chapter engages the theories of coloniality, especially historical trauma (Crawford, 2014) and othering theory, to analyse the conditions of names and naming persons in Africa. It argues that African anthroponyms have been othered through the imperial processes of slavery, colonialism and neo-colonialism. Slavery, education, urbanisation, Christianity and colonialities have resulted in the proliferation of European names and surnames for Africans. African names have been othered as unpronounceable and heathen, and European names have been forced on Africans through slavery, baptisms and schooling. The exclusion of African names in the different colonialities instantiates crude othering. Madsen and Vallentin (2018, p. 1) posit that 'The concept of othering is used to describe processes of distancing, stereotyping, alienation and dehumanisation in social relations.' Canales (2000) states that the identified other is defined as inferior due to some of its (real or imaginary) traits. The alienation of colonials included alienating their names and naming systems, and in so doing, African culture, history, religion and world view were obliterated to establish the new colonial culture.

The chapter argues that the processes of slavery, colonialism, urbanisation and Christianisation were traumatic and that the structures that enabled them remain in place today to perpetuate the trauma. Anthroponyms are one such historical and persistent trauma. Historical trauma, according to Crawford (2014), is generational trauma stemming from a traumatic historical event or process, affecting descendants who were not present during the past traumatic event or process. However, Kirmayer et al. (2014) reason that the trauma cannot be based on a past event or process but on the continuation of the traumatic structures. In other words, Africans are not traumatised by the past events of slavery and colonialism; they are traumatised because these traumatic processes never really ended in the past. The structures that facilitated these traumatic processes are still in place, and that explains the present trauma.

Using data on names gathered from newspapers, magazines, internet sites, literature, names of celebrities and unstructured telephone interviews, this chapter demonstrates how colonialism affected and changed African naming and names. It argues that the changes were done forcefully through slave, colonial and church names, and the force left a lasting effect as Africans continue giving colonial names. The chapter identifies slavery, colonialism, Christianity, colonial education and acculturation as the main causes of the othering of African names for colonial ones. The aim is to collect European names used to name Black Africans and analyse the causes for abandoning African names and how this affects African identity. The chapter further demonstrates that coloniality of anthroponyms extends to toponyms and the landscape. It also affects heritage in the form of surnames and totems. Realising the anthroponym-identity nexus, some prominent Africans have reverted to their African names. The identity crisis created through applying African cultural naming conventions on English names creates unique English names that are not acceptable in English naming conventions, yet they are not fully African names.

## 7.1 Colonial christening to other African identity

Slavery, colonialism and Christianity changed African names and bestowed on Africans European names. These changes were done through slave baptisms and church and school names. The alienation of African names and naming practices continue as a function of coloniality in the postcolonies. Names and renaming Africans were used to colonially other African names and alienate Africans from the culture imbedded in their names. Hitchcock (1993) highlights that European colonisation and globalisation are processes of othering the so-called third world. He further notes that western cultural critique fosters othering of the so-called third world subjects. Renaming Africans had psychological effects on their legacy, perpetuating historical trauma. Fitzpatrick (2012, p. 40) posits that:

> Certainly, this was one of the ways those in power sought to keep their feet on the backs of African and African Diasporic peoples through what psychologists, today, define as the labelling theory and self-fulfilling prophecy, by negatively penetrating the psyche of Africans.

Analysing Shona naming systems in Zimbabwe, Pongweni (2017, p. 103) states, 'Before colonialism the Shona gave their children culture bound names. However, the European settlers associated such names with heathenism and therefore insisted that converts to the new faith abandon or be given new ones.' This section focuses on how Christianity and colonial education alienated African names and established the tradition of European names in Africans.

### *7.1.1 Baptismal name changes*

Early missionary work in Africa entangles itself in slavery and colonialism. Matikiti (2020) describes colonial era missionaries in Africa as surveillance mechanisms for colonialism. Christianity facilitated acculturation. This was an important step towards political and mental colonisation. Christianity is somehow obsessed with changing the culture of those who convert. Onaiyekan (2001) ridicules the way they stretch their Christianisation when he argues that even the Jews from whom Christ came are supposed to change their culture when they become Christian. According to Igboin (2014, p. 26):

> the cultural complexities in Africa are further ossified by the wide spread establishment of missionary religions – Christianity and Islam – which have added their own cultural peculiarities to indigenous cultures, particularly names that many Africans have to bear.

Kimeria (2017), writing in *Quartz Africa*, observes that for a long time it never bothered her that all her classmates in Kenya had names such as Rose, Catherine, Jeffrey and Lawrence. She knew these to be Christian names, which guaranteed their place in heaven. Thomas (1997, p. 398) also identifies links between slavery and Christian names and baptisms:

> In the early seventeenth century, it became customary for slaves in Africa to be baptised before their departure from Africa. This requirement was first laid down by King Philip III of Spain (II of Portugal) in 1607 and confirmed in 1619. The slaves had, as a rule, received no instruction whatever before this ceremony, and many, perhaps most, of them had no previous indication that there was such a thing as a Christian God. So, the christening was perfunctory.

European missionaries who came to Africa understood the divine power of naming. They exercised it on Africans because they understood Africans to be sub-humans, without names. Borkfelt (2011, p. 117) argues that:

> Naming, thus, is symbolic of the unequal power relations inherent to our relationship with other species. And indeed, commentators throughout history have most often taken this inequality for granted. Martin Luther, for instance, also comments on the act of naming the animals as something showing a great wisdom naturally inherent to man (but not to the other creatures).

This European theology on the inequalities of species is demonstrated in fallacies such as eugenics and the evolution of species as applying to race differentiation. It is clear that the baptism and renaming of Africans demonstrated Europeans' authority over 'their animals', the Africans – more so because the Christian names were meant to disconnect Africans from their perceived heathenism and usher them into heaven. Such a belief can only be explained in the context of eugenics whereby Africans needed to be like Europeans to qualify for heaven.

According to Okello (2020), the Luo of Kenya name their newborns by the name of the living-dead, the ancestors, who visit the parents in a dream to reveal the name. The ancestors are actually the namers in this case. Judeo-Christian scripts exhibit similar naming conventions whereby names come from God even before the child is born. The introduction of Christian names, now coming from missionaries, from different spirits, othered African religion, which was practiced through the naming conventions. Christianity and the baptismal names did not only other African names at the level of language hegemony, but the alienation goes deeper than the morphology of the names to symbolise cultural and religious alienation. African religions are alienated in colonial names; characters in the Christian Bible were used to replace names linked to African religion, as these were perceived to be evil. Christianity introduced 'purifying names' of biblical saints, such as, Peter, John, Jacob, Abraham, Joseph, Matthew, Israel, Mary, Martha, Ruth, Rebecca and Eve. These names were intended to disconnect Africans from their voodoo religion, which was associated with their African names. Even biblical toponyms are used as anthroponyms for Africans in names such as Judea, Canaan, Egypt, Jericho and Israel. Christianity is here imagined as the religion through the erasure of African names for Christian ones. The missionaries usurped the divine power to name in Africa, and they took the place of the ancestors, effectively othering African gods and the religion through naming.

African names and naming systems are characterised by religious onomastic practices such as taboo names and naming. Likaka (2009), for example, notes that in Congo, people were given first names which linked them to their ancestors and second names for secondary referential purposes. The first name carried the identity of the person, and it was concealed from strangers. Baptisms are publicly done, and the sacredness of names which characterised Africa before colonisation is rendered obsolete. It is common practice that there are certain names that are not supposed to be public, or at least they are not supposed to be known by some people. In Nguni cultures, names of in-laws, names of parents and names of elders are sacred; however, Christian missionaries demystified these names. The breaking of name taboos in Africa also othered African naming conventions and replaced them with European circular naming. The missionaries also doubled up as teachers in the early colonial schools. They established mission schools, and part of the mission was to change African names.

### *7.1.2 School name changes*

Having two names was not a new thing to Africans. Ngubane (2013) gives the example of Zulu parents giving two names to a newborn, the father's name and the mother's, *igama likayihlo* and *igama likanyoko*, respectively. Colonialism created three possible namers, the parents, the teacher and the priest creating home name, school name and church name for one African. Neethling (2003, p. 47) states that:

> With the introduction of Christianity and education as practiced by mission schools to Xhosa speakers in the early 19th century, came a new development. English names were bestowed upon Xhosa children by the

missionaries (at baptism) and by teachers (at school). These were often referred to as 'church' and 'school' names.

Teachers arbitrarily allocated European names to African learners, Mandela (1994, p. 13) describes his first encounter with the name Nelson:

> On the first day of school my teacher, Miss Mdingane, gave each of us an English name. . . . Miss Mdingane told me that my new name was Nelson. Why she bestowed this particular name on me I have no idea. Perhaps, it had something to do with Lord Nelson, but that would only be a guess.

Mabasa (2014), writing in *The Herald*, narrates a similar experience of colonial school name changes in Zimbabwe:

> One of my uncles went to a mission school. His name was Nyikadzino. This name was very difficult for the White teacher to pronounce and after several weeks of trying and never getting it right, he gave up. Then, he said to uncle Nyikadzino, 'Hey, do you mind if I called you Joseph?' That is how my uncle got the name Joseph. He was Joseph to the school community, but at home he answered to Nyikadzino.

Kimeria (2017), writing in *Quartz Africa*, describes how the British colonialists could not pronounce Kenyan names and replaced them with Christian names. She gives the example of them failing to pronounce Mount Kirinyanga and changing it to Mount Kenya. In addition to the English school name, Catholics acquired a European saint's name during baptism.

Missionaries relied on bible names and names of Christian saints, while teachers consolidated the colonisation by renaming Africans using European names as a way of civilising them. It is mostly at school that names such as George, Rose, Caesar, King and Dorothy were given. These names were either names of famous Europeans or common names in European cultures. It is clear that most European names are meaningless beyond being tags, because they were randomly appropriated to Africans. This phenomenon of meaningless names is un-African and others African naming practices. I went to school eight years after the end of colonial rule in Zimbabwe, but some of my schoolmates had their African names changed by a Black headmaster. He either argued that they were too difficult for people at the registry office, or they were 'too loaded' with meaning. The headmaster followed the trend of renaming students with English names, such as Mary, Peace, Dorothy and David. It is evident that English Christian and school names are still bestowed on Africans today by Black priests and Black teachers.

## 7.2 European onomastics in African anthroponymy

Colonising Europeans brought with them names from their own cultures and environments, and they used these exotic names to rename Africans. Names are closely related to culture. Wamitila (1999) observes that one of the most basic qualities about a name is the relationship with a particular culture. He terms this relationship the social contextuality of naming. He further notes that the choice of names can reveal the ethnic society. Africans now bear names that attest to Europe and European culture and heritage, yet the bearers, in the majority, have not set foot in Europe. European politicians, monarchies and toponyms have been used to name Africans.

Western monarchs and their titles were imposed on African anthroponymy, to the exclusion of local titles. In Zimbabwe, for example, the British monarchy found a place in the anthroponyms of Africans. Royal titles such as King, Queen, Prince, Princess and Duke were used and continue to be used as personal names. These names replace African names; in Ndebele, for example, the titles are also used as names, and their translation into English others the Ndebele names such as Nkosi 'King', Nkosana 'Prince' and Nkosazana 'Princess'. The obsession with the British royal family in Zimbabwean anthroponyms was extended to mimicking the names of persons in the royal family. The reigning British monarch at the time of colonisation, Queen Victoria's name was used to name many African women, and her son King George's name was also widely used to name many a man in Zimbabwe and other British colonies. The name of King George's daughter, Queen Elizabeth, is also a common name in former British colonies, as are Charles and William. The names of African royals disappeared from the onomastic conventions after colonial conquest.

Prominent historical figures in Europe have had their names used to name colonials, too. The names of William Shakespeare, both name and surname, are used as personal names. Other European figures such as David Livingstone had their surnames used as first names; this trend meant alienating African luminaries, replacing their legacy with foreign legacies. This pseudo-European superiority was engraved into the African psyche until they saw it as truth. Koopman (2002) observes that prior to democratisation in South Africa, Zulu people avoided using their indigenous names in formal settings, opting instead to use names of European origin. This scramble for European names meant that there was high demand. Some people were then named using European toponyms. The paradox is in naming an African as belonging to Europe, not Africa. Table 7.1 gives some European toponyms used as anthroponyms in Zimbabwe.

Africans were colonially acculturated to glorify the West as a better place, the utopia, and Africa as its dystopia. Colonialism fostered a false belonging to the colonial power in Africans, hence names describing Africans as Europeans such as Welshman, Norman and Scotch. European places became the subject of education, history, geography and even the arts. I remember at primary school singing the song, *London is burning look yonder, pour water.* For a Zimbabwean whose city, Bulawayo, was burnt at the colonisation of the country, it would make sense to sing, 'Bulawayo is burning' not London, which I did not know. This indoctrination with European environs resulted in some people being named after European countries and cities.

*Table 7.1* Euro-American toponyms used as anthroponyms in Zimbabwe

| *Euro-American toponym* | *Derived Zimbabwean anthroponym* | *Appellative meaning* | *Anthroponomastic reference in Zimbabwe* |
|---|---|---|---|
| Britain | Britain | European country | Female first name |
| Wales | Welshman | A man who is an indigene or citizen of Wales | Male first name |
| Italy | Italy | European country | Male first name |
| Scotland | Scotch | One from Scotland | Female first name |
| Normandy | Norman | Citizen of Normandy or of Norman descent | Male first name |
| Washington DC | Washington | The capital city of the United States; named after George Washington, former president | Male first name |
| Detroit | Detroit | City in the United States | Male first name |

## 7.3 African anthroponyms reflective of colonial material and social culture

Early missionaries confirm that Africans name their newborns to reflect social, emotional, environmental and other realities. Tyler (1891, p. 33), who was a missionary, alludes to the fact that:

> The names of persons in Zulu are derived from circumstances connected with their birth. For instance, if a small snake happens to be seen or killed when a boy is born, he is called *Unyokana* 'A little snake'. Should the infant be a large one, he receives the appellation *Ungangomuntu* 'As large as a man'.

The changed environment brought about by colonial realities meant new realities were now available as sources for names. Ngubane (2013) states that changes in culture, economy and social factors have transformed the naming of newborns in Zulu culture. Okello (2020) observes that urbanisation alienated Africans from their extended families, communities and culture into a colonial urban landscape characterised by individualism and lack of community. Suzman (1994) observes that changes in society affect naming. Some names now describe changed environments such as urban and European life and culture. Githuri (2020), writing in *Microsoft News* (MSN), discusses new name trends inspired by the new colonial life in South Africa and Zimbabwe. In South Africa, he identifies the names *Two-rand, Matric* and *Captain*, while in Zimbabwe there are *Sixpence* and *Settlement*. Table 7.2 juxtaposes Nguni

*Table 7.2* Nguni anthroponyms derived from African culture, and English colonial culture derivatives

| **Nguni anthroponyms from traditional culture** | |
|---|---|
| **Cultural concept** | **Derived anthroponyms** |
| *Amadlozi*: ancestral spirits | Female: Nomadlozi (mother of good spirits), male: Madlozi |
| *Sithebe*: grinding mat | Female: Sithebe |
| *Mkhonto*: spear | Male: Mkhonto |
| *Mqhele*: head band | Female: Nomqhele (mother of head band), male: Mqhele |
| *Sihlangu*: Sandals | Unisex: Sihlangu |
| *Nduku*: knobkerrie | Male: Vikinduku (dodge the knobkerrie) |
| **Anthroponyms derived from colonial culture** | |
| **Colonial concept** | **Derived Zimbabwean anthroponyms** |
| Border | Male: Border |
| Passport | Male: Passport |
| Democracy | Male: Democracy |
| Museum | Male: Museum |
| Psychology | Male: Psychology |

names derived from African culture and those derived from the changed colonial culture.

The sample Nguni names from African culture represent African religion in *amadlozi*, material culture in the utensils, military and hunting life in the names derived from weapons. The coming of colonialism introduced urbanisation and separation and demarcation of African nation states. This culture proliferated immigration concepts such as passports and borders, and these are now used to name Africans. Globalisation concepts such as democracy and tourism derive names such as Democracy and Museum. All the Africans bearing names derived from European culture could be bearing African names, expressing and representing Africanness. However, these African names were replaced by European and globalisation trends.

## 7.4 Colonial morphosemantics and African 'funny' names

African English names are sometimes derived from common English lexis using English affixes. Some of these affixes are now common name-deriving strategies; however, some have imperial and violent origins. The English affixes and common lexis appropriated as names, especially in Southern Africa, derive names that are a cultural shock to the British, although the names are in English. Africans also use African naming conventions on English names, creating an identity crisis whereby the culture and meaning intentions are African, yet the names are in English script.

There are some tags which were used in slavery and colonialism which are still used to derive African English names today. Such names and affixes other

Africans to perpetual coloniality and replace African names with tags used in slavery and colonial othering of African identity. Fitzpatrick (2012, p. 40) argues:

> In the subsequent years, enslaved Africans oftentimes went nameless, and were objectified by the slave masters, and identified in terms of numbers e.g., slave #1, slave #2 strictly for the benefit of the slave master and book-keeper so that they could keep count of their human stock or simply, enslaved Africans were referred to as 'boy' or 'girl'. Very rare were they allowed to keep their indigenous names. Later, during the twentieth century, these assigned slave names were used as derogatory and racist slurs among Whites when addressing African Americans, these would include names such as 'nigger', 'boy' and 'sambo'.

The use of the English words 'boy' and 'girl' as affixations in deriving African English names is derogatory naming reminiscent of slavery and inhuman colonial labour. Just as Africans were labelled boy or girl in slavery, they were called *garden boy* and *house girl* as they worked for colonial masters during colonial eras. While Africans seek to describe their children using *boy* and *girl* as adjectives, they unconsciously slide back to slave and colonial phaulisms attendant to the adjectives as exemplified in Table 7.3.

The names *Boy* and *Girl* recall *slave boy, slave girl, garden boy* and *house girl*, derogatory and othered labelling of Africans used instead of their African names. What is more disturbing is that these names were used on grown-up Africans; old men and women were called boys and girls, respectively. The names imply that maturity is impossible in Africans; even their adults are called children. In Southern Africa, 'boy' describes the coloniality of labour, and a slave or aid is called *ibhoyi*, which in Nguni has come to mean an abused

*Table 7.3* Slavery and colonial connotations in naming Africans as *boy* or *girl*

| *African English personal name* | *Intended descriptive function* | *Unintended historical trauma* |
|---|---|---|
| Boy/Bhoyi | Boy child: *Fanyana* (Nguni) | Slave/gardener or primitive |
| Bigboy | Big at birth: *Ngangomuntu* (Nguni) | Big slave man or big and primitive |
| Newboy | New boy child: *Mfanomutsha* (Nguni) | New slave man/gardener or new primitive |
| Zuluboy | Zulu boy child: *Mfanomzulu* (Nguni) | Zulu slave man/gardener |
| Girly | Girl children: *Mankazana* (Nguni) | Slave woman/house girl |
| Beautygirl | *Ntobenhle* (Nguni) | Beautiful slave woman/domestic worker/cleaner |
| Prettygirl | *Nakai* (Shona) | Pretty slave woman/domestic cleaner |

labourer. African culture is juxtaposed to modernity as *chibhoi* in Shona, depicting primitivity. To use the word *boy* to name Africans is a colonial phaulism. Joe Devney, writing on the *Quora* blog (2020), narrates similar occurrences after slavery, 'Upon emancipation in the 1860s, many African Americans took on new names. Sometimes they chose something like "Freeman" or "Newman" because of their new status.' The use of the adjective 'man' is, like 'boy', reminiscent of the same slavery they sought to shake off from their identity crisis.

The continued dominance of English and French in Africa creates cultural coloniality, which produces foreign experiences used to name African newborns up to this day. Devney argues on the Quora blog that it made sense for freed slaves in America to choose English names, since they lived in an English-speaking society. Kimeria (2017), writing in *Quartz Africa*, argues that, in the psyche of Kenyans, Christian names came to be associated with formal contexts, official usage, education, Christianity and being modern. However, according to Suzman (1994, p. 253), 'Children in many African societies have meaningful names – unlike their western counterparts, whose names are primarily labels.' This is why they try by all means to capture meaning and emotions, even in 'homemade' English names. To them, names such as George, John, Mary and Janet are labels of persons and their sex and cannot capture the African essence of naming, which incorporates, history, family, community, feelings and wishes of the namers and so on. Suzman (1994) further states that in western consumerism, some names such as Caroline are considered old fashioned, and they make way for new popular-culture-inspired ones such as Marlene. A name that is trending at the time can be chosen for a newborn not because of any meaningful symbolism. Africans value names and cannot just follow trending names; in Zimbabwe they would rather infuse meaning in those English words and combine them to come up with meaningful and expressive Zimbabwean English names.

The urge to have descriptive names has seen Africans use the adjectives, **-more, -ness** and **-well** to derive names such as *Thankmore, Passmore, Givemore, Hopewell, Donewell, Givewell* and *Loveness*. The Nguni use the prefix **no-** to derive feminine names, as it adds the meaning 'mother of' to the name. This has also been stretched to English names, deriving names such as *Nolizzy, Nomatter, Noplease* and *Norest*; however, the prefix **no-** is used for negation in English, and the African meanings are overshadowed, creating meaningless or negative names.

Analysing the colonial effects on Malawian naming practices, Moyo (2012, p. 10) argues that:

> Personal names, in particular, could be humorous, idiosyncratic and at times nonsensical to native speakers of English and weird to most people, e.g., *Spoon, Hinges, Bywell, Goodness, Loveness, Whisky, Advocate, Gift*, etc. However, they may tend to be consistent with social and linguistic formations of New Englishes.

In South Africa, Suzman (1994) identifies names such as *Stophi*, 'traffic stop' (born at the stop light); *Nomasonto*, 'mother of Sundays' (born on Sunday);

and *Paseka*, 'Passover' (born during Easter). The admin of Zimbabwean-names blogspot identifies these 'funny' English names as homemade Zimbabwean English names. He further notes that:

> Some Zimbabweans prefer 'homemade' English names that are not taken from a typical English Dictionary of Names. These are creative names, coined to express a meaning, gratitude, feelings or record an event, memories and experiences. Unlike British names such as George or Christine which do not have a meaning, Zimbabwean English names are self-explanatory.

*The Standard Newspaper* identifies the list of Zimbabwean refugees in South Africa having names such as '*Swagger* and a *Bigboy*, a *Brain* and a *Confidence*, but also a *Decent*, a *Pardon*, and three *Blessings*. There was an *Innocence*, an *Endless* and a *Future*.'

Africans were coerced to give English and French names through the long processes of colonialism and imperialism. However, they, in the majority, maintained the symbolic naming conventions and translated them into the European languages; this creates ridiculous names in the conventions of the colonisers. Most English names in Zimbabwe, for example, are direct translations or approximations of indigenous names, Table 7.4 gives some of the approximations.

The conventional English names do not fulfil the naming conventions of Africans. The creation of the 'strange' names is a way of Africanising English names. Mabasa (2014), writing in *The Herald*, states, 'Zimbabwean names in English are very weird because we often try to use the same philosophy behind African names. Unfortunately, we at times end up with very strange and sometimes hilarious names like *Avoid, Shame, Someone Lightfoot*.' He goes on:

> Out of context, a lot of names given by the Shona in English are very strange, but if you investigate the reason or story behind a name, you will come to a conclusion that the same names in the Shona language are not weird. Here are examples of strange names of Shona people in English and what they possibly mean in Shona: Reason = *Chikonzero*. Shame = *Nyarai/Nyadzisai*. Rise = *Simukai/Mukai*. Wonder = *Shamiso*. Clever = *Ngwaru/Ngwarai*. Shine = *Chiedza*. Steady = *Dzikamai*. Nomatter = *Hazvinei*. Godknows = *Kuzivakwashe/Mwarianoziva*.

The English still expect Zimbabweans to stick to the old names of Christian saints, and these meaningful Zimbabwean English names are weird to them. The names are in English, and the meaning is in African culture, creating an identity crisis of a kind. Igboin (2014, p. 36) posits that 'names have much to do with identity-determination as well as identity-crisis.' Mavaza (2017), writing in the *Patriot*, narrates how Zimbabwean English names alarm the former colonisers in the United Kingdom. He identifies Zimbabweans with names

*Table 7.4* English translations of some African names

| *Indigenous name* | *Language* | *Meaning and context of appellation* | *English approximate translation* |
|---|---|---|---|
| Mandla (enkosi) | Nguni | Male: God's power, thanking God for the miracle son | Power: references physical power |
| Jongumbuso | Nguni | Male: watch over the kingdom, an encouragement to be a good soldier | Kingdom: watching is elided to mean kingdom, especially heaven |
| Nkumbulo | Nguni | Male: remembrance, named in remembrance of someone or something | Memory: now a female name |
| Thulani | Nguni | Male: hold your peace, usually parents talking to other people | Silent: the name now describes the bearer as silent |
| Taurai | Shona | Male: challenging people to talk, usually those who thought the child would not be born | Talkmore: encouraging to continue talking |
| Rudo | Shona | Female: love, an expression of the parent's love for each other or for the baby | Loveness: the quality of being love, making the word love an adjective |
| Sekai | Shona | Female: talking back to those who were laughing at the parents' childlessness | Smile: a call to happiness |

such as *Danger, Trouble, Oneday, Innocent* and *Nevermind* living in the United Kingdom, and he states that these 'loaded' names give their bearers a difficult time. He notes that these 'funny' names are due to direct translations of indigenous names into English due to the love of English. He further states that the police, for example, have problems when they ask one's name and the reply is *Nevermind.* Githuri (2020) identifies the names *Don't worry* and *Very-important-person* in South Africa, and in Zimbabwe, he identifies, *Have-a-look* and *Heavy-weight.* These names carry history and aspirations of Africans only expressed in a colonial language.

## 7.5 Effects of othering African anthroponyms on identity and nomen de-coloniality

The othering of African personal names for colonial ones has had adverse effects on African heritage, identity and the linguistic landscape. In most African traditions, names of grandparents and parents are bequeathed to the younger generation as personal names or as surnames. Once an African is given a colonial name, the effects could be hereditary. The colonial names have derived colonial surnames for Africans, and these affect the identity of the whole clan, not just an individual. The colonial names of saints also mark the landscape with colonial identities through naming churches, schools and parishes after European saints. The colonial names also hamper efforts to decolonise the linguistic landscape through renaming, as some African icons used to rename spaces already have colonial names.

Surnames were also affected by these colonial name shifts and changes. Surnames express identity more than first names; they are more collective and cultural than first names, and they are shared by many people, whom they also unite. Surnames in Africa are usually the name of the great-grandfather of the clan, *ukhokho* in Nguni (Ngubane, 2013). African surnames have been othered in some cases, and people now pass on English and French surnames from one generation to the other. The generational bequeathing of names is common in Africa; for example, in the Kenyan Kikuyu culture, the second daughter is given the name of her maternal grandmother (Kimeria, 2017). These names are also passed on as surnames.

The after-life of slavery can be read in the surnames of African Americans. The majority of African Americans bear English and French surnames. Joe Devney, writing on the *Quora* blog (2020), states that these English surnames are remnants or effects of slavery; they are names of former slave owners; names given by the slave owner; the name of the plantation the slave worked on; expressions of freedom from slavery; and names of prominent Americans such as Washington, Jefferson and Howard. Some Nigerians have English surnames. The origins of these sparked debate on Nairaland.com. The commenters had different theories, all pointing to slavery and colonialism; some linked the surnames to returning slaves, and others linked these to Christian first names of fathers and grandfathers used by their progeny as surnames. One commentator on the platform states, 'I just asked my mother. She said some Nigerians use a Christian saint's name, and these names are used by their grand children as surnames.' Feelings of historical trauma appear to be affecting some who bear these English surnames, as one person comments thus, 'I never liked my English surname. I have often wanted to discard it like Malcolm X did.'

English or European surnames are also common in Southern Africa. Slavery and colonialism both affected African surnames, although the intensity differs. There are people who answer to English surnames in Zimbabwe, and this is more surprising than an English first name. People are bound to ask you why you have an English surname in Zimbabwe, yet English first names no longer surprise anyone. Some examples of English surnames in Zimbabwe are in the public domain, as some celebrities bear these, such as *Knight, Scott, Fourpence, Billiat* and *Lantern*. Some of the European surnames could be a result of translating African surnames into European languages; for example, in South Africa there are Black people, some very prominent, with the surname *Grootboom*, Afrikaans for 'Big tree'. Suffice it to says that there is a similar Nguni surname, *Mthimkhulu*, 'Big tree', *Grootboom* may have been a translation of *Mthimkhulu*. It is a very common trend to find Africans who translate their surnames to English, especially on social media platforms. I have encountered the Shona surname *Moyo* translated to English 'Heart' and the various animal totems rendered in English translation.

Anthroponyms are also used as toponyms; in this function, they mark space as belonging to the language and culture of the names used. Language on public spaces, including names, is the linguistic landscape. Landry and Bourhis (1997), as well as Spolsky and Cooper (1991), posit that LL functions as an informational marker and as a symbolic marker communicating the relative power and status of linguistic communities in a given territory. The colonial names of saints used on Africans also characterise the religious landscape in Africa. The othering of African anthroponymy affects other nomen heritages. The exclusion of African names in Christian baptisms has created an English bias on the naming of parishes and church institutions in Africa. The names that dominate the African religious landscapes are, for example, *Saints John, Peter, Paul, Joseph, Mary, Mark, Patrick, Luke, Thomas, Andrew, Columbus, Jude, Theresa* and *David*. In Zimbabwe, several churches, schools, colleges and parishes are named using these names across the country, and there is no indigenous name used.

Names of Europeans were used to name towns, monuments, countries and streets in Africa. At the dawn of political independence, African governments sought to decolonise the LL by using names of African liberation icons, especially to rename spaces. According to Moll (2009, p. 305):

> An important strand is the call for uhuru and the development of an ethos of Afro-centrism which was reflected in the riddance of the so-called 'colonial hangovers' and the changing of the names of places, towns and cities, leaders and events in truly national terms.

However, the othering of anthroponyms affects decolonial nomen renaming in Africa. Most of the icons used in the renaming have English names, and this does not change the LL to reflect African culture, languages and ethos. The renaming perpetuates English hegemony and culture.

Realising the power of names, some African luminaries changed their names. These changes facilitate decoloniality in the case when their names are used to rename spaces in Africa such as streets. Several prominent Africans have changed their names as a way of tracing their footsteps back to their culture; popular Kenyan author James Ngugi changed to Ngugi wa Thiongo, 'Ngugi son of Thiongo', Nigerian author Albert Chinualumoga changed to Chinua Achebe, and Malawian political activist John Lupenga Mphande changed to Lupenga Mphande (Moyo, 2012). Elsewhere, among South African politicians, Ben Alexander changed his name to Khoisan X, Arnold Stofile changed to Makhenkesi Stofile and Patrick Terror Lekota changed to Mosioua Lekota (De Klerk, 1999). The former president of the DRC, Joseph Desire, also changed his name to Mobutu Sese Seko (Igboin, 2014). Anti-colonial fighters such as Nelson Mandela, Kenneth Kaunda, Joshua Nkomo, Oliver Tambo, Julius Nyerere and Sam Nujoma, to pick just a few, have English names, and these names now dominate street, town, airport and other names. The decolonial effort cannot be complete, as some of the decolonial icons did not decolonise their own names.

## 7.6 Conclusion

African naming conventions for newborns are sacred. The names of newborns are believed, in some African cultures, to be gifted by the gods. Naming people expresses aspects of African religion and belief systems. The use of some names is also tied to religious taboos. Africans had names given in their languages capturing elements within the cultures. Most names describe circumstances, environments and events, and some communicate wishes. The coming of Europeans to Africa for slavery, colonialism and Christianisation altered the naming conventions of Africans. Africans were forced to abandon their names as a way of alienating them from their perceived heathen culture. Christian missionaries aided both slavery and colonialism, and they facilitated acculturation. African names were othered, and Africans were renamed through baptisms into the colonial culture. Priests and teachers replaced elders and the spirits as namers. Names of Christian saints were forced on Africans, and African anthroponymy resembled Christian Bible characterisation. At school, African names were changed because they were difficult for the European teachers and were replaced by European ones. Africans were exposed to a new culture; they exploited this new culture to derive descriptive names, as is their naming system. The new colonial culture derived names describing colonial culture, and African cultural concepts were further othered. The use of African naming conventions on European culture and languages created unique names, which are neither European nor African. The effects of othering African anthroponyms have a hereditary problem, as these colonial names are then passed on from generation to generation as names or surnames. Colonial anthroponymy has had an effect on toponyms too. Colonial anthroponyms are then used to name or rename spaces, creating European identity on African spaces. Most of the African icons used in decolonial renaming exercises have European names, and this thwarts the achievement of total decolonisation of the LL. However, some African luminaries, although very few, have decolonised their names so that they reflect the African ethos. When such names are used in renaming, the renamed spaces become truly African.

## References

Agyekum, K. (2006). The sociolinguistic of Akan personal names. *Nordic Journal of African Studies*, *15*(2), 206–235.

Anim, N. O. (1993). *Names as factor in cultural identity among the Akan, Ga and Ewe tribes of Ghana*. Centre for Development Analysis.

Ayantayo, J. K. (2010). The phenomenon of change of name and identity in Yorùbá religious community in the light of social change. *ORITA: Ibadan Journal of Religious Studies*, *42*(1), 1–16.

Borkfelt, S. (2011). What's in a name? Consequences of naming non-human animals. *Animals, 1*(1), 116–125. https://doi.org/10.3390/ani1010116

Canales, M. K. (2000). Othering: Toward an understanding of difference. *Advances in Nursing Science, 22*(4), 16–31.

Crawford, A. (2014). The trauma experienced by generations past having an effect in their descendants: Narrative and historical trauma among Inuit in Nunavut, Canada. *Transcultural Psychiatry, 51*(3), 339–369.

De Klerk, V. (1999). Beauty or Buhle? On changing one's name. *Nomina Africana, 13*(1), 1–17.

Devney, J. (2020). Why do Black people in the USA have English last names? *Quora.com.* www.quora.com/Why-do-black-people-in-the-USA-have-English-last-names

Dube, S., Makoni, S., & Mashiri, P. (2007). Naming practices in Zimbabwe. *Current Issues in Language Planning, 8*(3), 1–31.

Echekwube, A. O. (2005). Good name and chieftaincy titles in Nigeria today: An ethical insight. In P. Iroegbu & A. Echekwube (Eds.), *Kpim of morality: Ethics: General, special and professional* (pp. 278–287). Heinemann Educational.

Fitzpatrick, L. A. (2012). *African names and naming practices: The impact slavery and European domination had on the African psyche, identity and protest* [Doctoral dissertation, The Ohio State University].

Githuri, J. (2020, May 6). Funny names you can only find in Africa. *Microsoft News.* www.msn.com/en-xl/news/other/50-2b-funny-names-you-can-only-find-in-africa/ar-BB14eZXR

Heller, M. (1975). *Black names in America: Origins and usage.* G. K. Hall & Company.

Herbert, R. K. (1999). Personal names as social protest: The status of African political names. *Names, 47*(2), 109–124.

Hitchcock, P. (1993). The othering of cultural studies. *Third Text,* 7(25), 11–20.

Igboin, B. O. (2014). An African religious discourse on names and identity. *Filosofia Theoretica: Journal of African Philosophy, Culture and Religions, 3*(1), 26–40.

Kimeria, C. (2017, July 30). It took moving to America for me to change my colonised name. *Quartz Africa.* https://qz.com/africa/1039890/colonial-name-taking-back-my-african-name-as-a-kenyan-woman/

Kirmayer, L. J., Gone, J. P., & Moses, J. (2014). Rethinking historical trauma. *Transcultural Psychiatry, 51*(3), 299–319.

Koopman, A. (2002). *Zulu names.* University of Natal Press.

Krige, E. J. (1936). *The social system of the Zulus.* Longmans Green.

Landry, R., & Bourhis, R. Y. (1997). Linguistic landscape and ethnolinguistic vitality: An empirical study. *Journal of Language and Social Psychology, 16*(1), 23–49.

Likaka, O. (2009). *Naming colonialism: History and collective memory in the Congo, 1870–1960.* University of Wisconsin Press.

Mabasa, I. (2014, November 4). Strange, sometimes hilarious names of Zimbabweans [correspondent]. *The Herald.* www.herald.co.zw/strange-sometimes-hilarious-names-of-zimbabweans/

Madsen, S. O., & Vallentin, S. (2018, July). The processes of othering in public organization. *Academy of Management Proceedings, 1,* 17597. https://doi.org/10.5465/AMBPP.2018.17597abstract

Mandela, N. R. (1994). *A long walk to freedom: The autobiography.* Macdonald Purnell Press.

Matikiti, R. (2020). We know our Africans: Missionaries as torchbearers of the colonisation in Zimbabwe. *Decolonising Science, Technology, Engineering and Mathematics (STEM) in an Age of Technocolonialism: Recentring African Indigenous Knowledge and Belief Systems, 175.*

Mavaza, M. (2017, October 5). Zimbabweans struggle with unusual English names in the United Kingdom [correspondent]. *The Patriot*. www.thepatriot.co.zw/old_posts/zimbos-struggle-with-unusual-english-names-in-uk/

Mbiti, J. S. (1969). *African religions & philosophy*. Heinemann Educational.

Moll, J. (2009). Colonial names of countries in Africa before and after uhuru. *Tydskrif vir Geesteswetenskappe, 49*(2), 305–320.

Moyo, T. (2012). Naming practices in colonial and post-colonial Malawi. *Inkanyiso: Journal of Humanities and Social Sciences, 4*(1), 10–16.

Nairaland.com. (2010, August 11). *Nigerian English surnames*. www.nairaland.com/495459/nigerians-english-surnames

Neethling, S. J. (2003). Perceptions around the English names of Xhosa speakers. *Nomina Africana, 17*(2), 45–65.

Ngubane, S. E. (2000). *Reclaiming our names: Shifts in post-1994 in Zulu personal naming practices* [PhD thesis, University of Natal].

Ngubane, S. E. (2013). The socio-cultural and linguistic implications of Zulu names. *South African Journal of African Languages, 33*(2), 165–172.

Okello, B. A. (2020). What's in a name? Reinventing Luo naming system in Kenya's ethnopolitical landscape. *African Identities, 19*(1), 77–90. https://doi.org/10.1080/14725843.2020.1791687

Okello, B. A., & Nyakwaka, D. (2016). Missionaries' rivalry in Kenya and the establishment of St. Mary's school Yala. *African and Asian Studies, 15*(4), 372–392.

Onaiyekan, J. O. (2001). *Christianity: A foreign religion?* Gaudium Et Spes Institute.

Pongweni, A. (2017). The impact of English on the naming practices of the Shona people of Zimbabwe. *Nomina Africana, 31*(2), 101–116.

Spolsky, B., & Cooper, R. L. (1991). *The languages of Jerusalem*. Clarendon Press.

The Standard Newspaper. (2015, May 31). *What's in a name: Zimbabweans' craziest names* www.thestandard.co.zw/2015/05/31/whats-in-a-name-zimbabweans-craziest-names/

Stewart, J. (1996). *1001 African names*. Carol Publishing Group.

Suzman, S. M. (1994). Names as pointers: Zulu personal naming practices. *Language in Society, 23*(2), 253–272.

Thomas, H. (1997). *The slave trade: The story of the Atlantic slave trade, 1440–1870*. Simon & Schuster.

Tyler, J. (1891). *Forty years among the Zulus*. Congregational Sunday School and Publishing Society.

Wamitila, K. W. (1999). What's in a name: Towards literary onomastics in Kiswahili literature. *Swahili Forum, 6*, 35–44.

Zimbabwean Names Blogspot. (2013, January 19). *Zimbabwean homemade English names*. http://zimbabwe-names.blogspot.com/2013/01/Zimbabwean-Homemade-English-Names.html

## Section Three

# Names as exhibits of gendered, disablist, exclusion and sexist subalternities in African contexts

# 8 The woman other in African names and naming

## 8.0 Introduction

Culture and language represent social realities, and names and naming are one of the avenues of language used to express social structure and power relations. It has been established that the world is named by those who own or control it (Borkfelt, 2011), and the named is subordinate to the namer in one way or the other. This chapter argues that the othering of women in African societies can be seen through the window of onomastics. The structure and semantics of names given to boys and girls tell a patriarchal story. Girls are named to reinforce their 'women other' status, and boys are named into the echelons of social power structures. The chapter further argues that the exclusion of women from the economy can be read from the names used to name businesses and that the disparities between men and women in commemorative names reflect patriarchal political power structures. Boys and girls are named differently to prioritise the boys (Ngubane, 2013). Women's names are conspicuously fewer in business names and brands (Ndlovu, 2014) and in toponymy. Bosworth (2012) enquires, 'A tiny proportion of streets in Rome are named after women, while nearly half are named after men – and it is a similar story in other major cities around the world. Outrageous sexism, a simple fact of history, or both?' Spender (2000, p. 195) answers this question by stating that:

> those who name the world have the privilege of highlighting their own experiences – and thereby identify what they consider important. Thus, groups that have a marginal status are denied the vocabulary to define (and express) their own experiences.

The chapter engages and blends the views of patriarchy from Marxist materialists (Dallas & James, 1972), radical feminists (Firestone, 1972) and postmodernists (Walby, 1992). Materialists argue that women are confined to unpaid domestic work, and when they do get work outside the home, they get low-paying jobs because they are socialised and structurally confined to such jobs. Radical feminist reasoning is that women are not an economic class but a sex class; their oppression stems from sexualisation and reproduction. The postmodernists

DOI: 10.4324/9781003170761-11

think the subordination of women is culturally constructed through language. They have argued that language affects the psyche and helps construct the gendered inequalities. The three views do not independently adequately address the gendered othering of women in names. However, they complement each other to create a succinct argument for the othering of women in personal naming conventions, business names and commemorative naming on the linguistic landscape. The combined arguments resonate with critical feminist political economy (Estes, 2004). In feminist theory, women suffer injustice in patriarchy because such a system is built on sexism, objectification of women and misogyny (Jeffreys, 2014). Feminist political economy advocates social change in society for gender equity, focusing on the three concepts of social reproduction, patriarchy and gender. Estes (2004, p. 23) states that:

> A major goal of a critical feminist political economy . . . is understanding how the state and social security policy work in tandem with capital and sex and gender system in ways that render women vulnerable and dependent throughout their life course.

Patriarchy in Africa and elsewhere has been responsible for the othering of women from power, money and social space, and this is expressed and reflected in naming conventions. Defining patriarchy, Makama (2013, p. 117) states that 'The term has been defined as a system of male authority which oppresses women through its social, political and economic institutions.' The system of patriarchy exploits the othering process through stereotypes which assign women to subordination and men to agentive roles. Gender stereotypes are linked to traditional social roles and power disparities between men and women (Eagly, 1987). Cendra et al. (2019, p. 46) state that:

> Gender stereotypes divide women's and men's roles into masculine and feminine. For example, women are mostly stereotyped as warm and caring. Therefore, women are mostly required to be warm and caring. In contrast, men are labelled as strong and agentic; thus, in the real life, they should be strong and agentic.

Foka (2015) observes that it is a common stereotype that women are uncontrollable when left alone outside patriarchy; they need to depend on men. The stereotype is a belief that women are a danger to themselves and to others if left uncontrolled. Patriarchy is obsessed with controlling women such that it sees any challenge by women as unfeminine. Women are then kept out of their families, family businesses, politics, economy and memory. Stereotypes even keep women away from public life and discourses. Adoko (1999, p. 71) recounts:

> When we looked further, we found a number of other reasons why women were being excluded, many of them linked to cultural taboos. A number of women said that their husbands did not want them to participate in public

> meetings because a woman who always joins the company of men will fall in love with other people's husbands.

Names exhibit verbalised hostilities and exclusions of women. The verbalised hostilities to women emanate from the social oppression of women in societal structures of power (Hollander et al., 2011).

The chapter is a critical discourse analysis of names in African communities to establish gendered othering of women in social practice. CDA is a framework that is useful in analysing the nexus between language and social phenomena (Jorgensen & Phillips, 2002), and names are part of language. CDA helps us understand how language is used to construct identities and social relations (Berger, 2016). Names are related to social phenomena, economy, culture, power, politics and relations. The data for the research were collected mostly from Zimbabwe, as the researcher is Zimbabwean, and Nguni personal names dominate the section on anthroponyms. Document analysis was also used as a source for the data. These included magazines, newspapers and literature on names and gender. Unstructured interviews were also done over the phone to establish facts on the meaning and etymology of some names. Google maps were sources for street names in Abuja, Nairobi and Harare. Company names were retrieved from the Zimbabwe stock exchange and online business sites in Zimbabwe and South Africa. *Unirankings* and *Skyscanner* websites were sources for the names of universities and airports, respectively. The analysis of the names follows the three-dimensional model of CDA: description, interpretation and explanation (Fairclough, 2003). Under description, the names are analysed linguistically and etymologically to get their meanings; at the level of interpretation, the analysis shows how the names represent patriarchy; and at the level of explanation, the analysis relates the names to patriarchal power systems. The analysis of names in the public domain is also aided by the linguistic landscape. Blommaert and Maly (2016, p. 4) opine that LL is:

> an ethnographic and historical project, in which we see signs as indices of social relationships, interests and practices, deployed in a field which is replete with overlapping and intersecting norms – not just norms of language use, but norms of conduct, membership, legitimate belonging and usage.

Sankaranarayanan (2015) posits that urban spaces named after personalities indicate social hierarchies within a city, and their prestige is linked to the legacy of the person they are named after.

## 8.1 Patriarchal morphosyntax in some African anthroponyms

Patriarchy is a social system that undermines women and establishes them as second to men. The power relations within patriarchal systems are observable in language. A CDA of language usage has the potential to expose masculinities. Women are usually objects in a male-dominated patriarchy. Only men are perceived to be the self actors, while women are not given such opportunities. Names reflect patriarchy, and they represent gendered African societies. Some social activities are expressed with men as actors and women as objects of the actions of men. According to Bailey et al. (2013), one of the feminine stereotypes is that women should be physically attractive. This creates objects of beauty to be 'used' by men, who themselves have no need to keep up appearances. The expected beauty makes women objects of sexualities. In Nguni, for example, verbs relating to marriage and reproduction allocate the agentive positions to men, while women are allocated the object position. McFadden (1994, p. 64) observes that 'cultural practices such as *lobolo*, *ukungena* (the levirate) and *inhlanti* (sororate) indicate that the African woman is not recognised as a person with rights in herself.' Women are judged in a sexualising and objectifying manner; they are valued for their attractiveness to fulfil men's needs (Lisdiantina, 2013).

Human beings are essentially male, and in the event that a female is born, a male name has to be used with an indication that this is a female child. In Nguni kinship, for example, the suffix *-kazi*, which inflects the meaning female, is appended to masculine roots to derive female kinship terms. Father is *ubaba*, and the paternal aunt is called *ubabakazi*, 'female father'; grandfather is *ukhulu*, and his sister is *ukhulukazi*. A son is *indodana* 'young man', diminutive of *indoda* 'man', while a daughter is *indodakazi*. Marriage and reproduction are also expressed using gendered verbs whereby men do everything, while women are passive recipients. Table 8.1 gives the semantic argument structure of verbs denoting marriage and reproduction and their relation to men and women arguments.

Men are the agentive actors and causers of gendered social and reproductive action, while women are the passive recipients of the actions or are caused by men to do these very important social activities. Femininity is stereotypically associated with being incompetent, characterised by being passive, illogical and emotional, while masculinity is stereotypically competent through being active and logical (Felmlee et al., 2020; Ellemers, 2018). The reproductive

*Table 8.1* The agentive status for men and object position of women in Nguni social verbs

| *Agentive/causer (subject), verb for men* | *Gloss* | *Passive/cause (object), verb for women* | *Gloss* |
|---|---|---|---|
| *thatha* | marry | *thathwa* | to be married |
| *lobola* | pay dowry | *lotsholwa* | to be paid dowry for |
| *mithisa* | cause to be pregnant | *mitha* | caused to be pregnant |
| *vela* | engage to marry | *velelwa* | engaged to be married |
| *zalisa* | cause to reproduce | *zala* | reproduce |

verb argument structure in language tells a lot about social structure. Women are referred to in the passive voice, while men are referred to using the active voice. This sexist quality of many African languages extends to their naming conventions. Active words are used to name boy children, while passive voices are used for girl children. Table 8.2 gives some Nguni active names for boys and the passive derivatives for female names.

Some of the names confirm the exclusion of women in celebrating social and political activities such as liberation. This can as well explain why there are fewer women used to name aspects of toponymy. Males are named to be the actors, while females benefit from the actions of men. *Sikhululi*, for example, makes the boy child the soldier who liberated people from colonial rule, as the name derives from the verb *khulula*, 'liberate'. ***si-*** is the agentive prefix. The feminine name Khululiwe, for example, implies that the girl was liberated, as it is the passive voice of *khulula*, making the girl an object beneficiary. Such naming praises men as the ones who fought against colonialism and women benefited from this action. Names like Sipho for men concretise the sexist belief that boy children are more valuable than girl children; therefore, they are gifts, while Siphiwe has connotations of accepting what you are given. Siphiwe is not a gift but an expression of dissatisfaction at what the parents have been given.

It is very common in Africa to use affixes to derive names for female newborns from roots used to name males. Cameron (1992, p. 367) declares that 'Feminist commentators on language have notated in many contexts that the world has been "named" from a male and male-dominant perspective and that lexico-grammatical features in languages often reveal important underlying cultural (male) assumptions.' Ngubane (2013) posits that in Zulu, a boy's name can be made feminine by adding either the tense marker suffix ***-ile*** or the prefix ***no-***. Nguni has clear prefixes which inflect sex into word stems, and these are usually ***so-*** for male, inflecting the meaning father, and ***no-*** inflecting female; it means mother. However, it is interesting to observe that the male prefix is seldom used to mark names as masculine. The natural roots are assumed to be masculine and only inflect femininity when used to name girls. Mufema (1999, p. 98) reinforces the negative stereotypes against women when he quotes an

*Table 8.2* Active and passive names in naming boys and girls in Nguni

| *Active names for boys* | *Passive derivatives for girls* |
|---|---|
| Sikhululi – liberator | Khululiwe – liberated |
| Khumbula/Nkumbulo – remember/memory | Khunjuliwe – remembered |
| Sipho – gift | Siphiwe – we have been given |
| Thando – love | Thandiwe – beloved |
| Sibusiso – blessing | Sibusisiwe/Busiswa – we have been blessed/ blessed |

Egyptian taxi driver as saying, 'a man is worth two women . . . women were born of Adam, born of his rib.' Ngubane (2013, p. 170) further declares that:

> In the mind of the name giver, the concept starts with a male name, as males are the most desired children among most Zulu families. For example, the noun *imfundo* 'education', which is in class 5 may be used to name a boy by changing it into class 1; *imfundo* thus becomes uMfundo. If the child happens to be a girl, a prefix ***No-*** will be added to the noun, which then becomes uNomfundo.

The simple present tense is usually used in Nguni to name male children, and to derive female names, the past perfect and perfect tense suffix **-ile** is used. For example, *themba*, which means 'trust' in the simple present tense, is used to name boys Themba. The suffix **-ile** is used to derive Themekile, 'trusted', which is a girl's name. The non-usage of the masculine prefix **so-** on natural roots gives the assumption that the roots are naturally masculine and can only be made feminine by affixation. Males become the natural selves, and females are derivatives. This disparity in social power structures can be read in the uses of prefixes to derive feminine names. The past perfect and perfect tenses also imply the naturalness of male and the imagined inferiority of women. The boy child is the real concept in the present life of the name givers, yet the girl is named to be away from the present wishes.

## 8.2 Women others in African business nomenclature

Men dominate businesses as owners and managers, while women are still fighting for parity, which is still far from being achieved across the globe. Makama (2013, p. 116) argues that 'The patriarchal society sets the parameters for women's structurally unequal position in families and markets by condoning gender-differential terms in inheritance rights.' Capitalism is built on patriarchy to further exclude women. Estes (2004, p. 12) observes that 'under capitalism, women's role historically has been in reproduction, seen as a 'complement' of men's role in production.' The field of economics has not been spared as far as othering of women is concerned. Ferber and Nelson (1993, p. 1) state that:

> if we instead recognise that the discipline, we call economics has been developed by particular human actors, it is hard to see how it could fail to be critically influenced by . . . the social, cultural, economic and political milieu in which it has been created.

This is why Rai and Waylen (2013) argue that economic policies are issues of women's rights. A look at names used to name businesses confirms certain gender stereotypes on women. Their names are used to name small businesses linked to domestic chores, they are excluded in family businesses due to their perceived transitory nature through marriage and all these prejudices can be read in the naming of some companies in Africa.

The elevation of Whites through names in Africa clearly focuses on males. Names such as *uMlungu, iNgamla, uMkhiwa* and *Aboforo* are usually qualified when they reference women, for example, *umama woMlungu*, White woman, and *umfazi weNgamula*, the boss's wife. The boss is idealised to be a man and not a woman. Women are also stereotyped to be homemakers. The Industrial Revolution in 19th-century Europe divided gender roles between men and women, assigning industrial roles to men and confining women to the home, taking care of the children (Cendra et al., 2019; Brannon, 2011). This industrial exclusion of women was extended to Africa through colonialism, as Ndlovu (2014, p. 44) notes that 'capitalism and the Judaeo-Christian civilisation brought extended public life and more public-sphere gender roles.' Schmidt (1991, p. 733) further postulates that 'As a result of state policy, African women and children were forced to stay behind in remote rural reserves, undertaking subsistence cultivation to feed themselves and to subsidise the men's wages.' Stereotyping women as homemakers and their exclusion from industrial work influences the types of businesses women own in Africa. A look at company and business names in Zimbabwe reveals that male names dominate transport, fuel, hardware and construction, while female names can be seen in catering and tailoring businesses. Masculine first names used to name some businesses in Zimbabwe include *Mark's Garage, William Surveyors, Max Hardware, Stanley and Livingstone Hotel and Safari, Ian and Co Real Estate* and *Anderson Motors*. There are no female names in these types of businesses, an indication that women do not own such businesses. Women are confined to the periphery of the economy. Makama (2013, p. 121) reiterates that 'Women are mainly involved in petty trading, selling wares in the market and street hawking in urban areas. According to statistics 78% of women are mostly engaged in the informal sector, which are farming and petty trading.' The businesses that bear feminine names are, for example, *Sis B Restaurant, Floe Restaurant* and *Zoe Tailors*. *Mansa Digital Business Magazine* (2018) identifies two fashion and apparel companies in Johannesburg, South Africa, named using women's first names, *Kim and Kimberly*, www.kimandkimberly.co.za, and *Lumka Hlobo Fashions*, www.lhbylumkahlobo.co.za. These types of companies are linked to homemaking and are indeed small businesses compared to those named after men.

Women are the majority in most countries, yet there are fewer women than men in business. The *Mansa Digital Business Magazine* (2018) notes that:

> Women are still in the minority when it comes to South Africa's entrepreneurial landscape. According to Small and Medium Enterprises (SME) South Africa, more than half of South Africa's population is female, yet only 34% of SMEs are women-led, according to a survey conducted by Facebook in partnership with the World Bank and OECD.

Women face double resistance as they try to venture into business: capitalist and cultural masculinities.

Women are not excluded from business by capitalist and state policies only, but they are also excluded by their own families. More value and belonging are placed on boy children, and the girl child is viewed as a member in transit. As such, boys are incorporated into the family businesses, and girls are less likely to be included. The domination of women by men in marriage makes it difficult for families to invest their businesses on daughters who will be married away and be subordinate to a foreign man. Ncube et al. (1997, p. 67) argue that 'in African law and custom, property acquired during a marriage becomes the husband's property whether acquired by him or his wife. To this rule there are few exceptions.' This influences parents to include sons and leave out daughters in family businesses, and names expose this patriarchy, as exemplified in Table 8.3.

It is difficult to find a business named after a parent and daughters in Africa, all because of sexist stereotypes which other and exclude women, even from their own family businesses. Most of the names incorporating sons are in the transport sector, and Ndlovu (2014, p. 44) argues 'a combination of traditional patriarchy, Christian gender roles and capitalism influence gender roles in the automobile industry in Zimbabwe.' This negative influence has kept women out of the automobile industry. Brothers also tend to come together, some after the father dies or from their own initiative to partner in businesses. They also do not include their sisters in the partnerships; hence, it is common in Africa to hear companies named brother partnerships. Table 8.4 gives some examples of Zimbabwean companies named to indicate brother partners.

Suffice it to say that I did not encounter any company names that were sisters' enterprises. However, the gender inequalities found in businesses today as reflected in the names are not necessarily a result of the fact that women have poor business acumen but are a result of negative stereotyping which excludes them. Bolzendahl and Myers (2004) argue that, with the same level of education, men and women have the same capabilities, supporting the social feminist belief that women are as capable as men, and daughters can run the family business just as well as sons.

*Table 8.3* Names of Zimbabwean family businesses which exclude daughters

| *Company name* | *Type of business* |
|---|---|
| Coufinan and Sons | Property/real estate |
| Tanda Tavaruva and Sons | Transport |
| Mavako and Sons Buses | Transport |
| Matsikidze and Sons General Dealer | Retail/grocery |

*Table 8.4* Zimbabwean business nomenclature indicating brother partnerships

| *Company name or brand* | *Type of business* |
|---|---|
| MAP Ndlovu Brothers | Construction and haulage |
| Brothers Coaches | Transport |
| Mutsvangwa Brothers | Transport and farming |
| Mutema Brothers | Retail shops |
| Mahendere Brothers | Entertainment |

## 8.3 Women others in the African commemorative toponomastic landscape

The othering of women in commemorative toponymy is a global patriarchal problem. Bosworth (2012) notes that, as a geography teacher in Rome, Maria Pia Ercolini was writing about the role of women in the cultural history of the city, and she realised that far more streets were named after men than women. She undertook research to quantify this toponomastic sexism, and she is quoted as saying, 'During the research I realised that you never see traces of women. History just cancelled the women – they are not here.' To evaluate the hodonym gender imbalances, her research teams went through every one of Rome's 16,550 streets and discovered that 7,575 (45.7%) were named after men and 580 (3.5%) after women. Bosworth further states that a similar survey was done in the Spanish city of Madrid, and there, too, 27% of the streets were named after men and 7% after women.

The commemoration of the liberation of Africa from colonialism is heritagised in names of key state spaces such as streets, stadia, airports, water bodies, towns, heritage sites and key state buildings. The patriarchal nature of African communities and the new Abrahamic religions they adopted influence national memories. Patriarchy justifies the marginalisation of women in education, economy, the labour market, politics, business, family, domestic matters and inheritance (Salaam, 2003). State power has been, and still is, controlled by men in all African countries, and these have the mandate to name and rename spaces of national importance. According to Bhabha (1990, p. 319), 'national memory is always the site of hybridity of histories and the displacement of narratives.' Men have tended to dominate the linguistic landscape as they commemorate their own heroics and exclude women.

The tendency or trend to exclude women from toponomastic commemorative naming and renaming is also very common in Africa, and the reasons are the same. African metropoles are very much masculine in their toponymy. The names used to name urban streets in Africa were predominantly masculine during the colonial era, and after the renaming exercises after political independence, the names of men are still commemorated by these street names far more often than women. A Google Maps (2021c) street view of Abuja, the capital of

Nigeria, reveals that the main street names are in memory of men to the exclusion of women, as demonstrated in Table 8.5.

Power in Nigeria has been exchanged militarily, and the street names of Abuja represent this phenomenon. The names used to name Abuja's main streets derive from power structures within Nigerian politics and military. The fact that out of 17 main street names, 16 are named in memory of men and only one commemorates a woman shows that women are excluded from the power structures which make history and have had the power to name. The army generals, diplomats, parliamentarians and ministers are predominantly men. The only woman in the list had to make global impact based in America and led a global body. It would appear that she needed to head the World Trade Organisation (WTO) for her influence to equal that of male African chiefs, parliamentarians and ministers.

*Table 8.5* Gendered naming of key streets of Abuja, Nigeria

| *Personal names used to name Abuja streets* | *Memorial* | *Sex* |
|---|---|---|
| Ahmadu Bello Way | Ahmadu Ibrahim Bello, Sardauna of Sokoto – former premier and statesman | Male |
| Kur Mohammed Avenue | Colonel Kur Mohammed – executed coup leader | Male |
| Sani Abacha Way | Former military ruler | Male |
| Herbert Macaulay Way | Olayinka Herbert Samuel Heelas Badmus Macaulay – founding nationalist | Male |
| Samuel Ademulegun Avenue | Samuel Adesujo Ademulegun – former brigadier general | Male |
| Ibrahim Babankida Way | Ibrahim Badamasi Babankida – former army general and president | Male |
| Kashim Ibrahim Way | Sir Shettima Kashim Ibrahim – former minister | Male |
| Nnandi Azikiwe Express way | Nnandi Benjamin Azikiwe – former president | Male |
| Solomon Lar Road | Chief Solomon Daushep Lar – former parliamentarian | Male |
| Shehu Yar'adua Way | Shehu Musa Yar'adua – former president | Male |
| Augustus Aikhomu | Augustus Akhabue Aikhomu – former vice president | Male |
| Obafemi Olowo Way | Chief Obafemi Olowo – politician | Male |
| Olusegun Obasanjo Way | Olusegun Matthew Okikiola Aremu Obasanjo – former president | |
| N Okonjo-lweala Way | Ngozi Okonjo-Iweala – first African (Nigerian) and woman to be director general of the World Trade Organisation | Female |
| Obafemi Ogundipe Boulevard | General Obafemi Ogundipe – former Nigerian diplomat | Male |
| Umaru Musa Yar'adua Road | Former president | Male |
| Abdulasalami Abubakar Road | Former president | Male |

In East Africa, the situation is no different. Views from Google Maps (2021b) street names of Nairobi in Kenya, and Kanyeki (2014), writing in the *Kenya Standard*, expose the masculinities of the street names. The ten major roads in the city of Nairobi are also predominantly named in memory of men, as represented in Table 8.6.

The names are derived from anticolonial stalwarts, presidents, politicians and leaders of other African countries. In all these categories, it can be concluded from the street names that women are excluded; their absence makes a mockery of their struggles to liberate Kenya and Africa. The only woman in the list is the former first lady, and I wonder whether this is to her memory, or it is to the memory of her husband? In patriarchy, women are subordinate to men, and the only woman used to name a major street in Nairobi is a wife and not an independent politician. The *Standard* indicates that the street was named to commemorate Jomo Kenyatta's wife. She is not credited with possessing influential power beyond being a wife to the powerful former president.

The capital of Zimbabwe, Harare, representing Southern Africa, totally excludes women from the prime linguistic landscape of the city. Viewing the city from Google Maps (2021a) and from intuition, the 11 main streets in the central business district are all named after men, as shown in Table 8.7.

There are several women, like Queen Lozikeyi Dlodlo, Ruth Chinamano, Victoria Chitepo and Orpah Muchinguri, who fought for the liberation of Zimbabwe, and it is expected that one or more of them should be commemorated in Harare's prime streets. Just like Kenyatta, Mugabe could have named one of the streets after his late wife Sally Mugabe, but he did not. A revered host of a popular spirit medium in Zimbabwe, Mbuya Nehanda, is commemorated on a street that is at the periphery of the city. Women are pushed to the periphery, that is, when they are lucky to be commemorated. The same applies in metropoles outside Africa. Sankaranarayanan (2015) declares that,

*Table 8.6* Patriarchal naming of Nairobi's major streets – Kenya

| *Personal names used to name Nairobi streets* | *Memorial* | *Sex* |
|---|---|---|
| Kenyatta Avenue | Mzee Jomo Kenyatta – first president of independent Kenya | Male |
| Kimathi Street | Field marshal Dedan Kimathi – anticolonial fighter | Male |
| Muindi Mbigu | Samuel Muindi Mbigu – anticolonial protester | Male |
| Koinange Street | Chief Koinange wa Mbiyu – anticolonial protester | Male |
| Wabera Street | Daudi Dabasso Wabera – first African district commissioner | Male |
| Tom Mboya Street | Anticolonial politician | Male |
| Moi Avenue | Daniel Arap Moi – former president | Male |
| Ronald Ngala | Former opposition politician | Male |
| Haile Selassie | Former Ethiopian emperor | Male |
| Mama Ngina Street | Wife to the former president Jomo Kenyatta | Female |

*Table 8.7* Male domination in naming Harare's main streets – Zimbabwe

| *Personal names used to name Harare streets* | *Memorial* | *Sex* |
|---|---|---|
| Robert Mugabe Road | Former president | Male |
| Simon Muzenda Street | Former vice president | Male |
| Jason Moyo Avenue | Anticolonial politician | Male |
| Robson Manyika | Anticolonial politician | Male |
| Herbert Chitepo Avenue | Anticolonial politician | Male |
| Leopold Takawira Street | Anticolonial politician | Male |
| Julius Nyerere Way | Former Tanzanian president | Male |
| Samora Machel Avenue | Former Mozambican president | Male |
| Kenneth Kaunda Avenue | Former Zambian president | Male |
| Nelson Mandela Avenue | Former South African president | Male |
| Sam Nujoma Street | Former Namibian president | Male |

after studying the cities of London, Paris, San Francisco, New Delhi, Chennai, Mumbai and Bengaluru, they were not surprised that streets named after men were more numerous and more centrally located than streets named after women. The irony in Harare is that the government of Zimbabwe could not erect Nehanda's statue on Nehanda street because the street is less important and not very visible. They instead erected her statue on Julius Nyerere way, which is an irony since there is already a street named after her in the city.

Commemorative naming in Africa is also prevalent in the naming of institutions of higher learning. Several universities are named to commemorate individuals who have made an impact in the societies or Africa as a whole. Unirankings' (2021) top 200 universities in Africa features some names derived from personal names of historical figures. The list of 200 universities has several named after people, and of these none is named after a woman. Table 8.8 is a sample of African universities named after men.

The naming of universities after men and none after women is indicative of the patriarchal attitude of excluding women and girls from education. The names also confirm that women are not in positions of power and influence. Those who are in such positions are not commemorated. Two universities in Kenya are named after Kenyatta, yet none is named after a woman, not even his wife this time. Nelson Mandela also has two institutions named after him, but no women are commemorated in the names of universities in Africa.

Another key institution in the pride and identity of nations is the national or main airport. These airports have been subjects of the decolonisation agenda through renaming to make sure they reflect the character of the culture and histories of African people. Airports are the gateways to countries, and in Africa, these gateways are masculine in nomenclature. According to Skyscanner (2021), 17 countries in Africa have their main airports named after people, and it is not surprising that not even a single one of the 17 is named after a woman, as shown in Table 8.9.

*Table 8.8* Some African universities named after men

| *African university* | *Country* | *Named after* | *Sex* |
|---|---|---|---|
| Nelson Mandela University | South Africa | Former president of South Africa | Male |
| Nelson Mandela African Institution of Science and Technology | Tanzania | Former president of South Africa | Male |
| Mongosuthu University of Technology | South Africa | South African politician Chief Mongosuthu Buthelezi | Male |
| Rhodes University | South Africa | Cecil John Rhodes, British colonialist in Southern Africa | Male |
| Kenyatta University | Kenya | Former Kenyan president | Male |
| Jomo Kenyatta University of Agriculture and Technology | Kenya | Former Kenyan president | Male |
| Moi University | Kenya | Former Kenyan president | Male |
| Kwame Nkrumah University of Science and Technology | Ghana | Former Ghanaian president | Male |
| Ahmadu Bello University | Nigeria | Former Nigerian statesman | Male |
| Obafemi Olowo University | Nigeria | Former Nigerian politician | Male |
| Universidade Eduardo Mondlane | Mozambique | Former Mozambican freedom fighter | Male |
| Universite Cheikh Anta Diop | Senegal | Former Senegalese historian and politician | Male |
| Universite Freres Mentouri de Constantine 1 | Algeria | Former Roman emperor | Male |
| Universite Mohammed V | Morocco | Former king of Morocco | Male |

Women are excluded from traditional power structures such as monarchies, and this is why we see male monarchs and chiefs featuring in the names of airports. The same names decorate and in some cases litter African commemorative naming of streets, universities, airports, towns, bridges and so on, yet women are not allowed in the memory. It is clear that currencies of power are guns and money in Africa. Men dominate these to consolidate power and use the same power to impose their names on the major linguistic landscapes in Africa. Commemorative naming in Africa confirms and reinforces patriarchy.

## 8.4 Conclusion

Patriarchy and its attendant stereotypes of women create disparities in the treatment of men and women in African societies. Gender stereotypes influence power structures and limit women's access to resources and power. Girls and boys are even named differently to express and reinforce the subordinate position of women in society. Men are named to be the norm and women the men's other. The naming of businesses also reveals the deep-seated patriarchy and exclusion of women in business. Women are excluded from businesses by state and capitalist

*Table 8.9* The woman other in naming African international airports

| *International airport* | *Country* | *In memory of* | *Sex* |
|---|---|---|---|
| Mohammed V | Morocco | King Mohammed V | Male |
| Nnandi Azikiwe | Nigeria | Former president | Male |
| Diori Hamani | Niger | Former president | Male |
| Roberts | Liberia | Joseph Jenkins Roberts – African-American colonial president | Male |
| Leopold Sedar Senghor | Senegal | Former president and academic | Male |
| Modibo Keita | Mali | Former president | Male |
| Amilcar Cabral | Cape Verde | Former Guinea Bissau and Cape Verde anticolonial politician | Male |
| Jomo Kenyatta | Kenya | Former president | Male |
| Sir Seewoosagur Ramgoolan | Mauritius | Former governor-general | Male |
| Julius Nyerere | Tanzania | Former president | Male |
| Kenneth Kaunda | Zambia | Former president | Male |
| Hosea Kutako | Namibia | Chief Hosea Komombumbi Kutako – former anticolonial politician | Male |
| Robert Gabriel Mugabe | Zimbabwe | Former president | Male |
| Sir Seretse Khama | Botswana | Former president | Male |
| King Mswati III | eSwatini | Past king | Male |
| Moshoeshoe I | Lesotho | Past king | Male |
| OR Tambo | South Africa | Anti-apartheid politician | Male |

policies, and they are also excluded from family businesses, as expressed in some family business nomenclature. There is need for a feminist psyching of African power structures to help them fight for the cause of women as exposed by gendered naming patterns. Advocacy helps the fight for women. Meier (2015) notes that some French women sought to redress the woman other in the Paris landscape, since only 2.6% of the streets are named for women. In August of 2015, the feminist activist group *Osez le Feminisme*, 'Dare to be Feminist', installed guerrilla signposts renaming streets and parks after prominent women such as singer Nina Simone, sailor Florence Arthaud and author Simone de Beauvoir. This action motivated interest in characterising gender disparities in naming within the world's metropoles. Cameron (1992, p. 212) argues:

> In the end, though, feminism cannot afford a theory that tells us only how women are oppressed; it must convince women also of the strength and potential of their own language. But potential is a very important word here. Women's 'difference' cannot be celebrated uncritically; it needs to be redefined in the pursuit of liberation and justice.

It is not only women who lose out by being excluded from business, but business itself loses, too. Wittenberg-Cox (2010, p. 3) points out that 'The

Organisation for Economic Cooperation and Development (OECD) has declared that gender equality strengthens long-term economic development.' It would be a welcome development in Africa to see companies named after a father and his daughter or all his children or companies named after brothers and sisters. Commemorative naming and renaming overlooks women. This is partly because they are already overlooked in positions of influence for them to be icons. The low percentage of women commemorated in African toponyms is indicative of the plight of women in patriarchal power asymmetries.

## References


Adoko, J. (1999). Representative systems and accountability structures in refugee settlements in Ikafe, Uganda. In F. Porter, I. Smyth, & C. Sweetman (Eds.), *Gender works: Oxfam experience in policy and practice* (pp. 68–75). Oxfam.

Bailey, J., Steeves, V., Burkell, J., & Regan, P. (2013). Negotiating with gender stereotypes on social networking sites: From "bicycle face" to Facebook. *Journal of Communication Inquiry, 37*(2), 91–112.

Berger, A. A. (2016). *Applied discourse analysis: Popular culture, media and everyday life*. Acid-Free Paper.

Bhabha, H. K. (1990). Dissemination: Time, narrative, and the margins of the modern nation. In H. K. Bhabha (Ed.), *Nation and narration* (pp. 291–322). Routledge.

Blommaert, J., & Maly, I. (2016). Ethnographic linguistic landscape analysis and social change. *Language and Superdiversity, 191*(211), 207–227.

Bolzendahl, C. I., & Myers, D. J. (2004). Feminist attitudes and support for gender equality: Opinion change in women and men, 1974–1998. *Social Forces, 83*(2), 759–789.

Borkfelt, S. (2011). What's in a name? Consequences of naming non-human animals. *Animals, 1*(1), 116–125. http://doi.org/10.3390/ani1010116

Bosworth, M. (2012, April 11). Are our street names sexist? *BBC World Service*. www.bbc.com/news/magazine-17203823

Brannon, L. (2011). *Gender: Psychological perspectives* (6th ed.). Pearson.

Cameron, D. (1992). *Feminism and linguistic theory* (2nd ed.). St. Martin's Press.

Cendra, A. N., Triutami, T. D., & Bram, B. (2019). Gender stereotypes depicted in online sexist jokes. *The European Journal of Humour Research*, 7(2), 44–66.

Dallas, C. M., & James, S. (1972). *The power of women and the subversion of the community*. Falling Wall Press.

Eagly, A. H. (1987). *Sex differences in social behaviour: A social-role interpretation*. Erlbaum.

Ellemers, N. (2018). Gender stereotypes. *Annual Review of Psychology, 69*(1), 275–298.

Estes, C. L. (2004). Social security privatization and older women: A feminist political economy perspective. *Journal of Aging Studies, 18*(1), 9–26.

Fairclough, N. (2003). *Analysing discourse: Textual analysis for social research*. Psychology Press.

Felmlee, D., Rodis, P. I., & Zhang, A. (2020). Sexist slurs: Reinforcing feminine stereotypes online. *Sex Roles, 83*(1), 16–28.

Ferber, M. A., & Nelson, J. A. (1993). The social construction of economics and the social construction of gender. In M. A. Ferber & J. A. Nelson (Eds.), *Beyond economic man: Feminist theory and economics* (pp. 1–22). University of Chicago Press.

Firestone, S. (1972). *The dialectic of sex*. Paladin.

Foka, A. (2015). Gender subversion and the early Christian East: Reconstructing the Byzantine comic mime. In A. Foka & J. Liliequist (Eds.), *Laughter, humour, and the (un)making of gender: Historical and cultural perspective* (pp. 65–84). St. Martin's Press.

Google Maps. (2021a, April 15). *Harare road map and street view*. www.google.com/maps/place/Harare,+Zimbabwe/

Google Maps. (2021b, April 15). *Nairobi road map and street view*. www.nationsonline.org/oneworld/map/google_map_Nairobi.htm

Google Maps. (2021c, April 15). *Abuja road map and street view*. www.maps-streetview.com/Nigeria/Abuja/roadmap.php

Hollander, J. A., Renfrow, D. G., & Howard, J. A. (2011). *Gendered situations, gendered selves: A gender lens on social psychology*. Rowman & Littlefield Publishers.

Jeffreys, S. (2014). *Beauty and misogyny: Harmful cultural practices in the West*. Routledge.

Jorgensen, M., & Phillips, L. J. (2002). *Discourse analysis as theory and method*. Sage.

Kanyeki, W. (2014, April 3). Nairobi street names over the years [correspondent]. *The Standard Newspaper*. www.standardmedia.co.ke/home-away/article/2000108495/nairobi-street-names-over-the-years

Lisdiantina, A. (2013). *An analysis of the occurrence of sexism in blonde joke websites* [Undergraduate thesis, Sanata Dharma University, Language and Arts Education].

Makama, G. A. (2013). Patriarchy and gender inequality in Nigeria: The way forward. *European Scientific Journal*, *9*(17), 115–144.

Mansa Digital. (2018, July 2). *List of female owned construction companies in South Africa*. https://mansadigital.co.za/list-of-female-owned-construction-companies-in-south-africa/

McFadden, P. (1994). Gender, power and patriarchy. In *Changing families, changing laws* (pp. 58–67). Working Paper 9. Women and Law in Southern Africa (WLSA) Trust.

Meier, A. (2015, November 6). Mapping the gender imbalance in city street names. *Hyperallergic*. https://hyperallergic.com/251819/mapping-the-gender-imbalance-in-city-street-names/

Mufema, E. (1999). Empowerment and development of women in Egypt: Salient challenges of the 1990s. In P. McFadden, M. R. Galloy, M. G. Ntarangwi, & K. N. Abraham (Eds.), *Reflections on gender issues in Africa*. SAPES Books.

Ncube, W., Stewart, J., Dendu-Zvobgo, K., Gwaunza, E., Kazembe, J., & Nzira, T. (1997). *Paradigms of exclusion: Women's access to resources in Zimbabwe*. Women and Law in Southern Africa (WLSA) Trust.

Ndlovu, S. (2014). Automobile-based gender discrimination in Zimbabwe. *South African Journal of African Languages*, *34*(1), 43–50.

Ngubane, S. (2013). The socio-cultural and linguistic implications of Zulu names. *South African Journal of African Languages*, *33*(2), 165–172.

Rai, S. M., & Waylen, G. (2013). Feminist political economy: Looking back, looking forward. In S. M. Rai & G. Waylen (Eds.), *New frontiers in feminist political economy* (pp. 1–18). Routledge.

Salaam, T. (2003). A brief analysis on the situation of women in Nigeria today. *Democratic Socialist Movement (DSM)*. www.socialistnigeria.org/women/1-3-03.htm

Sankaranarayanan, A. (2015, November 3). Mapping female versus male street names. *Mapbox*. https://blog.mapbox.com/mapping-female-versus-male-street-names-b4654c1e00d5

Schmidt, E. (1991). Patriarchy, capitalism, and the colonial state in Zimbabwe. *Signs*, *16*(4), 732–756.

Skyscanner. (2021, April 15). *Airports in Africa by country*. www.skyscanner.de/airports/f/airports-in-africa

Spender, D. (2000). The politics of naming. In M. Curtis (Ed.), *The composition of ourselves* (pp. 195–200). Kendall, Hunt.

UniRankings. (2021, April 15). *Top 200 universities in Africa.* www.4icu.org/top-universities-africa/

Walby, S. (1992). Post-post-modernism? Theorising complexity. In M. Barrett & A. Phillips (Eds.), *Destabilising theory: Contemporary feminist debates* (pp. 108–128). Polity Press.

Wittenberg-Cox, A. (2010). *How women mean business: A step by step guide to profiting from gender balanced business.* John Wiley & Sons.

# 9 Disablist, homophobic and sexist nomen othering in Africa

## 9.0 Introduction

Names and naming have been deployed and continue to be deployed on social and bio-medical conditions to other people. This chapter deals with names, slurs and terms used by African societies to reference disability, homosexuality and femininity. It argues that non-disabled, heterosexual and masculine social structures are the ones that have the power to name, and they display their disablist, homophobic and sexist attitudes in the way they name disabled people, homosexual people and femininity, respectively. African societies claim to have a totalising African culture, which is usually abused as the source of misogynistic, homophobic and disablist philosophies. Naming these social categories appears to be modelled on medical frameworks which view disability and homosexuality as sicknesses and femininity as a biological weakness. There have been pleas for social models based on and emphasising inclusivity; these, too, have proven lacking in addressing the plight of the ostracised, prompting resistance movements fighting for rights, not just inclusion. Duckitt (2001) suggests that efforts to reduce prejudice can be organised around four causal levels of intervention; cognitive, individual, interpersonal and societal. African people and societies still need to do away with the disablist, homophobic and sexist prejudices which are attested by some names.

Children born with disabilities were ostracised or eliminated in early African societies (Choruma, 2007). They were considered bad omens. Up to the present day, people with albinism are hunted because of cultural myths in various African communities. Musere and Byakutaga (2000, p. 9) argue that 'in some African societies infants born with defects, or atypical features, or those born in a way considered very strange, including albinos and cripples, are treated as sacred and are even given names that relate to supernaturalism.' I remember growing up, I believed that people with albinism do not die. I viewed them not as human beings but some spirits because of the community beliefs I was exposed to, and I wonder how many Africans like me grew up with such evil mythology on other humans. This is not peculiar to Africa only: in 17th- to 19th-century Europe, disabled people with visible differences and impairments were displayed in public gaze shows which came to be known as 'freak shows'.

DOI: 10.4324/9781003170761-12

From these absurd shows came a plethora of slurs describing the displayed others. The public shows were called 'freak shows' because freak means strange and abnormal. This led to the word's use to describe disability (Shade of Noir, 2021). While freak is now taboo as it is offensive, many words describing and naming disability have been offensive. Disability became a spectacle because people denied that it is part of them. There was a need for social inclusion, a transition from modelling disability medically to modelling it socially. The *Nottinghamshire Disability* blog (2019) disambiguates the social and medical models of disability:

> The social model of disability says that disability is caused by the way society is organised, rather than by a person's impairment or difference. It looks at ways of removing barriers that restrict life choices for disabled people. When barriers are removed, disabled people can be independent and equal in society, with choice and control over their own lives. Disabled people developed the social model of disability because the traditional medical model did not explain their personal experience of disability or help to develop more inclusive ways of living.

Those advocating a paradigm shift from seeing impairment from medical lenses to social lenses have argued for inclusivity in dealing with disability. Barnes et al. (2002) opine that models on disability should address culture, difference and impairment, while Corker (2000) proposes the fusion of politics, language and social policy in theorising disability. The medical model of disability informed social structure against disabled people, and society is structured to other people with impairments. The disabled have tried to negotiate with a non-disabled society for inclusion, but this has not changed their fate, as society is structured to other disability. Donoghue (2003) is of the opinion that structural resistance is key in fighting societal disablism. Shakespeare and Watson (2001, p. 19) concur that:

> disability is the quintessential postmodern concept, because it is so complex, so variable, so contingent, so situated. It sits at the intersection of biology and society and of agency and structure. Disability cannot be reduced to a singular identity: it is a multiplicity, a plurality.

The medical and spiritualised disablist concept is also used to politicise sexualities in Africa. Homosexuality is argued to be un-African and something that came from the West. This totalised Africanness, coupled with born-again African Christian Pentecostalism, has been used to oppose homosexuality and incite homophobic hate speech and even physical attacks. Asante (2020) describes how a vigilante group in Ghana by the name 'Gay Killers' identifies gay men and lynches them, all because homosexuality is un-African. However, Chimakonam and Agada (2020) avow that homosexuality always existed in African societies. The names given to homosexual people are hostile homophobic slurs because they are derived by a society that is hostile to homosexuality. Ndjio (2013) recounts that in Africa, sexuality is now used as political strategy. He outlines four political strategies deploying sexuality in Cameroon: (1) exaltation and glorification of procreative sexuality, (2) essentialisation and racialisation of African sexuality, (3) othering of gay and lesbian people and (4) criminalisation and demonisation of same-sex practices.

While many scholars have proved that homosexuality existed in Africa before its contact with the West, their arguments also add to stigmas associated with homosexuality. Gelfand (1979) argues that homosexuality was not prevalent in Shona societies because they groomed their children well; such an argument criminalises homosexuality as delinquency. Some have argued that it existed in Africa but was only limited to situations were men had no women, such as in the army, in mines and among herd boys (Swindler, 1993; Murray & Roscoe, 1998). This also creates the impression that it is a choice out of desperation and cannot be condoned where women abound. Gay men are imagined as women; this is itself evidence of the sexist images of femininity in Africa. Naming is part of the sexist strategies available for masculinities to undermine women in social and cultural practice. Felmlee et al. (2020, p. 18) opine that 'institutional sexism creates the social situations in which gendered stereotypes are established, and, in return, the perpetuation of stereotypes preserves and reinforces the social culture of sexism and dominant masculinity.' In India, for example, names given to boy children indicate their value and appreciation, while those for girls indicate that they are not the preferred child (Shijith & Sekher, 2017). Buberwa (2018) also discovers sexist practices in naming Haya children in Tanzania whereby boy child names exalt them as holding the future of the family and community, while girl child names express their attractiveness and that they are marriageable.

This chapter analyses names and naming of disability, homosexuality and femininity in Africa from a qualitative dimension. It engages the theories of othering (De Beauvoir, 1997; Brons, 2015) and how deployment of medical, biological and social models around disability, homosexuality and femininity ostracise these categories. Ostracism is framed on the concept of coloniality. The affected are colonials of the African social structures. Martinot (2011, p. 1) establishes that:

> It is not only our labour, or our sexualities and genders that mark colonial relations; it is not only the wars, the mass murder and death squads organised by imperialist classes, nor the sub colonies formed by women, African-American communities, or ethnic identities; it is also the hegemonic mind, the white, or masculinist, or heterosexist, or national chauvinist mind that constitutes and is constituted by coloniality.

The colonialities exhibited in names are analysed using the lenses of critical discourse analysis, According to Van Dijk (2001), CDA is an interdisciplinary approach focusing on power relations. Here, language is both cultural and social practice whereby social context is central in language analysis. Social power structures and inequalities can be reflected in discourse. The chapter investigates the semantics and pragmatics of sexist, homophobic and disablist names and slurs and deploys theories on expressive and descriptive content (Kaplan, 1999; Hedger, 2012, 2013; Croom, 2014). While Kaplan and Hedger argue there are no offences in truthful descriptive content, arguing that offence comes from expressive content with no truth value, it is strange to describe sexes, sexual orientations and disabilities which you are not. Croom (2014) argues that any argument for a definition of slurs based on a purely expressive content analysis is an attempt to account for the inoffensiveness of descriptive content slurs. This chapter demonstrates how those outside certain differences imagine their superiority by describing the differences as inferiorising conditions. Data for the chapter were gathered through document analysis and unstructured telephone interviews with purposively selected interviewees in Zimbabwe, Malawi, Ivory Coast, South Africa, Zambia and Botswana. Some of the names were collected from social media platforms and from intuition, since the researcher is exposed to several cultures in Southern Africa. The chapter argues that the names are constructed to express societal hostilities, while some which appear to be well-meaning become pejorated and taboo because social structure taboos the referents.

## 9.1 Disablist nomenclature in Africa

The term disability itself is not wholly acceptable; however, its antonym, able-bodied, is considered outright offensive. The National Centre on Disability and Journalism (NCDJ) (2015) notes, 'Some members of the disability community oppose the use of the term able-bodied as it implies that all people with disabilities lack "able bodies", they may prefer "non-disabled" or "enabled" as being more accurate.' Purcell (2018) argues that:

> Throughout history and the generations, disabled people have been referred to in a variety of ways. Even in society and the media today, there are still disagreements and misunderstandings as to which words and phrases are acceptable, and which most certainly are not.

Terms referencing disability are usually pejorated by etymologies and their reference to visible difference by those outside the difference, such as cripple and handicap. The equivalents to 'cripple' in Nguni and Shona are *isilima* and *chirema*, respectively. These are clearly derived from the verbs *limala* and *remara*, respectively, which mean getting injured. These names are medically modelled to paint physical and mental impairment as sicknesses, and those without these are healthy. The *Shades of Noir* (2021) journal on disability states that the word 'cripple' comes from the verb 'creep', which is synonymous with crawl and is extremely offensive. The designation of the names *izilima* or *zvirema*, 'the injured', are instances of crude othering of disability, especially because statements such as *ungabozenza isilima*, 'do not act like a cripple', are common insults among non-disabled people. Purcell (2018), living with physical disability herself, declares that 'Personally, I would be offended if a non-disabled person or stranger called me a cripple, but I am happy to use it in a humorous context among my peers.' I recall one old man in my rural village whose name was *Sigoga*, 'cripple', and indeed, the man limped as he walked. He was born in the early 1920s and was named most likely for his crippled leg, and the name lived with him until his death in the year 2000. Disability is commonly referred to in Nguni as *ubulima*, which loosely translates to 'the state of being injured'; it references 'handicap' as a general term incorporating all disabilities.

The term 'handicap' as a hypernym for all disabilities, just like *ubulima*, is insulting to disability. Disability has been known as 'handicap' for a long time. *Shades of Noir* (2021) identifies two possible etymologies for the word, both relating negatively to 'hand' and 'cap/hat'. The first etymology links the word to Italian horse racing; here, good riders are said to have ridden with one hand as the other hand held their cap to make the race more equal for bad and learner riders. The other etymology is linked to the belief in Europe that disabled people were sinners and hence excluded from society, and they had to survive by begging. To approach would-be alms givers, these beggars would remove their hats and hold them in their hand: they begged 'cap in hand', hence the descriptive name 'handicap'.

The various disabilities, just like their hypernyms, are also referred to in othering terms clearly labelled by people who are themselves non-disabled. Mental disability has been named crudely to isolate and banish the 'patients' as dangerous and suspicious. *Thesaurus.com* (2021) gives the following as synonyms for mental hospital in English and slang: *asylum, chaos, loony, pandemonium, madhouse, nuthouse, snake pit, laughing academy*. These ideas of a psychiatric hospital are used to other the institutions and their 'patients', and at times the nurses, as dangerous and non-human. The meaning scope of the names used to name the institutions are derived from social practices and attitudes. The Nguni word describing mental disability is *ukuhlanya*, 'madness', and the name for the patient is *uhlanya*, 'mad person.' The word *uhlanya* is similar to the English and slang terms *lunatic, bonkers* and *crazy*. These names are also used in ordinary discourse to describe or chastise people against exhibiting behaviour akin to that of patients in these institutions. Namasasu (2020, p. 9) postulates that:

> Some of the terms used to refer to persons with disability that have been incorporated into Zimbabwe's informal lexicon carry the same connotation as the word *idiot* and are generally used as insults. *Sascam* is an example of such a term. It is derived from the acronym *Salisbury Association for the Care of the African Mentally Handicapped*.

The tendency to idealise mental disability as subnormal and not to be included in society comes from the images institutions for mental health people have. The *Collins* dictionary (2019), for example, defines asylum thus: *asylum*: in

British English. a safe or inviolable place of refuge, especially as formerly offered by the Christian Church to criminals, outlaws, etc; sanctuary. And *Sanitarium* is defined as an institution for the care of invalids or convalescents. These are generic names for institutions that cater to mental disability. Already society has named these as the other. Mental hospitals are stigmatised as banishments for the patients, and they are used negatively in common metaphorical expressions. The idea of a mental hospital I conjured up from general talk as I was growing up was similar to that of a maximum-security prison, where society banishes its malcontents. This stigmatisation of mental hospitals is fronted by their names, and these names are extended to cover the patients.

It is common for the institution's name to be used to name people with a certain condition treated or housed in it. In Zimbabwe, for example, there are names that reference people with mental illness that are derived from the names of psychiatric hospitals. The Ndebele vernacular term for a mentally disabled person is *insayi*, from the English word asylum, while *sascam* is now the Zimbabwean vernacular for mental disability. *Sascam* is also used as metaphor. Namasasu (2020, p. 9) states that it is common to hear people saying '*Handidi zveuSascam pano*, 'I do not want foolish behaviour here', literally: 'I do not want behaviour associated with mentally retarded people here'. Another institution for mental disability is the *Sibantubanye* school for children with Down's syndrome. The name itself is a call to society to accept the students, as will be discussed later. The name is now used in Ndebele to refer to someone with the syndrome as *isibantu*; you hear statements such as *lowana oyisibantu*, 'that one who is a *sibantu* (with Down's syndrome)'. The institution is already named an asylum, meaning a place for those who do not belong, and then the name of the institution is extended to the 'inmates'. This basically extends banishment to the individuals. The people are also known as *amadawuni*, 'the Downs', from Down's syndrome, a term that came to Zimbabwe through English, loaded with its own prejudiced etymologies.

Langdon Down, a medical doctor working in a London hospital in the 1860s, noticed cases of what has come to be known by his name, Down's syndrome. He noted that the patients' features reminded him of Mongolian people. He then reasoned that there was a genetic hierarchy of races. He believed races are ranked in descending order from Europeans–Asians–Africans and then Mongols. Each, he thought, was genetically inferior to the group above them (Stiles & Isoun, 1966; Estreich, 2016). From this almost impish theorising, people with Down's syndrome came to be called Mongols and the syndrome, mongolism. Down christened the syndrome Mongolian idiocy in 1866 (Balwan et al., 2008; Trent, 2013). This history warrants that even his name be removed from naming the condition, as now, it continues to be associated with someone who popularised it as idiocy and even waded into race theories of eugenics.

Imagining people with disabilities as degenerates with poor genes and assigning them lower human ranks also happens to people with albinism in most African societies. This comes from cultural stigmas and beliefs about albinism such as their being witches and a bad omen (Schuhle, 2013); if a pregnant woman looks at them, she should spit or else she will bear a child with albinism (Mwiba, 2018). The word 'albino' has gained negative connotations over the years; the NCDJ (2015) observes that the term 'albino' has been used throughout history in a hateful way; therefore, many prefer the people-first term, 'person with albinism'. In Nguni, people with albinism are called *inkawu*, the same noun used to designate monkey. In some cultures, they are described using their skin colour, something that is already a slur in race relations. In Shona, they refer to them as *musupe*, a term which describes the skin as bleached. People living with albinism are also mocked in Shona as *varungudunhu*, which means 'fake White people'. According to Mwiba (2018), in Malawi they are called by names such as *mizukwa*,'ghosts'; *mzungu osauka*, 'poor White person'; *nzungudala*, 'fake White person'; or *napweri*, 'white patches on a diseased tomato leaf'. He further states that women with albinism are called *machilitso*, 'cure', from the belief that having sex with them cures HIV/AIDS. These stereotypes expressed in naming have resulted in ritual killings of people living with albinism.

Another disability that has been named derogatively in Zimbabwe is height disability. Through folklore and usage, the word 'dwarf' came to reference shortness of stature and has a negative connotation. NCDJ (2015) cautions that use of the word 'dwarf' is considered acceptable when referring to the genetic condition, but it is often considered offensive when used in a non-medical sense. People with this condition are referred to variously by the Ndebele of Zimbabwe; one such term is *Abathwa*, which means 'Khoisan' people, a double slur to disability and to the San community. They are also popularly known as *oGodknows*, from a character in a Ndebele television dram which was aired on Zimbabwe television. The character had the condition of dwarfism, and his persona is now used as onomastic synecdoche to reference people with this condition.

Most of the terms for disability are offensive, as they are framed on the medical understanding of disability. However, movements and theories in disability issues morphed into social models which sought to include disabilities in society. The movement saw the establishment of institutions and schools for disabled people. In Zimbabwean universities and the education sector, such institutions and programmes are called special programmes or institutions, and some are known as special needs. The term 'special' comes with its own controversies. Purcell (2018) points out that 'The phrase came about as an attempt to be less negative, labelling disabled children's educational needs, rather than their condition. In my opinion, special needs describes a group of people who are unwanted, not accepted and ridiculed.' Namasasu (2020, p. 4) concurs:

> Even where a *special* class of children with disability is provided, this does not necessarily translate to inclusive education. The notion that children with disability are *special* and require separate *special education* has been critiqued as a violation of the human rights of children with disability and a

form of 'apartheid' and therefore contrary to the principles of social justice and democratic citizenship which schools ought to be teaching.

Exclusion is thus not simply the absence of inclusion but the product of social forces and environments that work against inclusive education and turn children with disability into second-class citizens (Chataika, 2007; Slee, 2001). According to Kearney (2011), inclusive education requires all children, irrespective of disability, to belong and meaningfully participate and learn at their local school. The special institutions are also named to other people with disabilities. The social model of disability has negative effects of creating objects of mercy in disabled people, which in itself is disabling. Society works to include the disabled because they feel pity for them, not because they are individuals with rights. The care of people with impairments is usually credited to those without the impairments, and this is expressed in the names given to disability centres the world over. Non-disabled philanthropists are credited for their 'mercy' on the disabled by having their names used to name disability centres and in some cases disability itself. Langdon Down, for example, has his name immortalised in the name Down's syndrome; the name suggests that it is his syndrome, yet we all know that he never had the condition. If he had wanted, and had understood his patients to be equal beings, he could have named the syndrome after one of his patients. However, non-disabled society which others disability sought to honour a non-disabled person for his 'mercy' and service to the disabled.

Several philanthropists and medics who obviously were informed by medical models of disability have shown benevolence to the cause of the disabled and donated either their services or resources to build centres for various impairments. In Zimbabwe, for example, several disability schools are named after benefactors who never had disabilities, as demonstrated in Table 9.1.

*Table 9.1* Names of non-disabled people used to name disability centres in Zimbabwe

| *Non-disabled person used to name a disability institution* | *Etymology* |
|---|---|
| Sir Humphrey Gibbs school – Bulawayo | He was patron of the Hoplands Trust, which funded the building of the school for mentally disabled children |
| King George VI (KGVI) school and centre – Bulawayo | Funded by the KGVI Foundation, in honour of King George VI of the United Kingdom |
| Naran Centre: Gweru | Mr Prag Naran, a businessman, donated the centre to Jairos Jiri for the care of children with various disabilities |
| Henry Murray School for the Deaf: Masvingo | He was principal at Morgenster School when sign language was introduced |
| Margaretha Hugo School for the Blind: Masvingo | Wife to Reverend Andrew Hugo, who helped establish the Braille school at Capota Mission |
| Jairos Jiri centres | Zimbabwean philanthropist who established various disability centres across the country |

The names point to people without disabilities doing something to help the disabled, which is part of the social model for disability. The fact that disabled people are not commemorated in the names of institutions which purport to serve them is telling of the social structures which other disability. According to Marungudzi (2016), Margaretha Hugo and her husband were approached for help in 1915 by a visually impaired boy called Dzingai who was rejected by his parents. Out of compassion for the boy, she started teaching him Braille, and this is how the school started. The memory of Dzingai as a person with a disability was never commemorated, but that of the benefactor was. I am not for ingratitude; I am simply looking for the memory of disabled people in naming the very institutions which serve them. It could as well have been named Margaretha-Dzingai school to include the disabled.

Some of the disability institutions in Zimbabwe were also named to specify the nature of the disability they deal with (Marungudzi, 2016). Some of the names included and some still include terms such as *blind, deaf, dumb* and *crippled*, which are now considered offensive; this includes names such as *Margaretha Hugo School for the Blind*, and *Henry Murray School for the Deaf*. Such names other disabled people by focusing on their disability. Some even specify the body organ which is disabled in the name, such as in the name *Nzeve Deaf Children's Centre* in the Zimbabwean town of Mutare. *Nzeve* is Shona for ear. This evokes medical modelling of disability whereby the centre looks at the organ of the ear to treat it, not the social integration of the disabled people. Such names give the impression that the terms used are not hate speech, when in actual fact they are. In his study of societies' attitude towards disability in a Zimbabwean school Namasasu (2020, p. 7) discovered that:

> Terms considered offensive to persons with disability such as *the crippled, the deaf, and the dumb* were freely used in class by both teachers and pupils to refer to persons with physical, hearing and speech impairments. Emphasis was on pity and charity for persons with disability rather than their empowerment, self-reliance and integration into the wider community.

Social inclusive education developments have seen most of these schools drop the reference to a specific disability and are just referred to as school or centre (Marungudzi, 2016; Mariga et al., 2014). The new trend of names for these institutions, though exhibiting some semblance of social modelling and inclusivity, still exposes some societal prejudices on disability. The majority of the new names express the desperate case of disabled people who are at the mercy of the non-disabled, while some are calls for inclusivity, an indication that society is still hostile to disability. Table 9.2 gives some of the new names and their implied or expressed othering of disability in Zimbabwe through envisaging them as alms cases.

The names are a call to a society which has not embraced disability; this is evidence that the names reveal underlying social hostilities to disability. The names portray people with disabilities as passive objects at the mercy of those

*Table 9.2* Begging implications in the meanings of some names of disability centres in Zimbabwe

| *Name of special disability institute* | *Implied semantics of begging* |
|---|---|
| Batsirai School: Harare | Shona: call for help |
| Rubatsiro School: Kadoma | Shona: assistance/help |
| Chengetai School: Mutare | Shona: call for people to care |
| Ratidzo School: Masvingo | Shona: demonstration or display |
| Mudavanhu School: Gweru | Shona: one who loves people |
| Sibantubanye Centre: Bulawayo | Ndebele: we are one people/we are the same |
| Simanyane Centre: Bulawayo | Ndebele: let us unite |

non-disabled in society. The names span the two models of medical and social disability. They give a picture of medical cases at the same time; some are a call to society to be inclusive. Gabel and Peters (2004) trace disability theorising from the traditional medical model to how disabled people changed the paradigm to model their conditions in relation to society. Relating impairment to society is an attempt at integrating disability into society, otherwise known as inclusivity. They further note that dealing with the otherness of disability demands a transition from the social model to agency and resistance models. There is no name for a disability centre in Zimbabwe which asserts disability rights and resistance to social exclusion.

## 9.2 Names exhibiting homophobic tendencies

Medical modelling in disability is extended to, or is also prevalent in, African views on homosexuality. Homosexuals are seen as people who have a sickness which can be physical or spiritual, and a balm can help restore and readjust their 'unnatural' situation (Asante, 2020). The negative discourses on homosexuality are further bolstered by theories of a precolonial Africa without homosexuality (Gelfand, 1979) and the puritan sexualities of Christianity and Islam (Klinken, 2014). These views are the basis for homophobia in Africa, and as a result, only 2 countries out of the 55 have legislation protecting same-sex unions. In the other countries, homosexuality is actually a crime of a serious nature, attracting up to 15 years imprisonment (Chimakonam & Agada, 2020; Klinken, 2014). The language and names given to homosexual people are usually slurs, indicating the social and legislative disapproval of the unions. There are several homophobic slurs societies use to express their contempt towards homosexuality. Finlay (2005, p. 19) questions, 'Why would a speaker call a person a "faggot" rather than homosexual . . . ? This choice of terminology is explained by the intention to express contempt towards a group.'

Homophobia in Africa is partly based on the belief that it is un-African and that it goes against principles of the dominant religions in the continent, Christianity and Islam. These positions have been heavily challenged by scholars arguing for African homosexuality before contact with Europeans (Dlamini,

2006; Chimakonam & Agada, 2020). African discourses on homosexuality are situated in colonial discourses. Homosexuality is seen as a form of cultural coloniality whereby the West is forcing its cultural sexualities on otherwise conservative African sexualities (Klinken, 2014). The language describing homosexuality is negative in most of Africa because, it, like colonialism, should be resisted for African cultural independence. According to Ndjio (2013, p. 126):

> In many African countries, sexuality has become a political and social landscape of privileged intervention by the postcolonial state seeking to purify the body of the nation. . . . It has also become a key site where the myth about African cultural unity is enacted by those who see a complex continent and its diverse populations through the lens of homogeneity and uniformity. In addition, sexuality has been made a cultural tool through which Africanity is expressed, and nativist ideologies are dramatised.

Just like the discourses on disability, whereby non-disabled people call themselves able bodied in contrast to and dehumanisation of disability, sexualities are also described as straight or homosexual. Heterosexuality in Africa, and indeed in many regions, is described as 'straight'; this is the basis for the imagined intervention on homosexual people to reorient and readjust them to 'straightness'. Naming heterosexuality as straight implies that homosexuality is crooked and therefore deviant. This name mirrors the medical modelling of homosexuality as a deviation from health which can be medically adjusted. The homosexual person is viewed as the crooked other. In Nguni, homosexual people are called *amambuka* (Sigamoney & Epprecht, 2013), 'cultural delinquents', derived from the verb *phambuka*, which means to take a turn from a road, typically into the bush. They further identify some names for homosexuality in South Africa, relating it to taboo, such as *umhlolo* and *meleko*, Nguni and Tswana for 'taboo', respectively. It is also referred to as *umkhuba* in Nguni, which is a synonym for *umhlolo*.

The association of homosexuality with deviant culture and taboo has seen some African languages designate animalism to homosexuality. In Nguni, for example, homosexual people are called *inkonkoni*, 'wildebeest', especially the 'Blue' sub species, *Connochaetes taurinus*. The scientific name derives from the Greek word *konnos*, meaning beard or mane. While the species clearly has sex dimorphism, it is in terms of the male being bigger; otherwise, both males and females have symmetric appearances (Van Heerden, 2018). Both sexes have the 'beard', and they have horns. In other species like lions, only the male has the mane, and in kudu, for example, females do not have horns, but wildebeest females have horns and the mane just like their male counterparts. It is this sex symmetry in appearances that is mapped onto gay people, whereby two people with beard fall in love. This name appears to be an old name for gay men in Nguni, and this has prompted speculation that homosexuality is no recent phenomena in Africa.

Another name for homosexual people with animalising undertones is *izitabane*. This is a term of Nguni origin popular in Southern Africa denoting hermaphrodite (Sigamoney & Epprecht, 2013). While humans are classified scientifically as gonochoric, whereby there are distinct male and female gametes and gonads, there are other non-human organisms, especially invertebrates and plants, which are hermaphroditic. A homosexual person is called *istabane*, 'hermaphrodite', to indicate their deviation from the normal sexualities of the human species. Common hermaphrodites are snails, earthworms, and slugs, crawly and creepy animals that are also disgusting. This makes the name an instance of crude othering of homosexuals. The name hermaphrodite was used in medicine to designate humans of ambiguous genitalia and gonadal mosaicism. It became offensive, and intersex is now its euphemism. The names associate sexuality with procreation through reference to male and female gametes. This is one of the strategies used to disqualify homosexuality in Africa as non-productive. In South Africa and Zimbabwe, lesbians are also called *izinyumba* (Sigamoney & Epprecht, 2013), 'the barren', because of the reproductive bias of African sexualities. The name is similar to other homophobic slurs such as *sisi-bhuti*, 'sister-brother'; *ndoda-mfazi*, 'male-female'; and *two-in-one*. These names imply dual sexuality, and there is no place for the third sex as in homosexual or queer.

There is a tendency to reduce homosexuality, especially gay practices, to the anus. Gay people are named for the anus and faecal matter associated with the rectum. Such names portray gay people as dirty and heterosexual people as clean. For example, there is no need to identify heterosexual men with the vagina because that is the perceived norm. Urine and gonads are also not associated with heterosexuality, but the anus and faecal matter are used as descriptors to name gay people. Homosexuality is narrowed to the anus as a way of expressing homophobia and othering homosexuals in Malawi. Interview data indicate that homosexuals are called *amathanyula*, 'those who engage in anal sex'. A similar homophobic name for homosexuals linking their identity to anal sex is found in the Ivory Coast, where, according to interview data, in Baoule language, homosexuals are called *PD* or *di huntuan*, 'ass fucker [sic] or simply one who has anal sex'. Sigamoney and Epprecht (2013) identify some labels for homosexuality, especially gay people in South Africa, linking them to the anus or faeces such as *skiki* and *poowes*, which both separately mean chamber pot. They further identify *chocolate pops* as another slur for gay people because the type of pop resembles a penis browned with faeces after anal sex. Ndlovu (2018) identifies the use of the term *imanyuwa*, 'manure', for anal sex and gay people being referred to as *abemanyuwa*, 'manure people.' The South African gay celebrity Somizi branded himself *Somgaga* inspired by the American pop diva Lady Gaga. He did this by blending his name with Gaga, ***Som- + -Gaga = Somgaga***. However, he is trolled on social media as *Somdidi*, a vulgar blending of his name, Somizi, and *umdidi*, 'anus' in Nguni, as in ***So[mizi] + [u]mdidi= Somdidi***. Gay people are also trolled on Zimbabwean social media as *analists*, a blend of ***anal-*** and the suffix ***-ist***. Gay people are othered as dirty and anus people; the names identify them as people considered outcasts by African societies.

Homosexual people, especially celebrities, have their names used to name homosexuality in some cases. In South Africa, where homosexuality is legal, there are more gay and lesbian people who come out publicly, and some of these people's names are used as names for gay and lesbian people. Gay people are known is Southern Africa as *oSomizi*, 'the Somizis', after the South African gay socialite Somizi Mhlongo, while lesbians are also called *oCaster*, 'the Casters', after the world-renowned lesbian South African athlete. The former Zimbabwean president Canaan Sodindo Banana was gay and served time in prison for sodomy. He is trolled as Canaan '*Sodomy*' Banana, which is a slur. His names Sodindo and Banana are now common lingua franca for gay people in Zimbabwe. Sigamoney and Epprecht (2013) identify the name Banana used to reference gay people in South Africa as well. Persons who play homosexual roles in popular television series are also used to name homosexuality. In most Southern African countries that watch South African Television through digital satellite television, gay people are called Senzo or Jason. These two are same-sex-attracted characters from the South African soap opera *Generations* (Sigamoney & Epprecht, 2013).

## 9.3 Sexist nomen othering in Africa

Biological labelling and subalternity experienced by homosexual people are also prevalent in language relating to women. Women are expressed as the other through sexist language which represents sexist social strata. According to Fromkin and Rodman (1993), language reinforces sexist speech habits. There are words for women with abusive and sexual implications, which are used consciously and unconsciously. Women are represented as sex objects through naming them or aspects of their sexuality, while men are imagined as the sex norm.

Some sexist images of women are extended to gay men in Africa, whereby they are referred to as women in an objectifying sense. Sigamoney and Epprecht (2013) identify the name *mattress* used to refer to gay men in South Africa. This term derives from sexist imagining of coital positions where the woman is under the man and therefore his 'mattress'. The image of a mattress and a man lying on it represent the sexual disempowerment of women prevalent in many African societies. Women are not expected to be active in sexual matters but are to be passive for the satisfaction of men. Men are the ones who go out looking for women, not the other way round; as a result, in Nguni, the words for proposing love and for sexual intercourse are *ukukhombisa* and *ukubhebha*, respectively. When they relate to women noun phrases, it is always the passive forms, *ukukhonjiswa* and *ukubhejwa*, respectively. In colloquial Nguni, having sex for men, is called *ukudla*, 'eating', while for women it is *ukudliwa*, 'they are eaten', even when the very act of heterosexual penile penetration resembles the women eating. Naming gay men other men's 'mattresses' implies they are stooping to the sexual level of women who are the passive objects of sex.

Society has created social sex stigmas for women which do not apply to men. There are certain sexualities that are defined socially to subordinate women to masculinity; for example, in many African languages, a prostitute is a woman, and there is no name for male prostitution. This is to be expected because polygamy is accepted and polyandry is not; in fact, the word for polyandry is prostitution. In Shona culture in Zimbabwe, a woman who has a child before marriage is called *mvana*, meaning 'a body from which a child has been removed'; ***bva-*** 'remove' + ***-mwana*** 'child'. Such a woman fetches less on the 'lobola market' (Ndlovu, 2021). In Nguni, such a woman is called *imitha*, 'one who has been pregnant before'. There is no Shona male equivalent for *mvana*; neither is there a Nguni male equivalent for *imitha*. If a woman builds her own home without a man, she is called *umazakhela*, 'one who built for herself'. In Nguni, this implies that men are expected to build for women, and *umazakhela* is a despised name. These names are given to women deriving from misogynistic society which values women as procreation objects. It is common to sexually objectify women in Africa. Murugi (2003) establishes that in Nairobi, Kenya, women are abused through the use of certain terms in English, Kiswahili and Sheng. Men in public transport and universities portray female passengers and students as sex objects and subordinate to men.

It is interesting to note that in some verbs denoting sexual relations and activities between men and women, men are the agentive subjects, while women are the passive recipients or are the arguments caused to act by men. However, when it comes to prostitution, there is an inversion of arguments whereby men exchange argument positions with women, and they become the objects of the verb prostitute. The appellative prostitute is therefore designated to women in a way that condones errant sexual behaviour by males. The name which describes prostitution is feminine, implying that it is an activity for females and males are just customers. The development of male prostitutes in the sex industry derived the retronym 'male prostitute' to categorise men who engage in the female enterprise of prostitution. Onomastic synecdoche is also employed in a gendered manner to derive nomen metaphors for prostitution in Nguni. Names such as *uJezebeli*, *uGoma* and *uDelila* from the Judeo-Christian script are deployed on women to describe them as prostitutes. The same script has examples of men who displayed worse errant sexuality such as David, Solomon and many others, but these are not used to reference men of errant sexual behaviour. Solomon is proudly remembered for his wisdom, while David was a great king, never mind their multiple sexual partners and encounters. There are many African men named after the two, and the motives for the naming exclude their sex escapades.

## 9.4 Conclusion

Names are a window into societies' attitudes and power structures, and a CDA of names can reveal the intricacies of power and disempowerment. In African societies, there are social hierarchies which privilege the non-disabled, heterosexuals and men over people with disabilities, homosexual people and women, respectively. These social structures are based on the fallacy of a united African culture, homogenous throughout the whole continent, and this culture has the desired universal characteristics of misogyny, heterosexuality and non-disability. African cultures created social structures that excluded disability, and they even eliminated disabled children. Some disabilities are associated with spiritism and the occult, and these myths have created certain hostilities and misconceptions about disability. These can be read in the names ascribed to disability in Africa. Disability is still viewed as a medical case which should get a medical, not a social, adjustment. The names for disabilities and institutions for disability are still disablist, as they emphasise disability as a case for the mercy of society. The institutions and some conditions for people with disabilities are named to commemorate non-disabled people, not those they serve. The myth of a puritan African culture was exacerbated by the conversion of Africans to puritan religions of Islam and Christianity, which have questionable records on women's rights and they also demonise homosexuality. Based on these two philosophies, African governments, most of which are dictatorial, have politicised sexualities and criminalised homosexuality as unproductive and colonial. This has prompted these societies to name homosexuality as disdained criminality or dirty sex and women as objects of procreation. Women are still viewed as sex objects, and the naming of gender and women is sexist in most of Africa. There is need for transition from social models of gender, disability and homosexuality to resistance models, and the naming should reflect rights and equality as influenced by changes in social practice.

## References

Asante, G. A. (2020). Anti-LGBT violence and the ambivalent (colonial) discourses of Ghanaian Pentecostalist-Charismatic church leaders. *Howard Journal of Communications*, *31*(1), 20–34.

Balwan, W. K., Raina, T. R., Kumar, P., Sharma, S., Raina, S., & Gupta, S. (2008). Down's syndrome: A chromosome study of 118 cases from Jammu & Kashmir, India. *Indian Journal of Endocrinology and Metabolism*, *12*(4), 5–8.

Barnes, C., Barton, L., & Oliver, M. (Eds.). (2002). *Disability studies today*. Polity Press.

Brons, L. L. (2015). Othering, an analysis. *Transcience*, *6*(1), 69–90.

Buberwa, A. (2018). Sexism in Haya language personal names selection. *JULACE: Journal of the University of Namibia Language Centre*, *3*(2), 87–98.

Chataika, T. (2007). *Inclusion of disabled students in higher education in Zimbabwe: From idealism to reality: A social ecosystem perspective* [Doctoral thesis, University of Sheffield].

Chimakonam, J. O., & Agada, A. (2020). The sexual orientation question in Nigeria: Cultural relativism versus universal human rights concerns. *Sexuality & Culture, 24*(6), 1705–1719.

Choruma, T. (2007). *The forgotten tribe: People with disabilities in Zimbabwe.* CIIR.

The Collins Dictionary. (2019). *Asylum.* Retrieved April 18, 2021, from www.collinsdictionary.com/dictionary/english/asylum

Corker, M. (2000). Disability politics, language planning and inclusive social policy. *Disability & Society, 15*(3), 445–462.

Croom, A. M. (2014). Remarks on "the semantics of racial slurs". *Linguistic and Philosophical Investigations, 13,* 11–32.

De Beauvoir, S. (1997). *The second sex.* Vintage.

Disability Nottinghamshire. (2019, February 14). *Social model vs medical model of disability.* www.disabilitynottinghamshire.org.uk/index.php/about/social-model-vs-medical-model-of-disability/differences

Dlamini, B. (2006). Homosexuality in the African context. *Agenda, 20*(67), 128–136.

Donoghue, C. (2003). Challenging the authority of the medical definition of disability: An analysis of the resistance to the social constructionist paradigm. *Disability & Society, 18*(2), 199–208.

Duckitt, J. (2001). Reducing prejudice: A historical and multilevel approach. In M. Augoustinos & K. Reynolds (Eds.), *Understanding prejudice, racism and social conflict* (pp. 253–272). Sage.

Estreich, G. (2016). An open letter to medical students: Down syndrome, paradox, and medicine. *AMA Journal of Ethics, 18*(4), 438–441.

Felmlee, D., Rodis, P. I., & Zhang, A. (2020). Sexist slurs: Reinforcing feminine stereotypes online. *Sex Roles, 83*(1), 16–28.

Finlay, S. (2005). Value and implicature. *Philosopher's Imprint, 5,* 1–20.

Fromkin, V., & Rodman, R. (1993). *Introduction to language.* Holt, Rinehart and Winston.

Gabel, S., & Peters, S. (2004). Presage of a paradigm shift? Beyond the social model of disability toward resistance theories of disability. *Disability & Society, 19*(6), 585–600.

Gelfand, M. (1979). The infrequency of homosexuality in traditional Shona society. *Central African Journal of Medicine, 25*(9), 201–202.

Hedger, J. (2012). The semantics of racial slurs: Using Kaplan's framework to provide a theory of the meaning of derogatory epithets. *Linguistic and Philosophical Investigations, 11,* 74–84.

Hedger, J. (2013). Meaning and racial slurs: Derogatory epithets and the semantics/pragmatics interface. *Language and Communication, 33,* 205–213. http://doi.org/10.1016/j.langcom.2013.04.004

Kaplan, D. (1999). *The meaning of ouch and oops: Explorations in the theory of meaning as use.* University of California.

Kearney, A. (2011). Exclusion from and within school: Issues and solutions. *Studies in Inclusive Education, 14,* 1–33.

Klinken, A. V. (2014). Homosexuality, politics and Pentecostal nationalism in Zambia. *Studies in World Christianity, 20*(3), 259–281.

Mariga, L., McConkey, R., & Myezwa, H. (2014). *Inclusive education in low-income countries: A resource book for teacher educators, parent trainers and community development workers.* Disability Innovations Africa.

Martinot, S. (2011). *The coloniality of power: Notes toward de-colonization.* San Francisco State University. www.ocf.berkeley.edu/~marto/coloniality.htm#:~:text=The%20%22coloniality%20of%20power%22%20is,the%20Americas%20to%20the%20present

Marungudzi, T. (2016). Special institutions for people living with disabilities in Zimbabwe: A socio-onomastic exegesis. *Scholars Journal of Arts, Humanities and Social Sciences*, *4*(3), 306–316.

Murray, S. O., & Roscoe, W. (1998). *Boy-wives and female husbands: Studies in African homosexualities*. Saint Martins Press.

Murugi, K. L. (2003). *Language as a tool of abuse against women: The case of the language of Matatu touts and university students in Nairobi* [Master's thesis, University of Nairobi].

Musere, J., & Byakutaga, S. C. (2000). *African names and naming*. Ariko Pubns.

Mwiba, D. M. (2018). Medicine killings, abduction of people with albinism, wealth and prosperity in North Malawi: A historical assessment. *Proceedings of the African Futures Conference*, *2*(1), 30–49.

Namasasu, O. (2020). Exclusion of children with disability from citizenship education at primary school: A Harare case study. *ResearchGate*, 1–11. https://doi.org/10.13140/RG.2.2.26522.47044

National Centre on Disability and Journalism NCDJ. (2015, September 12). *Terms to avoid when writing about disability*. Arizona State University. https://ncdj.org/2015/09/terms-to-avoid-when-writing-about-disability/

Ndjio, B. (2013). Sexuality and nationalist ideologies in post-colonial Cameroon. In S. Wieringa & H. Sivori (Eds.), *The sexual history of the global South: Sexual politics in Africa, Asia, and Latin America* (pp. 120–143). Zed Books.

Ndlovu, S. (2018). *A comparative analysis of metaphorical expressions used by rural and urban Ndebele speakers: The contribution of S'ncamtho* [Doctoral dissertation, University of Cape Town].

Ndlovu, S. (2021). Mutation of lobola and "othering" of women in Ndebele culture. In L. Togarasei & E. Chitando (Eds.), *Lobola (Bridewealth) in contemporary Southern Africa* (pp. 185–200). Palgrave Macmillan.

Purcell, E. (2018, July 23). What is acceptable disability terminology? *Disability Horizons*. http://disabilityhorizons.com/2018/07/what-is-acceptable-disability-terminology/

Schuhle, J. (2013). *Medicine murder of people with albinism in Tanzania – How casino capitalism creates rumorscapes and occult economies*. CAS (Center for Area Studies) Working Papers Series 2. Center for Area Studies, Freie Universitat Berlin.

Shades of Noir. (2021, April 16). *Examples of disablist language*. https://shadesofnoir.org.uk/journals/content/examples-of-disablist-language

Shakespeare, T., & Watson, N. (2001). The social model of disability: An outdated ideology? In S. Barnartt & B. Altman (Eds.), *Exploring theories and expanding methodologies: Where we are and where we need to go* (pp. 9–28). Emerald Group Publishing Limited.

Shijith, V. P., & Sekher, T. V. (2017). "Unwanted" is my name: Bias surrounding the Nakusa Girls of Maharashtra. *Sociological Bulletin*, *66*(1), 58–74.

Sigamoney, V., & Epprecht, M. (2013). Meanings of homosexuality, same-sex sexuality, and Africanness in two South African townships: An evidence-based approach for rethinking same-sex prejudice. *African Studies Review*, *56*(2), 83–107.

Slee, R. (2001). Driven to the margins: Disabled students, inclusive schooling and the politics of possibility. *Cambridge Journal of Education*, *31*(3), 385–397.

Stiles, K. A., & Isoun, M. F. (1966). Bibliography of mongolism (Down's syndrome). *Acta Geneticae Medicae et Gemellologiae: Twin Research*, *15*(3), 247–272.

Swindler, A. (1993). *Homosexuality and world religions*. Trinity.

Thesaurus.com. (2021, April 18). *Mental hospital*. www.thesaurus.com/browse/mental%20hospital

Trent, J. W. (2013). Downs: The history of a disability by David Wright. *Bulletin of the History of Medicine, 87*(2), 284–285.

Van Dijk, T. A. (2001). Multidisciplinary CDA: A plea for diversity. *Methods of Critical Discourse Analysis, 1*, 95–120.

Van Heerden, A. M. (2018). *Profiling the meat quality of blue wildebeest (Connochaetes taurinus)* [Doctoral dissertation, Stellenbosch University].

# 10 Socio-political onomastic exclusions in Africa

## 10.0 Introduction

Ideas have been espoused to exclude Africa from global development and to reduce it to a small country. Africans have also used the same shrinking strategy to imagine a homogenous Africa, united by its opposition to external coloniality. Socio-political names and commemorative naming in Africa index these totalising and shrinking concepts which include and exclude others. Bhatia (2005, p. 9) opines that 'each name will come with a surrounding set of associations, natures, motives and intents.' This chapter argues that the name Africa is immersed in continentalist discourses which can be read in names; it further opines that Africa is not as united as is imagined, because names and naming speak more to divisions of Africa than unity. Names also betray African continental and nation states' preferential politics, and some of the names confirm ethnic exclusions within individual countries. The chapter engages the theory of othering and postcolonial theory to analyse nomen exclusions and inclusion in African contexts. Othering theory discusses the social processes of exclusion and how culture and language can be used to actively exclude others. Cahoone (2003, p. 11) states:

> The apparent identity of what appear to be cultural units – human beings, words, meanings, ideas, philosophical systems, social organisations – are maintained only through constitutive repression, an active process of exclusion, opposition, and hierarchisation. A phenomenon maintains its identity in semiotic systems only if other units are represented as foreign or 'other'.

Naming space and social organisations in Africa exhibit exclusions of some key outsiders in the African struggles, and some countries exclude others from their commemorative naming. Borkfelt (2011) argues that even after political independence in Africa and elsewhere, naming still signifies inequality and dominance; it is merely questioned what humans should do with this God-given power. In some cases, postcolonial african countries are named to exclude other ethnicities and languages within the same country. These postcolonial exclusions

DOI: 10.4324/9781003170761-13

are engaged through othering theory which is part of postcolonial theory (Jensen, 2011). Li (1995, p. 171) posits that:

> A central characteristic of postcolonial theory is its exertion of a certain historical vigilance, a wariness of all monocultural discourses and their colonising imperative. Postcolonial theory's suspicion of western narratives of enlightenment and progress is matched equally by its resolve to not be taken in by imagined or invented national allegories of native authenticity. Postcolonial theory's critical vigilance, moreover, is directed against itself, such that its institutional and geopolitical locations, locutions, and interests are all brought into question.

Names exhibit certain colonialities of hierarchisation and exclusion. Martinot (2011, p. 1) opines that 'We all live within a multiplicity of colonialities; subjected in both body and mind.' Postcolonial theory helps us look at African colonialities from and by Africans.

The chapter is a qualitative study of names and their socio-political indices. Data were collected through document analysis of newspapers, magazines, journals and literature addressing African histories, naming, renaming and cultures. The data are analysed using critical discourse analysis and linguistic landscape to reveal the underlying indices. CDA is used as an analytic tool to identify the nuanced exclusions and inclusions in names. Van Dijk (2001) argues that CDA is an interdisciplinary approach focusing on power relations in society as represented in discourses such as names and naming. LL accounts for commemorative exclusions on the African toponomastic landscape. Blommaert and Maly (2016, p. 4) opine that LL is:

> an ethnographic and historical project, in which we see signs as indices of social relationships, interests and practices, deployed in a field which is replete with overlapping and intersecting norms – not just norms of language use, but norms of conduct, membership, legitimate belonging and usage.

This chapter analyses continentalist nuances in naming Africa and African politics and culture. It looks at global, continental and national exclusions in African commemorative naming and also looks at ethnic and linguistic exclusions within African nation states.

## 10.1 Nuances of the name Africa in continentalist discourses

Totalising ideologies and naming are problematic in that they are based on generalisations that favour the one giving them. Hall (1991) exemplifies the folly of totalising nomenclature when he looks at how the Greeks labelled everyone who did not speak Greek or who was outside the perceived Greek self as Barbarian. He points out that the appellation 'barbarian' referenced different cultures and languages which were not unitary or homogenous. The Greeks achieved the unity of the others in their own imagination by simply placing all of them outside the Greek self and never cared about the obvious differences within the group they called barbarians. Totalising names create collective superiority and inferiority and achieve selfing and othering. African identities are complex. Ndlovu-Gatsheni (2010) has even questioned whether Africans exist. The concept Africa is manipulated through naming to include and exclude others.

Africa was imagined as the other continent, dark and uncivilised. The othering continued through the various stages of colonisation and coloniality. What is interesting is that people outside Africa imagined and some continue to imagine Africa as a unitary state. Such a totalising view of the concept Africa others the nationhood of 55 countries which make up the continent. The East and the West relate to Africa as a country, not a union of countries like the European Union (EU), for example. Ryder (2021) writes of Africa-China relations this nomenclature gives the impression that the Chinese government has political and economic relations with the African government. She was writing about how Africans were racially brutalised in China in the wake of the COVID-19 pandemic in 2020 and how China is covering up by donating vaccines to Africa. The coloniality and superiority displayed in China's racism against people of colour is attested in its totalising of a whole continent into a nation. Afrique (2021) also uses similar naming in the name France-Africa Summit, while the United Kingdom's government (2021) named its investment summit with African leaders the UK-Africa Investment Summit, and the *Africa News* platform features the Russia-Africa Dialogue. The United States has several so-called US-Africa partnerships, such as the US-Africa Business Summit of 2019 (Corporate Council on Africa, 2019). All these countries name their interactions with Africa using unequal nomenclature, yoking singular states to a whole continent in pacts. This clearly shows that the singular states command more power than the continent. The names of various Africa partnerships exclude individual African countries. While super-power global policies and hegemonies dominate African states and group them together for easy management, the European Union, which purports non-aggressive influence such as its normative and soft power global policies, also overlooks African nation states (Scheipers & Sicurelli, 2008). The normative influences and structures which emphasise, among other things sovereignty, are violated by names such as EU-Africa Summit and EU-Africa relations. Suffice it to say that these global powers come first and Africa last in the syntax of the various names of pacts with Africa.

One of the nuances of the toponym Africa is imagining it as an antonym for Europe and modernity. This also is generalisation and exclusion motivated by global colonialities. Africa is colonially reducible into one poor state. Some pro-African critics have questioned the globalised links between Africa and poverty (Asongu & Kodila-Tedika, 2017). The designation African poverty is a common expression in economics and development literature. The name links African identity to poverty. Africa is not only reducible to a state, but a poor one. Such a reduction excludes rich and affluent areas within Africa from African identity. Most South African, Tunisian, Nigerian and Moroccan cities for example, are recognised as 'world class' cities, not 'African class' (Bafana, 2016). Africa is also reduced to disease and bad governance; this creates un-Africanness in countries that have vibrant democracies such as Botswana, Namibia, South Africa, Ghana and so on. These negative views of Africa lead to the conjuring up of names such as *African medicine, African culture, African religion, African leadership, African science* and so on. These names assume that culture is homogenous in Africa and is all definable by juxtaposing it with western modernity.

Another problematic nuance of Africa is its association with Black identity. Africa has been defined as Black by outsiders (Filippov, 2014), and this definition is divisive and excludes many Africans from Africa. There are many White people who have had several generations of African identity, and they do not know any other home apart from the African countries (Rigby, 2020). There are also many White Arabs in Africa, who are usually thought of as unbelonging because they are in a Black continent (Rodriguez-Flores et al., 2016). A Black Africa does not only exclude non-Blacks from Africa, but it also excludes Blacks from other continents and countries outside Africa. It is almost unheard of to hear designations such as Black-European, Black-Russian, Black-Chinese and Black-Japanese, all because Black has been fused into African identity. The generalisation of Africa as the Black continent led to 'Black Americans', for example, being denied full nomen identity in America. They cannot be fully American because their skin colour belongs to Africa. The ambiguous name African-American is an attempt at making them belong to both spaces. However, the name African-American creates aliens who are othered from both spaces: they cannot be fully African, neither can they be fully American, yet they are bona fide American nationals. The fact that other Americans are not called British-Americans, yet they came from Britain, is an indication that the name African-American serves to exclude Black people from enjoying full American identity. Those who can otherwise claim autochthony of America are also sometimes referred to as Indian (Red Indians) to create an ambiguous identity. Kearney (1998, p. 128) argues that 'being neither fish nor fowl and yet both at the same time, the alien is a highly ambiguous person.'

Africa is synonymous with Black, and one globalised generalisation is that all people of colour originate in Africa. African identity was also extended to all people of colour by pan-Africanist machinations; this essentially denies that there is blackness outside Africa. Several indigenes of colour are found in India, the Middle East, Australia, North America, South America and so on, and all these have to be excluded from their separate identities because 'Black is African.' However, some non-Black races have stretched the meaning of the identity 'Black' to fit in as self-styled Blacks. Affirmative action in South Africa sought to benefit Black South Africans as victims of apartheid segregation. The

Black Economic Empowerment (BEE) scheme and legislation were designed to achieve this affirmative action. Surprisingly, the scheme attracted unfamiliar Blacks into the identity, the Chinese (Harris, 2017). Because apartheid othered Blacks and selfed Whites, Chinese are most likely to have been White then, or at least non-Black, and now that affirmative action others Whites as a Black selfing strategy, Chinese expand the identity and name Black to include eastern Whites.

Africans have sought to liberate themselves from global colonialities by imagining a unitary African identity which they claim was interrupted by colonialism. Even the groups fighting against colonialism in the various states were named to portray an African identity, as in African National Congress (ANC), Kenya African National Union (KANU) and Zimbabwe African People's Union (ZAPU). Africa has had theories totalising the various experiences and cultures as one culture, even the many; some unrelated languages are called African languages, a term that assumes dialectical relation among all languages in Africa. The idea of pan-Africanism has led many to think that African people are not different. There are confusing names for concepts in culture such as African attire, African wedding, African healer, African religion, African Christology and so on. These names reduce Africa to a singular ethnicity which is homogenous from Cape Town to Cairo, yet there are several countries, ethnicities, languages and cultures that are strategically excluded by these broad nuances of Africa.

The name Africa is usually contracted to denote national identity in a belief that a united African country will be stronger than Europe (Janis, 2013). Nationalising Africa may be a noble dream, but the unity calls become more humorous than they are serious, because there are even louder calls for cessation in the continent. At the international level of politics, these calls are often made by African dictators seeking refuge in Africanness for their human rights abuses. Contracting Africa into a national identity serves Afrocentric scholarship as well, in that it makes all White people accountable for the African colonial past and its injustices (Hughey, 2020). The French, for example, cannot be absolved from colonial injustices in Zimbabwe just because they did not colonise it; as long as they colonised part of Africa, they colonised Zimbabwe as well. Such a naming and identity system by Africans creates a totalised African self and expands all western states to continental selves who committed atrocities on a united country called Africa. African victimhood and White racial privileges and sins are deployed strategically (Horwitz, 2018) in naming Africa and Africanness as a nation and nationality, respectively, to create a shared continental victim self and a continental White violating other.

It is very unfortunate that calls for a 'United States of Africa' (Nyerere, 1963) are and have been coming strongly from African leaders who have abused power and violated the very Africans they are speaking for (Olaopa & Amusan, 2018). The United States of Africa as a name and identity are indexical of human rights abuses and strategic othering of African people. The leaders use the name to evoke mythical and projected African prosperity to be achieved through pulling African resources together. The name creates imaginary

African selves who own the continent, yet, in actual fact, it is turning out to be a euphemism for the new colonialism by the East. The name serves to other the West and America because they seek to arrest and stop African dictators from violating Africans; in the process, the East is glorified and justified in looting Africa. The obtaining situation is that the United States of Africa as moniker others the West and America, but ironically, it is fashioned along the structure of the name for the 'United States of America' (Nyerere, 1963). The African dictators are abusing the name 'Africa' and the concept of a united Africa to speak for different people in Africa and the continent. Berger (2002, p. 276) observed a similar trend in Asia, where the historical power of the East-West dichotomy, and the fixed conceptions of culture/race to which it is linked, have increasingly allowed the national elites of the region to speak not only for their 'nations,' but even for Asia and Asians.

In the context of national inclusion and exclusion, the name Africa and what it identifies are contracted and expanded for the convenience of selves who want to be included or to exclude others. To South Africans, for example, who are under the pressure of excess immigrants from across Africa, the name denotes a continent of 54 or 55 countries. This continental definition of Africa is fashioned to exclude foreign nationals from South Africa. However, to the asylum seekers, the name Africa is contracted to mean South Africa so that they can belong (Akinrinde, 2020). Forcing South Africa to be Africa is to other bona fide South Africans who have to share their resources with the rest of the continent. In the majority of the cases, African countries are mismanaged by greedy and cruel dictators, and South Africa has to suffer for its democracy and human rights. They even claim a right to be in South Africa because they helped fight apartheid (Masenya, 2017). They appeal to pseudo-Africanness, claim that the xenophobia is actually Afrophobia and accuse the perpetrators of betraying the common African brotherhood. Immigrants from Somalia, Malawi, Zambia and Tanzania, for example, pass through Zimbabwe on their way to 'Africa'. Some are arrested, but no one wants to settle in Zimbabwe. To them, Zimbabwe is not their Africa; if anything, Zimbabwe is Zimbabwe, and they are going to 'Africa' down south. This is the argument of foreign nationals in South Africa: that they belong because they are Africans. To them, South Africa is theirs more than it belongs to White South Africans. They all want to belong to one country because Africa is one. Unfortunately, South Africans cannot move en masse to any part of Africa because the very dictators who popularise the African unity mantra have run down most African states. Defining South Africa as Africa others South Africans and justifies foreign nationals crowding and posing a strain on national resources under the banner of 'Africa'.

## 10.2 Political exclusions in African commemorative naming

Commemorative naming in Africa is characterised by inconsistencies and gaps which betray national and international preferences and power. Wanjiru-Mwita

(2020) opines that, although names are less imposing compared to statues, which have led to global rereading of history, especially in Europe, and 'Rhodes must fall' calls in Southern Africa, they are also very important in the memory of nations and people. She argues that toponyms such as street names help us remember and forget events and people. There are some global, African and national icons who are conspicuous by their absence in the commemorative naming of some African states. As much as African leaders like to portray a united Africa and willingness to unite under one supra-Africa state, they betray their glaring differences by failing to acknowledge their unity in commemorative naming. Ironically, African states commemorate regionalism and nationalism in names, not sterile African continentalism. Globally, Cold War politics and Africa's preferences are attested through commemorative names in individual states. The naming also exposes the coloniality which continues in Africa. Ruling elites in African states prioritise their allies and friends and exclude some important people whom they see as a threat to their own legacy.

African renaissance and pan-Africanist theories and mantras are based on the legacies of people such as Marcus Garvey and the Universal Negro Improvement Association (Lennon, 2020), William Du Bois, Malcolm X and Martin Luther King, American civil rights advocates and pan-Africanists (Meer, 2019); Kwame Nkrumah, pan-Africanist (Davidson, 2019); Emperor Haile Selassie, pan-Africanist (Asserate, 2015); King Shaka and King Lobhengula, anti-colonial fighters (Ndlovu, 2020); Queen Nzinga, precolonial ruler and anti-slavery fighter (Vellem, 2015); and many more. However, these people are not much celebrated in African commemorative naming. It is expected that an Africa proud of its culture and history would name key places such as cities, airports, stadia, dams, parks and so on after celebrated pan-Africanists such as Garvey, Du Bois, X and King, but this is not the case. The founder of pan-Africanism, Du Bois, does not even have a street named after him in Zimbabwe, for example, and it is no different in other countries. Wanjiru-Mwita (2020), writing in *The Conversation*, demonstrates how Kenya remembered the pan-African movement in its decolonial renaming of Nairobi streets:

> Additionally, in the spirit of pan-Africanism, other African leaders such as Kwame Nkrumah, Albert Luthuli and Julius Nyerere were celebrated through street names. Beyond the African continent, leaders who fought for Black liberation and civil rights in America, such as Ralph Bunche and William Du Bois were also honoured.

All the inspirations and Black consciousness in the legacies of Garvey, X and King are not celebrated in Africa. The exclusion of these civil rights and freedom fighters is telling of the abuses of power in African states; for African leaders, celebrating these rights campaigners will be going against their own stranglehold on power. Africans were assisted by countries such as China, Russia and Cuba during their struggle for political independence. This was due to the rift between the West and the East during the Cold War era. Even this East-Africa partnership is not visible in commemorative African toponymy. Names such as Lenin, Gorbachev, Stalin, Mao and Castro do not form a significant part of the African linguistic landscape to match the glorified 'Look-East-Policies'.

Africa is affected by regional onomastic heritagisation whereby international commemorations operate regionally not continentally. The Arab states in the North other Black histories in the South in their toponyms, and the Black South others the Arab North. Libya and Egypt, for example, did a lot for the liberation of Southern African states, but there is little or no Arab heritage commemorated in these states. It should not be uncommon to see a street named after Gaddafi or Nasser in Zimbabwe, for example, but the naming excludes Arab Africa. Even non-Arab regions outside of the SADC region are not included; East, Central and West African heritages are not considered in naming Southern African space.

Africans are not as united as they claim to be, at least from how they commemorate African culture and identities. Each country prioritises its own culture, history, people and religion in commemorative naming. The idea of a United States of Africa was forcefully campaigned for by former Libyan dictator Muammar Gaddafi (Ramutsindela, 2009); however, he is not commemorated in African toponyms. Instead, his name is used to name a stadium outside Africa, in Pakistan. Zimbabwean and Nigerian economic refugees flood South Africa and even claim to belong there as Africans, yet their countries do not commemorate South African history or culture. Apart from Nelson Mandela, whose popularity and relevance are more global than African, no other South African is commemorated in Zimbabwean toponymy. Even in the case of Mandela, the Zimbabwean government had to honour him after the fall of apartheid and after he was honoured outside Africa. Why wait for the fall of apartheid to name a street after Mandela when you are already free? The exclusion of ANC icons in Zimbabwe's commemorative renaming may confirm speculation that the ZANU government did not help the ANC fight apartheid.

Political and friendship alliances were the basis for inclusion in street toponymy in Africa. Ndlovu (2020) posits that in Zimbabwe's renaming, for example, African icons who were friends to ZANU had their names used to rename Zimbabwean streets, while those aligned with the rival party, ZAPU, were excluded as part of ZANU triumphalism. ZANU was aligned with Nyerere of Tanzania, who actually helped in its formation; Machel of Mozambique; and Nujoma of Namibia, while ZAPU was aligned with the ANC of South Africa, Kaunda of Zambia and Khama of Botswana. ZANU excluded Kaunda and Khama from street renaming after independence. Kaunda was only added years later after some complaints, while Khama was never honoured. Walter Sisulu of South Africa is commemorated as far north as Nairobi in Kenya, yet Zimbabwe excluded him, although it is Zimbabwe which benefits from South Africa more than Kenya. It goes without say that ZAPU history and heroics are excluded in Zimbabwean commemorative naming, especially that of Father Zimbabwe, Joshua Nkomo, whose name was included after guerrilla posters were erected on streets pressuring the ZANU government to remember him (Mamvura, 2020).

## 10.3 Ethnolinguistic exclusions in naming and norming African others

Apart from political exclusion, African spaces, languages and cultures are also named to exclude national others. The ethnic exclusions are predominant within nation states whereby some ethnicities are named to belong at the exclusion of others. Some countries and territories within countries are named to exclude other ethnic groups and their languages, and some languages are labelled as inferior to others. Mamdani (1998) views the ethnic other as an ethnic stranger in the eyes of the selfing indigenes. Languages and names are used to exclude others. Levander and Mignolo (2011, p. 2) posit that:

> Disciplinary languages, frames of reference, and methods of inquiry – as much or even more than the languages and dialects that the world's peoples speak – can and do all too easily sustain and normalise the ways in which we parse power systems in an increasingly global age. But disciplinary languages have a history of upholding national boundaries, regional differences, and geopolitical hierarchies.

There are some country toponyms which are ethnically exclusive; this is one of the problems posed by plurality in Africa. African nation states usually present a facade of national and cultural unity formed on a homogenous national identity. The reality is that African countries are made of multiple cultures, languages and identities which cannot be expressed univocally. Naming a multicultural country using the language or heritage of one group others the various others. In Zimbabwe, for example, the name of the country derives from the Shona language and cultural history, and other ethnicities and languages are assumed in the Shona national self (Ndlovu, 2016). In this case, a country name is used to exclude other ethnicities and elevate one ethnic group in a country to the level of national self. Botswana also has over 28 languages and cultures, but the name of the country derives from one, the Tswana, and the name actually means 'land of the Tswana'. Other ethnicities are all living in a land that does not belong to them. Swaziland, now ESwatini, and Lesotho are other examples of one language and culture used to name spaces shared by many languages and cultures. These names create othered identities which are silenced in national onomastics, and the selfed ethnicity in a symbolic and physical sense owns the country.

Names of provinces and districts in some African countries overlook ethnic and linguistic composition within the provinces, and there is tendency to use demographics or assumed autochthony to come up with these names to the exclusion of others. The naming of Zimbabwean provinces, for example, was done by the colonial administration, and the toponyms are glaring ethnic divisions of the country. The provinces are named using Shona, Ndebele, Manyika and Karanga identities. These four ethnic identities selfed by the toponyms; *Mashonaland, Matabeleland, Manicaland* and *Masvingo* are occupied by other identities which the toponyms exclude. A similar trend obtains in South Africa, for example, Venda district, which includes Tsonga people, but the name excludes this identity.

The discourse and debates on language policies in Africa have created problematic labels which group some languages and ethnicities as othered minorities while elevating others to majority selves. Tollefson (1991, p. 2) argues that 'language has a fundamental importance in the organisation of human societies; it affects people's lives in more ways than the people themselves realise.' Many people are offended by domineering attitudes towards their languages in language policies. The name minority language is very common as a descriptor for sidelined languages in imagining post-independence national languages and cultures. There is a clearly expressed coloniality of power in the name *minority language* which is obviously proffered by those in power. Social and political hierarchies become evident when a group of people and their language or through their language is called minority by another group and language. To be minor is to be small or insignificant, yet to be major is to be big, visible and very significant. Majoritisation and minoritisation of languages are cunning political empowerment and disempowerment, respectively. The mathematics of adding and subtracting language speakers does not culminate in a quantitative glotto census but in power hierarchies which have nothing to do with language numbers. The discourse on minority is close to the vernacularisation of African languages whereby the colonial language is imagined as the language, and African languages are vernacular. In many churches today, people talk of an English bible or hymn book and its vernacular counterparts. It is very common in many Christian churches in Africa to hear a chorister giving out hymn numbers to a congregation referencing them as English and vernacular; for example, one says, for our opening song, we will make use of number 200 in the English hymn book; it is number 100 in the vernacular hymn book. Other languages suffer double colonialities in Africa, first as vernaculars to the colonial languages and second as minorities to the dominant African languages.

## 10.4 Conclusion

Names are deployed strategically to express and enforce global, political and ethnic exclusions in Africa. The name Africa itself is reduced to a country from its continent status, and this excludes the individual countries that form the continent. The global superpowers also relate to Africa as a country, and in so doing, they raise their own status to equal continental status. Africa is also imagined as Black. This designation others non-Black Africans, and it also others Black people outside the continent of Africa. While Africans glorify concepts such as pan-Africanism and the 'look-East' policies, they do not commemorate global pan-Africanist and eastern heritages. In fact, Africans are more nationalist than they are continentalist in their commemorations. The onomastic exclusions extend to ethnicities within nation states. Some countries and regions within countries are named using some languages and heritages to the exclusion of others, and this exclusion is extended to language planning and policies.

## References

Africa News. (2021, March 23). *The need for Russia-Africa dialogue*. www.africanews.com/2021/03/23/the-need-for-russia-africa-dialogue-agenda-set-for-the-international-interparty-meeting-with-the-energy-sector-to-play-a-role/

Afrique, J. (2021, April 8). France to host summit for African heads to give a big boost to those hit by COVID [correspondent]. *The Africa Report*. www.theafricareport.com/78627/france-to-host-summit-for-african-heads-to-give-a-big-boost-to-those-hit-by-covid/

Akinrinde, O. O. (2020). Africanity and the politics of African xenophobia: A study of two parallels. *Annals of Spiru Haret University: Economic Series*, *20*(4), 133–151.

Asongu, S. A., & Kodila-Tedika, O. (2017). Is poverty in the African DNA (Gene)? *South African Journal of Economics*, *85*(4), 533–552.

Asserate, A. W. (2015). *King of kings: The triumph and tragedy of Emperor Haile Selassie I of Ethiopia*. Haus Publishing.

Bafana, B. (2016, April). Africa's cities of the future. *Africa Renewal*, 3–5. www.un.org/africarenewal/sites/www.un.org.africarenewal/files/Africa_Renewal_EN_April_2016.pdf

Berger, M. T. (2002). The triumph of the East? The East Asian miracle and post-Cold War capitalism. In D. A. Borer (Ed.), *The rise of East Asia* (pp. 272–299). Routledge.

Bhatia, M. V. (2005). Fighting words: Naming terrorists, bandits, rebels and other violent actors. *Third World Quarterly*, *26*(1), 5–22.

Blommaert, J., & Maly, I. (2016). Ethnographic linguistic landscape analysis and social change. *Language and Superdiversity*, *191*(211), 207–227.

Borkfelt, S. (2011). What's in a name? Consequences of naming non-human animals. *Animals*, *1*(1), 116–125. https://doi.org/10.3390/ani1010116

Cahoone, L. E. (2003). *From modernism to postmodernism: An anthology* (2nd ed.). Blackwell.

Corporate Council on Africa. (2019, June 18). *US-Africa business summit*. https://cca.glueup.com/event/u-s-africa-business-summit-2019–11813/

Davidson, B. (2019). *Black star: A view of the life and times of Kwame Nkrumah*. Routledge.

Filippov, V. R. (2014). Francafrique: France on the Black continent. *International Affairs*, *90*(3), 170–188.

Hall, E. (1991). *Inventing the barbarian: Greek self-definition through tragedy*. Clarendon Press.

Harris, K. L. (2017). BEE-ing Chinese in South Africa: A legal historic perspective. *Fundamina*, *23*(2), 1–20.

Horwitz, R. B. (2018). Politics as victimhood, victimhood as politics. *Journal of Policy History*, *30*(3), 552–574.

Hughey, M. W. (2020). "The souls of White folk" (1920–2020): A century of peril and prophecy. *Ethnic and Racial Studies*, *43*(8), 1307–1332.

Janis, M. (2013). The United States of Africa: Afrofuturistic pasts and afropolitan futures. *Journal of African Cinemas*, *5*(1), 33–54.

Jensen, S. Q. (2011). Othering, identity formation and agency. *Quantitative Studies*, *2*(2), 63–78.

Kearney, M. (1998). Transnationalism in California and Mexico at the end of an empire. In T. M. Wilson & D. Hastings (Eds.), *Border identities – nation state at international frontiers* (pp. 117–141). Cambridge University Press.

Lennon, T. P. (2020). *Lower types of cranks, crooks and racial bigots? The universal Negro improvement association and Black political violence in the United States, 1918–1930*. Radical Americas.

Levander, C., & Mignolo, W. (2011). Introduction: The global South and world dis/order. *The Global South, 5*(1), 1–11.

Li, V. (1995). Towards articulation: Postcolonial theory and demotic resistance. *ARIEL: A Review of International English Literature, 26*(1), 167–189.

Mamdani, M. (1998). The politics of civil society and ethnicity: Reflections on an African dilemma. *Political Power and Social Theory, 12*, 221–234.

Mamvura, Z. (2020). Who does the Mugabe regime say that I am? Dissecting the toponymic commemoration of Joshua Nkomo in Zimbabwe's cultural geography. *African Identities*, 1–17.

Martinot, S. (2011). *The coloniality of power: Notes toward de-colonization*. San Francisco State University. www.ocf.berkeley.edu/~marto/coloniality.htm#:~:text=The%20%22coloniality%20of%20power%22%20is,the%20Americas%20to%20the%20present

Masenya, M. J. (2017). Afrophobia in South Africa: A general perspective of xenophobia. *Bangladesh Sociological Society, 14*(1), 81.

Meer, N. (2019). WEB Du Bois, double consciousness and the "spirit" of recognition. *The Sociological Review, 67*(1), 47–62.

Ndlovu, S. (2016). Transphonologisation of the toponym Zimbabwe: A Shibboleth ethnic identity marker in Zimbabwe. *Igama Journal of African Onomastics Studies, 1*(1), 39–51.

Ndlovu, S. (2020). Pathologisation and ostracisation of Ndebele history in imagining Zimbabwean heritage. In G. Ncube & L. Dube (Eds.), *Ndebele language and cultural productions in Zimbabwe* (pp. 140–157). Amagugu Publishers.

Ndlovu-Gatsheni, S. J. (2010). Do "Africans" exist? Genealogies and paradoxes of African identities and the discourses of nativism and xenophobia. *African Identities, 8*(3), 281–295.

Nyerere, J. K. (1963). A United States of Africa. *The Journal of Modern African Studies, 1*(1), 1–6.

Olaopa, O. R., & Amusan, L. (2018). The question of pan-Africanism and the problem of United States of Africa in Nigeria: Lessons for other African countries. *Journal of African Foreign Affairs, 5*(2), 109–122.

Ramutsindela, M. (2009). Gaddafi, continentalism and sovereignty in Africa. *South African Geographical Journal, 91*(1), 1–3.

Rigby, P. (2020). *African images: Racism and the end of anthropology*. Routledge.

Rodriguez-Flores, J. L., Fakhro, K., Agosto-Perez, F., Ramstetter, M. D., Arbiza, L., Vincent, T. L., & Mezey, J. G. (2016). Indigenous Arabs are descendants of the earliest split from ancient Eurasian populations. *Genome Research, 26*(2), 151–162.

Ryder, H. (2021, February 17). *Where is the Africa-China relationship headed in 2021?* Centre for Strategic & International Studies (CSIC). www.csis.org/analysis/where-africa-china-relationship-headed-2021

Scheipers, S., & Sicurelli, D. (2008). Empowering Africa: Normative power in EU–Africa relations. *Journal of European Public Policy, 15*(4), 607–623.

Tollefson, J. W. (1991). *Planning language, planning inequality*. Longman.

United Kingdom Government. (2021, April 21). *UK-Africa investment summit 2021*. Department for International Trade. www.events.great.gov.uk/website/3529/

Van Dijk, T. A. (2001). Multidisciplinary CDA: A plea for diversity. *Methods of Critical Discourse Analysis*, *1*, 95–120.
Vellem, V. S. (2015). Black ecclesiology: Uprising faith praxis for the blackness of humanity. *The Ecumenical Review*, *67*(4), 651–664.
Wanjiru-Mwita, M. (2020, June 30). Nairobi's street names reveal what those in power want to remember, or forget [correspondent]. *The Conversation*. https://theconversation.com/nairobis-street-names-reveal-what-those-in-power-want-to-remember-or-forget-141378

# 11 Conclusions and recommendations

## 11.0 Introduction

This chapter summarises conclusions from the three sections of the book. It demonstrates in summary how names are used to express otherness and how they represent othering structures in society. The deployment of names in African contexts betrays global, continental, regional, national, ethnic, social and economic colonialities. The chapter proffers some recommendations on problematic nomenclature.

## 11.1 Conclusion

Language expresses culture, identity and power relations (Hayward, 2020), and names are part of language. Africa is named in othering terms globally. Most of these names identify the continent as a poor and underdeveloped country (Pagel et al., 2014). Global designations of world spaces express economic and political discriminations through veiled direction descriptors such as Global North/South, North, South, East, West and sub-Sahara. These names are not genuine cartographical designations, as countries and spaces are uprooted from their cartographical points depending on their political and economic proximity to the global metropoles of power (Jolly, 2008). The South to which Africa is othered to belong is below the North, and in our body habitus, this signals the feet, not the head, which does the thinking. Global colonialities are exposed in names such as those describing Africa as underdeveloped, sub-Sahara and Third World and the West and North America as its opposite. When countries which have crowned themselves centres of global coloniality engage Africa, they group all 55 African countries into one small country which they can dominate. As the East and West fight for global dominance, Africa is their battleground, and there is no genuine equality when it comes to Africa for both blocks (Taylor, 2014). The othering of Africa as a 'heart of darkness' (Conrad, 1902) goes back to precolonial times which also othered African history, culture and heritage (Oyedemi, 2020). Europeans came to Africa and used their names to name African flora and fauna. They also named African culture as savage and wild. These names now exclude African

DOI: 10.4324/9781003170761-14

languages and histories, and the savaged cultures are further excluded from the global economy (Nhemachena, 2017). Savaging names are also common as ethnic and racial slurs (Ndlovu, 2017). Names which relate to skin colour are usually not objective descriptions, and these operate between races in Africa and globally. Black and White are part of eugenics and evolutionary theorising of race superiority, where Black is a degenerate (Schmahmann, 2020). Both Black and White people use skin colour to name and offend the racialised other. Indians and Arabs are also racially named in slurs to mark them as foreign to Africa. The exclusions are also found among Africans who refer to each other using some ethnic slurs to mark autochthony and modernity.

One area in which names betray unequal social structures is in the naming of colonised spaces and the colonials. The early African encounters with Europeans led them to name them dizzy wanderers through names such as *Mzungu*. However, as colonial and imperial evils unfolded, the naming changed to describe these evils through names such as *Mlumbi, Aboforo* and *Murungu* (Ochonu, 2019). As colonial privileges favoured White people, these names shifted to reference opulence (Spitzer, 2014). Colonialists named Africa to possess it. They used their own names to name African water bodies, towns, streets and countries. They also used their heritages to name African money. While there has been decolonial renaming across Africa, colonial nomenclature is still dominant, especially the colonial languages in the African linguistic landscape (Campbell, 2019). Some colonial states spread their religions to the colonials, and these were named to reference the colonial state; such names as Anglican church and Roman church are still used in African countries. Slavery and colonisation also affected African naming conventions. The priests and teachers became the new name givers, and they swayed Africans from purposeful and expressive naming into western names which meant nothing to the Africans (Okello, 2020). Faced with this othering onslaught on their naming conventions, Africans infused their conventions on western languages, in the process deriving what have been described as funny or strange names such as *Talkmore, Sixpence* and so on.

Onomastic othering is also prevalent in socio-political naming in Africa. The way Africans name men and women, disability and homosexuality and how they name their spaces and groups within Africa exhibits instances of othering. Men are named to be agentive and powerful, while girl children are named to be passive, beautiful and gentle from birth (Felmlee et al., 2020). Representation of women in the linguistic landscape through toponyms is an indication that women are not fairly represented in power politics and the economy. Treatment of disability in African cultures has always been shrouded in obscurity (Namasasu, 2020), and this is expressed in the way Africans name disability. Most names are instances of non-disabled people naming disability from the point of view of their abilities. African countries and cultures also disown homosexuality (Chimakonam & Agada, 2020), and this explains the prevalence of homophobic slurs used to reference homosexuality in Africa.

Apart from women, disabled people and homosexuals, Africans exclude each other regionally, nationally, ethnically and by language. African dictators will imagine Africa to be one so that they can unite to cover their own extremities. Africa is also identified as being Black, and this excludes many people from Africa and many Black people from other spaces outside Africa. While Africans pride themselves on being Black and glorify Black rights movements, they do not honour African Americans in their toponyms. Africans also pledge allegiance to the East, but they do not exhibit this allegiance in their commemorative naming. Africans are not as united as they preach. They do not commemorate African heritage; rather, each country commemorates its own. Even within these individual countries, there are intense ethnic and language exclusions where dominant ethnicities form their own local colonialities and exclude other ethnicities and languages in naming national heritages.

## 11.2 Recommendations

The various chapters discuss varieties of onomastic othering in African names and naming, and it is clear that there are several naming conventions that norm othering of people and their cultures, languages and spaces. There are some names that are widely used in literature which violate some sections of society through embedded and at times explicit colonialities. Some of the names appear to be formed by descriptive content, yet what they describe is now entangled in either exclusion or inferiorising the other. This section makes some recommendations on certain naming norms which have negative impact on Africans and other people and why these should be avoided.

While the designations First, Second and Third World have faced opposition, it is only the Second World which is obsolete as a name. The First and Third World continue to be used, and these create a globally favoured and disfavoured dichotomy. The precedence of the abolition of the name Second World is motivation that Third World can be overcome, too. While we cannot compel countries to name their groupings in certain ways, it is important for rich countries who partner with African states to be consistent in naming groups of partnering countries. Nomenclature such as China-Africa equates a whole continent to one country and may be rethought.

Efforts to categorise racial and ethnic slurs as hate speech are commendable; however, there are some slurs that have established themselves in certain discourses, especially in scientific research. Racial slurs such as Negro and Mongol are still used in literature. The use of the name Caucasian also has inverse racial slur references, as it is juxtaposed to Negroid and Mongoloid. These slurs can be better managed so that future generations will understand them as hate speech. The naming of some elements of African culture such as fruits, religion and animals gives away colonialities of history and culture. These names other African culture and exclude it from the global economy. Revising the names will help globalise African cultures.

While political coloniality is still expressed by many toponyms across Africa, it is encouraged to engage onomasticians in name changes so as to strike a balance between history and decoloniality. There are also some names, especially names of religious denominations, which should consider globalising by disassociating country names from religious nomenclature. While Africa is affected by western coloniality, it is clear that there are several social and local colonialities expressed in names and naming. There is a need to revisit the naming of disability and disability centres in Africa with the intention of ridding these of disablist nomenclature. Names reflect social structures and norms, and the prevalence of homophobic slurs in Africa points to homophobic societies in Africa. There are some names which intend to shrink Africa into a homogenous culture; such names other individual cultures and encourage ethnic and regional othering.

## References

Campbell, J. (2019, October 9). *The origins of African states, and their names*. www.cfr.org/blog/origins-african-states-and-their-names

Chimakonam, J. O., & Agada, A. (2020). The sexual orientation question in Nigeria: Cultural relativism versus universal human rights concerns. *Sexuality & Culture*, *24*(6), 1705–1719. https://link.springer.com/article/10.1007/s12119-020-09705-9

Conrad, J. (1902). *Heart of darkness*. Penguin.

Felmlee, D., Rodis, P. I., & Zhang, A. (2020). Sexist slurs: Reinforcing feminine stereotypes online. *Sex Roles*, *83*(1), 16–28. https://link.springer.com/article/10.1007/s11199-019-01095-z

Hayward, J. (2020). Orality in the digital age. In R. H. Kaschula & H. E. Wolff (Eds.), *The transformative power of language: From postcolonial to knowledge societies in Africa* (pp. 277–303). Cambridge University Press.

Jolly, M. (2008). The South in Southern theory: Antipodean reflections on the Pacific. *Australian Humanities Review*, *44*(1), 75–99.

Namasasu, O. (2020). Exclusion of children with disability from citizenship education at primary school: A Harare case study. *ResearchGate*, 1–11. https://doi.org/10.13140/RG.2.2.26522.47044

Ndlovu, S. (2017). Transphonologisation as ethnophaulism between the Ndebele and the Shona of Zimbabwe in selected toponyms and ethnonyms. *Nomina Africana: Journal of African Onomastics*, *31*(2), 117–125. https://journals.co.za/doi/abs/10.2989/NA.2017.31.2.2.1313

Nhemachena, A. (2017). *Relationality and resilience in a not so relational world? knowledge, chivanhu and (de-)coloniality in 21st century conflict-torn Zimbabwe*. Langaa RPCIG.

Ochonu, M. E. (2019). Looking for race: Pigmented pasts and colonial mentality in "non racial" Africa. In *Relating worlds of racism* (pp. 3–37). Palgrave Macmillan.

Okello, B. (2020). What's in a name? Reinventing Luo naming system in Kenya's ethnopolitical landscape. *African Identities*, *19*(1), 77–90. https://doi.org/10.1080/14725843.2020.1791687

Oyedemi, T. (2020). (De) coloniality and South African academe. *Critical Studies in Education*, *61*(4), 399–415. https://doi.org/10.1080/17508487.2018.1481123

Pagel, H., Ranke, K., Hempel, F., & Köhler, J. (2014, July 11). *The use of the concept "global South" in social science & humanities*. Symposium of the Global South, Humboldt University. www.academia.edu/download/38188278/pdf

Schmahmann, B. (2020). Senzeni Marasela's reworking of women's histories in *Beyond Booty: Covering Sarah Baartman and Other Tales*. *Textile*, 1–27. https://doi.org/10.1080/14759756.2020.1773612

Spitzer, H. (2014). *Mzungu, how are you? Reflections on the human element of North-South partnerships*. https://appear.at/fileadmin/Dokumente/appear.at/implementation_and_reporting/Gender/article_HelmutSpitzer_2014.pdf

Taylor, I. (2014). *Africa rising: BRICS-diversifying dependency*. James Currey.

# Index

*abeLungu* 67–6, **90–2**, *97–101*
*abeLumbi* 67, **94–6**, 98–9
*Aboforo* 67, **93–8**, *101–2*, 157, 200
Abuja 153, 159, **160**, 166
African: American 23, 66, 74, 164, 170, 189; culture 10, 39, 40–3, 46–8, 51–3, 55, 68, 78; fauna 40, 44–5; fruits 41–3, 55; languages 10, 45, 48–9, 53, 98, 101, 110, 113, 118, 130–1, 155, 178, 181, 190, 195; names and naming 10, 132, 134, 151, 201; names for white people 91, 101; religion 45, 50, 55, 134, 138, 145, 189, 190
agentive 152, **154–5**, 181, 200
Akan 38, 93, 97, 121, 129, 130
anthroponymy 45, 129, 135–6, 144–5
apartheid 2, 4, 20, 43, 60–1, 67, 75, 88, 100, 107, **112–113**, **164**, 175, 189–191, 193
Asia 20, 26–8, 69, 70, 191
Australia 17, 20, *26–8*, 122, 189
autochthony 70, 78, 189, 194, 200

Barbarian 2, 73, 188
baptism 133, 135
*Bhulu/Bhunu* 68
Black people 7, 61, 68, 70, 78, 87–8, 94, *96–101*, 143
Brazil 22, 30
BRICS 22, 30
British East Africa 112, 121
Bulawayo 107, **112–114**, **116**, 136, 175, **177**

Caucasian 49, 63, *64–*7, 68, 73–4, 201
centre-periphery 17, 31
China 22, 30–1, 33–4, 188, 192, 201
Christianity 24, 50–1, 55, 98, 123, 130–4, 140, 177, 182
church 51, **114**, 123–4, 131–2, 134–5, 144, 173, 200
civilisation 4, 6, 7, 21, 28, 34, 38, 42, 49, 68, 98, 157
colonialism 1, 6, 7, 9, 20–1, 34, 38, 43, 46, 50, 53–4, 60–1, 71–2, 74, 88, 90–3, 95–8, 101–2, 105, 107–8, 110, 112, 114, 118–121, 123, 125, 130–2, 134, 136, 138, 141, 143, 145, 155, 157, 159, 178, 190–1
coloniality: of being 7, 131; of power 3, 4, 98, 110, 195
commemorative naming 10, 152, 159, 162–3, 165, 186–7, 191–3, 201
critical discourse analysis CDA 8, 19, 40–1, 60, 89, 153–4, 170, 182, 187
cultural: authenticity 52–3, 68; identity 73; othering 38, 51–2

dark continent 38
decolonisation 4, 6, 21, 110, 145, 162
decoloniality 4, 6, 7, 9, 87–9, 144, 202
degeneration 64, 78
development: economic 165; global 28, 31, 33–4, 49, 53, 186
dictators 190–1, 201
disability 6, 9, 59, 168–178, 182, 200
disability rights 177
domestic worker 139

East-West dichotomy 19–20, 23, 191
Egypt 32, 49, 120, 134, 193
empire 5, 20–3, 27, 46, 49, 96, 118–119, 122
English culture 47, 54
eSwatini 7, 76, 89, 99, 111, **121**, **164**, 194
ethnophaulism 6, 59, 60, 65–7, 69, 71, 73–4, 76–7, 87–9, 92
etymological analysis 8, 19, 88–9

eugenics 4, 46, 63–4, 78, 133, 173, 200
European: culture 38, 47–8, 51–5, 68, 112, 131, 136, 138, 145; churches 51, 124; missionaries 124, 133
evolution of species 63, 78, 133

feminist political economy 4, 152
First World 18, 29, *31–2*
foreignising 73–4, 77–8, 88, 90, 92, 102
French West Africa 112

gay people 178–180
gazelle **44–6**
gendered naming 160, 164
Global: North 19, 24, 26–7, 29, 49, 199; South 18, 22, 24, 27
globalisation 3, 5, 9, 17, 25–6, 49, 130, 132, 138
G: names of country groupings; G5 33; G7 27, 33; G20 33; G77 33; G77 and China 33

heritage 6, 10, 106, 111, 116–120, 129, 131–2, 136, 142, 159, 193–4, 199, 201
historical trauma 4, 131–2, 139, 143
heterosexuality 178–9, 182
hodonyms 111–112, **114**, 125
homosexuality 168–170, 177–180, 182, 200
homophobia 61, 177, 179

identity: African 48, 65, 99, 132, 139, 189–190; crisis 123, 132, 138, 140–1; cultural 73; European 145
imperialism 1, 5, 20, 34, 46, 51, 55, 60–1, 92, 105, 107–8, 112, 119–121, 123–4, 141: cultural 107, 123; economic 107, 118, 125; political 107–8
indigenous: fruits 40; African 119, 121, 130; cultures 133, **142**
Islam 21, 133, 177, 182

Kenya 7, 32, 45, 89, 99, **109**, **111–113**, **120**, 130, 133, 135, **161–4**, 181, 190, 192–3
*Kwerekwere* 75

Left political spectrum 17, 19, 22–4

masculinities 154, 158, 161, 170
missionaries 87, 92, 95, 99, *101–2*, 123–4, 130, 132–5, 137, 145
*Mlumbi* 95, *102*, 200
*Mlungu* 2, 68, 88, *96–102*
modernity 3, 7, 38, 140, 188, 200
*Mulungu 98–102*
*Muzungu/Mzungu* 25, 87, 89–91, 93, 95–7, 99, *101–2*, 200
*Mwenye* 69–70

names and naming 1–2, 4, 6–7, 10, 73, 87, 92, 130–2, 134, 151, 168, 170, 186–7, 201–2
Ndebele 42–3, 48, 51, 53–4, 65, 67–9, **71–3**, 76–8, **112–113**, **116–118**, 136, 173–4, **177**, 195
Nigeria 7, 32, 96, 99, 111–112, **114**, **121**, 130, 160, **163–4**
Nigger 75, 139
Negroid 64, 201
North-South dichotomy 17–18, 24–6

*Oburoni* 67, 87, 91–2, 97–9
*Oboforo* 87
onomastics 10, 85, 106–7, 111, 135, 151, 194
onomastic: erasure 99; synecdoche 174, 181
othering theory 4, 5, 19, 60, 131, 186–7
other: ethnic 6, 39, 71–2, 117, 194; racial 97; economic 120; woman 151, 164

patriarchy 4, 7, 10, 151–4, 156, 158–9, 161, 163
postcolonial theory 4, 5, 6, 18, 60, 107, 186–7
power: nuclear 28, 30–2; political 105, 151

Queen 89, 113, 136: Elizabeth 136; Lozikeyi 161; Nzinga 192; Victoria **113–115**, 136
Qweqwe 117

racism 2, 4, 39, 61–3, 67–8, 78, 97–8, 100–1, 188
Right political spectrum 17, 19, 22–4, 27
right to name 3, 44, 66
rural 27, 40, 47, 53–4, 98, 118, 157, 172
Russia 22, 30–1, 64, 188, 192

self othering 21, 40, **53–4**, 69
selfing 4, 19–20, 30, 33, 50, **51–2**, 66, 85, 93, 125, 188, 190, 194
sexist 10, 149, 155, 158, 168, 170–1, 180, 182
Shona **42–3**, **48**, 69, 71–3, 77–8, 90, 95, 100, 116–118, 124, 132, **139**, **140–3**, 170, 174, **176–7**, 181, 194–5
slavery 1, 4, 6, 41, 50, 60–2, 92, 94, 168–9, 171
slur: ethnic 10, 59–61, 71, 200, 201; homophobic 169–170, 177, 179, 200, 202; racial 61, 66, 88, 139, 200, 201

social Darwinism 4, 23–4, 46, 63, 87, 89, 100
South Africa 2, 7, 20, 22, *25–7*, 30–3, 42, 60, 67–8, 75–6, 79, 88–91, 97, 100, 102, **111–113**, 121, 123–4, 136–7, 140–3, 153, 157, **163–4**, 171, 178–9, 180, 189, 191, 193, 195
subalternity 3, 4, 6, 19, 180
surnames 10, 131–2, 136, 142–3, 145
Swahili 89, 99, 100, **121**

Tanzania 89, 99, **109**, 111, **120**, **163–4**, 170, 191, 193
Third Word 5, 6, 18, 22, 27, 30, 32–3, 52, 132, 199, 201
toponyms 19, 25, 34, 60, 67, 72–3, **105–112**, **115–117**, 123, 132, 134, **136–7**, 144–5, 165, 192–5, 200–2
traditional 23, 40, **46–50**, 52–3, 55, **124**, 129–130, **138**, 152, 158, 163, 169, 177
transphonologisation 9, 108, 115–6
Tswana **48**, 67, 71, 74, 76, **121**, 178, 194

urbanisation 53, 130–1, 137–8
*ubuntu* 68
*uMlungu* 68, 87–8, 90–1, 94, 97–8, 100, 157
underdeveloped 17, 25–6, 28–9, *31–2*, 47, 199

*vaRumbi* 67, **95–8**
Victoria: falls **115**; lake **114–115**; street **113**
violence 21, 61, 66, 87, **93–6**, 98, 101, 130

West 10, 17–22, 24, 29–30, 33–4, 49, 53–4, 70, 94, 121, 124, 136, 169–170, 178, 188, 191–2, 199
West Africa 32, 54, 87, 89, 91, 93, **108–9**, **112–113**, 120–1, 130
western: civilisation 4, 6, 7, 68; countries 109; culture 38, 98, 110; modernity 6, 189
witches 77, **94–6**, 98–9, *102*, 174
White people 2, 10, 25, 67–8, 74, 78, **87–99**, *100–2*, 118, 174, 189, 190, 200

xenophobia 59, 61, 76, 87, 89, 92, 191
Xhosa 68, 88, 91, 134

Zambia 7, 69–70, 89–90, 99–100, 111, **121**, **164**, 171, 191, 193
ZANU 193, 194
ZAPU 190, 193
Zimbabwe 7, 39, 41–3, 48–9, 53, 60, **69–73**, 76–8, 89–90, 95–7, 107, **111–114**, 116, **120**, 123–4, 132, **135–7**, 141–4, 153, 157–8, **161–2**, **164**, 171, **173–7**, 179–181, 190–4